TWENTIETH-CENTURY FICTION
BY IRISH WOMEN

In memory of Mella Carroll

Twentieth-Century Fiction by Irish Women

Nation and Gender

HEATHER INGMAN
University of Dublin, Ireland

ASHGATE

© Heather Ingman 2007

Published by
Ashgate Publishing Limited
Gower House
Croft Road
Aldershot
Hampshire GU11 3HR
England

Ashgate Publishing Company
Suite 420
101 Cherry Street
Burlington, VT 05401-4405
USA

Ashgate website: http://www.ashgate.com

British Library Cataloguing in Publication Data
Ingman, Heather, 1953-
Twentieth-century fiction by Irish women : nation and gender
    1.English fiction – Irish authors – History and criticism 2.English fiction – Women authors – History and criticism 3.English fiction – 20th century – History and criticism 4.Women and literature – Ireland – History and criticism – 20th century 5.Sex role in literature 6.Nationalism in literature 7.Ireland – In literature
    I.Title
    823.9'14099287'09415

Library of Congress Cataloging-in-Publication Data
Ingman, Heather, 1953-
    Twentieth-century fiction by Irish women : nation and gender / by Heather Ingman.
        p. cm.
    Includes bibliographical references and index.
    1. English fiction—Irish authors—History and criticism. 2. English fiction—Women authors—History and criticism. 3. English fiction—20th century—History and criticism. 4. Kristeva, Julia, 1941– 5. Ireland—In literature. 6. Nationalism in literature. 7. Women—Ireland—Intellectual life. 8. Women and literature—Ireland—History—20th century. 9. Feminism and literature—Ireland—History—20th century. I. Title.

PR8807.W6I54 2006
823'.91099287—dc22

ISBN-13: 978-0-7546-3538-3

2006018483

ernational Ltd, Padstow, Cornwall.

Contents

Acknowledgements

I would like to acknowledge permission from the editors of the *Yearbook in English Studies*, *Irish University Review* and *Irish Studies Review* to re-use some material from my articles first published in their journals.[1]

A study like this evolves over several years. At Trinity College, Dublin I have been fortunate to work in an English department which is committed to the study and teaching of Irish literature while my teaching in the Center for Gender Studies has enabled me to focus on issues concerning women. I have very much valued my contacts with students and staff in both departments. I would particularly like to thank my colleague, Eve Patten, for her interest in this project.

I would also like to thank my editor at Ashgate, Ann Donahue, for her patience and courtesy during the writing process. I am grateful to Ashgate's anonymous readers for their careful reading and helpful comments on the manuscript. The flaws remain my own.

I am, as always, indebted more than I can say to Ferdinand von Prondzynski for his unfailing support.

[1] <http://www.tandf.co.uk/journals/carfax/09670882.html>

'But that's not Ireland, the Irish said, that's only women'

(Evelyn Conlon, *Stars in the Daytime*)

Chapter 1

Irish Women in the Twentieth Century

Introduction

The decision to focus my study of Irish women's fiction on the theme of women and the nation arose directly from my reading of Irish women's writing. It seems to me that much Irish women's writing, from all parts of the twentieth century, implicitly or explicitly deals with women trying to find a place for themselves within the narrative of the Irish nation. Ireland is, at the start of the twenty-first century, a country undergoing a period of rapid change. The old rigid forms of nationalism are giving way to a more heterogeneous and multicultural vision of the nation. There is an as yet unresolved argument between revisionists and the so-called new nationalists as to whether this new pluralism is the result of bowing to globalization and market forces or genuinely arises from strands of resistance and progressive thinking already present in Irish culture (see Kirby, Gibbons, Cronin, 2002). If it is the case, as I believe it is, that tendencies towards heterogeneity have always been present in Irish society, it seems an appropriate moment to look back and examine the extent to which women, who have frequently been positioned as the other in the Irish nation, have contributed to the formation of this new Ireland.

Ann Owens Weekes' book, *Irish Women Writers: An Uncharted Tradition* (1990) was, as the title suggests, the first full-length study to bring together Irish women writers of fiction and employ feminist theory in order to determine whether there could be said to be such a thing as a distinctive Irish women's tradition of writing. Weekes pinpointed certain themes specific to Irish women's writing such as the link between domestic and political violence, the move towards an independent heroine and the revision of the myths, both Judeo-Christian and Celtic, which entrap women. Weekes' book deals with only six women writers and it appeared before much of the recent, ground-breaking work on Irish women's history, on which I have drawn for this introductory chapter, was published. Feminist theory in general has not stood still and Weekes' book pre-dates 1990s writing on nationalism and gender which can be so illuminating in an Irish context. Moreover, largely due to the setting up of feminist publishing houses in Ireland, there has been a substantial increase in the number of Irish women's novels published during the 1980s and 1990s. All these factors suggest that there are compelling reasons to look again at Irish women's fiction.

Unlike Weekes I have limited my study to the twentieth century, partly because it establishes a convenient narrative framework but partly because of the recent explosion of Irish women's writing which provides a larger number of texts for study than were available to Weekes. My book differs also from Christine St. Peter's recent survey of contemporary Irish women's fiction, *Changing Ireland: Strategies in Contemporary Women's Fiction* (2000). While providing a useful first reading of a range of contemporary women's novels, St. Peter deliberately eschews an overarching thematic focus such as I have tried to bring to this study. However her volume does highlight the richness of contemporary Irish women's fiction, a richness which suggests that the time is ripe for a new study of Irish women's writing in the twentieth century incorporating novels from the 1980s and 1990s as well as recent developments in feminist literary theory.

In these days of the deconstruction of gender roles it may seem naïve and even retrogressive to deal with women writers as a separate category. I believe however that there is still some value in a strategic essentialism for political purposes. If it is 'painfully premature' to talk of post-nationalism in an Irish context (Maley, 1999, 20), so, in an Irish context where, with one or two exceptions, women's fiction has rarely been examined on its own terms, it seems similarly premature to talk of post-feminism. It is arguable that while Irish women's history has proceeded apace, feminist literary criticism in the Irish context has lagged behind. In her article, 'Feminism, Postmodernism and the Subject of Irish and Women's Studies', Moynagh Sullivan laments the prolonged inability of Irish studies to listen to ways in which feminist theory might have an impact on our reading of Irish women's literature and its place in the canon (Sullivan, 2000, 243–51). Irish women's writing has too often been subsumed, and thereby swallowed up, in an Irish literary canon and an Irish critical tradition constructed mainly by male scholars, as the under representation of female authors in the first three volumes of *The Field Day Anthology of Irish Literature* attested.

To speak of women's difference may not always be essential or even desirable but, as Elaine Showalter argued thirty years ago, when women writers are studied as a group we may discover recurrent patterns, themes and images which are almost impossible to perceive if women are discussed only in relation to male writers (Showalter, 1977/1978, 11). Christine St. Peter makes a similar point in her introduction to *Changing Ireland* where she defends her decision to treat women writers as a separate category by demonstrating, in the light of the separate social conditioning of women, the importance of establishing a specific women's tradition of writing in order to foster women's creativity (St. Peter, 2000, 8–9). The argument extends back as far as Virginia Woolf's 'A Room of One's Own' and has been used since by women writers from many different cultures, notably by Alice Walker in her essay 'In Search of our Mothers' Gardens'. The necessity of establishing a tradition of women's writing is picked up in an Irish context by Eavan Boland in *Object Lessons*, a series of essays published in 1995 tracing her development as a poet and her struggles with a national poetic tradition which marginalized the female poet. As a young poet, Boland felt hampered by the lack of a tradition of women's poetry-writing in Ireland: 'I was a poet' she says, 'lacking the precedent and example of previous Irish women poets' (Boland, 1995/1996, 151). In her effort to establish the everyday lives of ordinary women as a suitable subject for Irish poetry, Boland had to look outside the Irish poetic tradition – to the American poets Sylvia Plath and Adrienne Rich – for inspiration.

The point about the separate social conditioning of women is especially relevant in the context of nationalism since feminist research, such as Nira Yuval-Davis' study, *Gender and Nation* (1997) and Tamar Mayer's *Gender Ironies of Nationalism: Sexing the Nation* (2000), has revealed that rigid gender constructs are often crucial to the building of a nation's identity. In *Gender Ironies of Nationalism*, Mayer argues that many nations construct their identity around fixed concepts of gender. One gender, usually male, becomes empowered at the expense of the other with the result that, whatever rhetoric of equality may be employed, the nation becomes the property of men. Drawing on Judith Butler's theories of gender performance, Mayer argues that through repetition of accepted gendered behavior, men and women help to construct the identity of their nation; at the same time, this repetition reinforces gendered constructs. Men become the nation's protectors, women its biological and ideological reproducers guaranteeing the nation's purity. Hence: nationalism becomes the language through which sexual control and repression (specifically, but not exclusively, of women and homosexuals) is justified and masculine prowess is expressed and exercised. (Mayer, 2000, 1).

In the case of Ireland, fixed concepts of gender became institutionalized in its juridical structure and women's position after 1922 saw a gradual erosion of their political rights. When considering the topic of Irish nationalism there is therefore a case for regarding women as a separate group and asking the question: did and do Irish women participate in the national project differently from men?

As early as 1988, John Wilson Foster put forward the suggestion that feminist theory with its stress on difference might provide 'a third force, a third Irish identity', capable of destabilizing the binaries (Catholic/ Protestant, nationalist/ unionist) on which Irish identity has long been built (Foster, 1991, 246). Foster does not mention Julia Kristeva by name but it will be one of the central arguments of this study that her writings provide a framework for exploring and understanding this destabilizing force. In *Sex and Nation: Women in Irish Culture and Politics* (1991), Geraldine Meaney argues that Irish feminism must engage in dialog with Irish nationalism if women are not to remain marginalized within the life of the nation:

> If women are to renegotiate their relation to Irish culture, much work needs to be done. The work of analysing and theorising women's relation to Irish culture, of criticising and changing that relation, of providing a critical, political and historical context for Irish women's writing is an exciting and necessary task which, as yet, has scarcely begun. (Meaney, 1991, 15–16)

She adds: 'The work undertaken by feminist scholars elsewhere can be of invaluable assistance in this task and can expand the horizons of Irish sexual and national identity' (Meaney, 1991, 16). By using the writings of Julia Kristeva on women and nationalism, this study hopes to place the dialog between Irish feminism and nationalism in a wider theoretical context.

The choice of Kristevan theory as a lens through which to consider fiction by Irish women was prompted by Kristeva's own interest, from the 1990s onwards, in nations and nationalism and by the place she grants to women in this topic. Given the perceived male bias in Irish literary criticism until recent times, the justification for using a female theorist to examine Irish women's writing may seem evident. However, Kristeva is a contentious choice of theorist to use for reading women writers since she has frequently been judged to be anti-feminist, essentialist and over-reliant on male theorists (see, for example, Stone, Kuykendall, Butler, Stanton, Weedon).[1] These criticisms have been contested (Oliver, Rose, Jardine, Chanter, Smith). Anne-Marie Smith, who summarizes much of this criticism in *Julia Kristeva: Speaking the Unspeakable*, points out that when Anglo-American feminists criticize Kristeva, it is not always Kristeva herself they are criticizing so much as the established rules of sexual difference in classical psychoanalysis to which she adheres. Smith explains: 'to argue that Kristeva is suffering from too close an identification with the symbolic father is a manner of defining oneself as a separatist feminist arguing with psychoanalytic thought' (Smith, 1998, 37). These criticisms in any case often belong to the earlier part of Kristeva's career: Kristeva's later writings on nationalism in fact privilege women, and the influence of female figures in her own life and work is attested by her recent three volumes on *Le génie féminin*, looking at the contributions of Hannah Arendt, Melanie Klein and Colette to twentieth-century politics, psychoanalysis and literature, respectively.

At the same time, in her concern for the particularity of the individual, Kristeva has often expressed herself suspicious of feminism's totalitarian impulses and its reliance on oppositional narratives. A central question in her work has been how can we continue the struggle for equal rights for women without homogenizing what women are? In *New Maladies of the Soul* (1995), she asks: 'As it stands today, is feminism not about to become a sort of religion? Or will it manage to rid itself of its belief in Woman [...] and support instead the singularity of each woman, her complexities, her many languages?' (Kristeva, 1995, 221). By applying Kristevan theory to fiction which delineates the struggles of particular women to reconcile their gender with their nation, this study hopes to keep faith with Kristeva's emphasis on the particularity of the individual woman.

The use of Kristeva seems especially appropriate for an analysis of fiction because of Kristeva's belief in the redemptive capacities of imaginative writing. In *New Maladies of the Soul*, Kristeva argues for the therapeutic value of art and literature as providing a space outside the relentless demands of linear time in which personal identity and its clash with society and culture may be explored:

> Along with psychoanalysis, the role of aesthetic practice needs to be augmented, not only to counterbalance the mass-production and uniformity of the information age, but also to demystify the idea that the community of language is a universal, all-inclusive, and equalizing tool. Each artistic experience can also highlight the diversity of our identifications and the relativity of our symbolic and biological existence. (Kristeva, 1995, 223)

---

[1]	In 1983, after the publication of *Powers of Horror*, Jennifer Stone stated baldly that 'Kristeva's work is no longer in women's interests', arguing that Kristeva was unable to theorize beyond Freud (Stone, 1983, 42).

In the light of this statement, literature, in an Irish context, may provide in general terms a space in which to resist the homogenization of the nation brought about by the discourse of Irish nationalism.

More specifically, Kristeva urges the marginalized in the nation's life, which in her analysis includes women, to speak out, as Anna Smith explains in *Julia Kristeva: Readings of Exile and Estrangement*:

> [...] unless those marginalised by culture *speak* their marginalisation, they remain trapped in narcissism. Women and aliens for instance have the potential to enrich cultural life because they stand for difference, yet without the resources of language creatively or analytically disposed, their potentially subversive signs of difference melt away. (Smith, 1998, 185)

By expressing their secret desires in writing women, Kristeva argues in *New Maladies of the Soul*, have the power to change the way society views itself:

> At the same time, women's desire for affirmation has emerged as a longing for artistic and especially literary creation. Why the emphasis on literature? Is it because when literature is in conflict with social norms, it diffuses knowledge and occasionally the truth about a repressed, secret, and unconscious universe? Is it because literature intensifies the social contract by exposing the uncanny nature of that which remains unsaid? (Kristeva, 1995, 220)

'Understood as such,' she adds, 'aesthetics takes on the question of morality' (Kristeva, 1995, 223). In *Revolt, She Said*, Kristeva reiterates her argument that she sees it as the task of the artist to represent contemporaries' anxieties in a way that may be creative and healing for society (Kristeva, 2002c, 106).

Over and above the general relevance of Kristevan theory to fiction by women, Kristeva's writings on nationalism seem especially applicable to the situation faced by Irish women in the twentieth century. In *Nations Without Nationalism*, published originally in French in 1990, Kristeva warns that even political movements which have freedom as their goal, as the Irish nationalists in the early years of the twentieth century may be said to have had, run the danger of becoming totalitarian if their ideals are constructed around exclusions. This is precisely the point made by Hanna Sheehy Skeffington during the early years of the twentieth century in her argument with Constance Markievicz over whether Irish women should prioritize their suffragism or their nationalism. In a pamphlet published in 1909, 'Women, Ideals and the Nation', Constance Markievicz argued that Irish women could not do without a nation of their own and that women's equal rights would naturally follow from their participation in the nationalist struggle (Ward, 1995, 33–5). Conversely, writing in *Bean na hÉireann* in the same year, Hanna Sheehy Skeffington urged Irish women to put the suffrage campaign first, arguing that unless they did, women would remain in a subordinate role and Irish nationalism would retain its roots in the patriarchy. 'It is for Irishwomen [...] to work out their own "Sinn Féin" on their own lines' she declared (Ward, 1995, 36) and she berated Sinn Féin for recognizing women only in the role of wives and mothers rather than as citizens. Subsequent events bore out Sheehy Skeffington's analysis: Irish nationalism, particularly as embodied in Eamon de Valera's 1937

Constitution, positioned Irish women as bearers of children and keepers of the home, excluded from political and public life.

So how then are the rigidities and exclusions of political discourse to be resisted? In 'Psychoanalysis and the Polis', Kristeva argues that psychoanalytic discourse may be used to analyze political discourse and mobilize resistance to it. Using psychoanalytic discourse, which is always concerned with the individual, Kristeva proposes a kind of negotiation between the individual and the nation. She replaces opposition with mediation, negativity with dialectic. Instead of arguing in terms of fixed categories which close down discussion, she emphasizes what will open up identity in an attempt to steer a middle way between rigidity and dissolution:

> My reproach to some political discourses with which I am disillusioned is that they don't consider the individual as a value [...] That's why I say that, of course, political struggles for people that are exploited will continue, but they will continue maybe better if the main concern remains the individuality and the particularity of the person. (Kristeva, 1984, 22–7)

Kristeva stands for political reform rather than for revolution; her idea of revolt, as outlined in *Revolt, She Said*, is a tentative process rather than one which entails violence and upheaval:

> Modern revolt doesn't necessarily take the form of a clash of prohibitions and transgressions that beckons the way to firm promises; modern revolt is in the form of trials, hesitations, learning as you go, making patient and lateral adjustments to an endlessly complex network. (Kristeva, 2002c, 54)

For Kristeva, revolt is slow, patient work since, in her view, revolt which aims at a complete rupture with the status quo risks the establishment of a different totalitarianism. As Anne-Marie Smith points out, Kristeva has always insisted on 'the need for dissidence and transgression to be contained within a structure' (Smith, 1998, 2). Kristeva's analysis seems, therefore, particularly well-suited to Ireland where, for much of the century, Irish women have been in a double bind, supporting their nation, yet wishing for a greater voice in it. Having participated in their country's fight for independence, women like Constance Markiewicz, Hanna Sheehy Skeffington and Rosamond Jacob did not wish to see the Irish nation destroyed but modified to include women. As we shall see, this was to be a slow process.

It is the contention of this study, then, that Kristeva's emphasis on diversity within the nation, on the rights of the individual and on moderate reform rather than outright revolution, allies her with the concerns of Irish women in the twentieth century. In *Nations Without Nationalism*, Kristeva argues that women are often particularly well situated to combat totalitarianism since they are frequently positioned as strangers and exiles within the public life of the nation. This notion of women as exiles within the public life of the nation has particular relevance for Irish women who, for a large part of the twentieth century, were imprisoned in stereotypes of Irish womanhood not of their making.

Fixed constructs of gender had always been central to Irish nationalism. On a symbolic level, going back to eighteenth-century Gaelic poetry, Ireland was constructed as a woman victimized by the colonizing English male. She was Hibernia, Mother Ireland, the Poor Old Woman, the Shan Van Vocht, Cathleen Ni Houlihan, Dark Rosaleen.[2] The Devotional Revolution of the mid-nineteenth century added the cult of the Virgin Mary and established constructs of masculinity and femininity which reflected Catholic doctrine. Women were to be passive embodiments of Irish virtue; men were Mother Ireland's sons who were to sacrifice their lives for her. These stereotypes of male and female behavior held sway in Irish literature far into the twentieth century and, as Eavan Boland points out in relation to women: 'Long after it was necessary, Irish poetry had continued to trade in the exhausted fictions of the nation, had allowed these fictions to edit ideas of womanhood' (Boland, 1995/1996, 137).

Nationalist symbols had material consequences. Irish men were supposed to, and did, lay down their lives for Ireland. Irish women, with the example of the Virgin Mary set before them, were to embody the purity of the Irish nation. Sexuality thus became bound up with nationality. A certain female behavior, based on chastity and purity, guaranteed the purity and alterity of the Irish nation. Nuala O'Faolain, leaving school in the late 1950s, was told by the head nun that she would not go far wrong if 'in whatever situation I might find myself I should think what the Virgin Mary would have done, and do the same' (O'Faolain, 1996, 58). Catholic social teaching, particularly in the area of sexual morality, defined the Irish nation in opposition to England. The sexually loose woman was not only shocking, she was seen as anti-Irish or 'foreign'. Very often she had to be expelled, if not from her country, at least from her family or her community. As David Cairns and Shaun Richards put it: 'The personification of Ireland as "Woman" and "Mother" necessitated that the purity of that image was maintained on all levels' (Cairns and Richards, 1988, 77).

It is arguable, therefore, that nationalism in Ireland disempowered women. National symbols obscured the reality of their lives and provided unhelpful and constraining standards to live by. The participation of Irish women in the suffrage movement and in the nationalist struggle in the early part of the twentieth century, fostered hopes for the status of women in an independent Ireland. These hopes seemed initially bright with the statement of 'equal rights and equal opportunities to all its citizens' in the 1916 Proclamation and its reaffirmation in the 1922 Free State Constitution. During the 1920s and 1930s, however, these bright hopes gradually faded as gendered legislation, brought in by successive governments and culminating in Eamon de Valera's 1937 Constitution, increasingly restricted women's lives to the domestic sphere. In order to set the theoretical discussion of nationhood and gender in Irish women's fiction against its historical background, this chapter provides a brief survey of Irish women's lives in the twentieth century. Its purpose is to illuminate the kind of marginalization Irish women suffered and

---

[2]   For the symbolic representation of Ireland as female see, among others, C. L. Innes, 1993, Part I; D. Cairns and S. Richards in O'Brien Johnson and Cairns, 1991, 128–37; and Weekes, 1990, 14–15.

which, as we have seen, is germane to Kristeva's analysis of women as strangers and exiles within the life of the nation.

Leading up to 1916

The early part of the twentieth century saw a ferment of political activity in Ireland, activity in which women played a crucial part. However, as has been suggested above, the relationship between feminism and nationalism at this time is complex and not easy to disentangle. In the early twentieth century many women participated in both nationalist and feminist movements. Constance Markievicz was involved in the labor movement, the women's movement and the nationalist movement and all these different strands came together in her membership of James Connolly's Irish Citizen Army which accepted women on equal terms with men. Hanna Sheehy Skeffington, who founded the militant Irish Women's Franchise League in 1908, very definitely identified herself as nationalist and for this reason did not want the IWFL to be too closely allied to the English suffrage movement. As Margaret Ward has shown, Sheehy Skeffington placed her suffragism in the context of Irish traditions of militant resistance in order to distance herself from English suffragettes (Ward, 1995, 86). Rosamond Jacob, Hanna's lifelong friend, combined nationalism and feminism when she became a member of the IWFL and also of Sinn Féin. Like Sheehy Skeffington, Jacob was aware of the dangers of identifying Irish suffragism too closely with the English movement: in her novel *Callaghan*, published in 1920 under the gender-free pseudonym F. Winthrop, Jacob has one of her characters protest, after listening to a speech by an Irish suffragist, that: 'She speaks as an Englishwoman throughout!' (Winthrop, 1920, 73). However, notwithstanding her nationalist sympathies, her heroine Frances Morrin, like Jacob herself, joins the suffragist movement.

There was thus nothing unusual at this time in being actively committed to both feminism and nationalism; it is only when the details of these women's pronouncements are examined that different emphases emerge. As we saw, Hanna Sheehy-Skeffington, writing in *Bean na hÉireann,* the first nationalist-feminist journal to be produced in Ireland, urged Irish women to put the suffrage campaign first while, in the same year, Constance Markievicz was arguing that nationalism should be women's priority. Rosamond Jacob was closer to Markievicz's position in that she declared herself prepared to countenance a delay in female suffrage if it meant she would receive the vote from an Irish government. Both Jacob and Markievicz joined Cumann na mBan (Irishwomen's Council), founded in 1914 as an auxiliary to the Irish Volunteers. Sheehy Skeffington never joined it, protesting that such an organization reinforced women's subordinate status.

When we survey the early part of the twentieth century in Ireland it seems impossible to make any sweeping generalizations about women's commitment to nationalism and feminism. There were as many different shades of both as there were politically active women and often they differed by only a hair's breadth. Constance Markievicz may have been President of Cumann na mBan but she was prepared to admit that the subordinate role they played to the all-male Irish Volunteers was demoralizing (Hayes and Urquhart, 2001, 59). Suffragism may have been Hanna Sheehy Skeffington's priority but she praised James Connolly's leadership during the 1916 Rising and she surprised Constance Markievicz by turning up, along with other members of the IWFL, to deliver food to the nationalists besieged in the Royal College of Surgeons (Ward, 1997, 156). The situation is further complicated by the fact that Irish nationalism at this stage was not the homogeneous discourse it later became. It was both more subversive and more fluid. What women like Hanna Sheehy Skeffington wished to ensure was that when the discourse eventually coalesced into a nation-state, women would not be treated as second class citizens. Unfortunately that did not happen.

Rosamond Jacob's novel, *Callaghan*, portrays the choices facing politically active women at this time when her heroine, Frances Morrin, an active suffragist, falls in love with Andy Callaghan, a militant for Irish nationalism. Though Frances supports Irish nationalism, she is not prepared to have a relationship with Callaghan unless he admits her equality. Callaghan takes a while to comprehend her seriousness on this point but eventually he manages to come to grips with: 'this idea that a woman might have public duties which seemed to her as important as a man's' (Winthrop, 1920, 174). Frances ends by marrying Callaghan and helping him in his work for the Volunteers at the same time as she continues her involvement with suffragism.

It would be wrong therefore to say that nationalism and feminism were opposed in this period; rather they were given more or less emphasis by each individual woman according to the perceived exigencies of a situation. In view of the complex interaction between the two movements, historians are divided as to whether the rise in Irish nationalism helped or hindered the feminist movement in Ireland. In *The Hidden Tradition: Feminism, Women and Nationalism in Ireland* (1993), Carol Coulter argues that the nationalist movement was an advantage to Irish women in that it gave them access to a public platform from which they could then also campaign for equal rights. Others, notably the critic Edna Longley in her pamphlet 'From Cathleen to Anorexia: The Breakdown of Irelands' (1990), have argued that the various nationalist movements in Ireland have been detrimental to women's equality because they have encouraged women to put nationalism before feminism. Political developments from 1912 onwards certainly placed a great strain on the unity of the women's movement in Ireland. Fear of endangering the Home Rule Bill caused many women to suppress or postpone their suffrage views while others set aside their support for suffrage in order to help in the First World War (Owens, 1984, 8–9). Survey of the period leading up to 1916 demonstrates that feminism often became subordinate to other political concerns in which women played an ancillary role. Only in the women's movement were women able to be leaders.

1920s and 1930s

The 1920s opened on a note of hope as far as Irish women were concerned. After the Easter Rising, while the men who had not been executed languished in English jails, it was the women who had kept the nationalist movement going by fund-raising for the Prisoners' Defence Fund and by securing representation for Ireland at the Peace Conference. In 1918 they received the vote on the same terms as British women, that is, property-owning women over thirty years of age were enfranchised. In 1922 the Free State granted all Irish women over twenty-one the vote. English women had to wait another six years for this privilege. In addition, the declaration of equal citizenship for women in the 1916 Proclamation was confirmed in Article 3 of the 1922 Free State Constitution which declared that: 'every person, without distinction of sex, shall enjoy the privileges and be subject to the obligations of such citizenship'.

The diminished role played by Irish women in political and public life after the establishment of the Free State partly reflected a general European period of reaction after the successes of the suffragette movement. This reaction intensified with the rise of fascist ideology which sought to thrust women back into the home. The 1920s and particularly the 1930s were grim decades for feminism in Europe as women lost the focus provided by the suffragist cause and their energies became scattered into a number of different pressure groups. Amongst these the campaign for peace seemed particularly urgent. But there were features in this anti-feminist backlash peculiar to Ireland. Many prominent female activists – Maud Gonne, Constance Markievicz, Hanna Sheehy Skeffington, Rosamond Jacob – opposed the Treaty and their uncompromising republicanism often alienated contemporaries and led to these women being sidelined in public life, not to mention imprisoned. Added to this was the growing influence of the Roman Catholic Church encouraging Irish women out of the public sphere and back into the home.

Irish women after 1922 experienced a gradual erosion of their political rights. In 1925 the government sought to bring in restrictions on women's employment in the civil service, thus excluding women from having a voice in shaping policy on economics, health and welfare. Maryann Valiulis has written extensively about the Juries Act of 1927 which exempted women from jury service and thus ensured only one gender's voice was heard in the legal process.[3] At stake was women's right to participate in the public life of their country. Were women to be allowed to be full citizens or were they to be confined to the roles of wives and mothers which was what the State seemed to be offering?

As Caitríona Beaumont points out in her article, 'Women and the Politics of Equality: The Irish Women's Movement 1930–1943' (Valiulis and O'Dowd, 1997, 173–88), a number of women's groups protested against the 1925 Civil Service (Amendment) Bill and the 1927 Juries Bill, among them the Irish Women's Citizens' and Local Government Association, the National Council of Women and the National University Women Graduates' Association. Despite the relative success of their campaign (the Civil Service Act was suspended and the Juries Act was amended), this did not prevent the government from bringing in further restrictions on women's professional lives in the following decade. Moreover, as Beaumont demonstrates, these Dublin-based, middle-class organizations failed to find widespread support amongst Irish women generally. Nor did these women's groups unite to protest against Section 17 of the Criminal Law (Amendment) Bill of 1934 preventing the sale and importation of birth control devices in the Free State.

---

[3]　　See M. Valiulis, 1992, 43–60. See also M. Valiulis, 2001, 152–8.

In employment, more restrictions were brought in. In 1932 the marriage bar was formally introduced for teachers. Already, in 1926, only six per cent of married women worked in Ireland, a figure which remained unchanged until the 1960s.[4] Working conditions for all women worsened with the Conditions of Employment Bill of 1935 which allowed the government to limit the employment of women in a given industry. Women were channeled into less influential professions such as nursing, typing, clerical work and shop keeping. Women like Dorothy Macardle, who had been active in the nationalist movement, protested against the Bill and Hanna Sheehy Skeffington likened the attitude of the minister responsible for the Bill to that of a fascist dictator (Ward, 1995, 163). The marriage bars had the double effect of discouraging women from investing too much energy in their careers and employers from promoting them. They were also in clear contravention of Article 3 of the 1922 Free State constitution granting women citizenship on equal terms with men.

These efforts to restrict women to the domestic sphere culminated in Eamon de Valera's 1937 Constitution founded on the family unit. Article 41.1 of the Constitution states:

> The State recognizes the family as the natural primary and fundamental unit group of Society, and as a moral institution possessing inalienable and imprescriptible rights, antecedent and superior to all positive law.

Carol Coulter provides one explanation as to why the family played such a central role in the Constitution and in the life of the Irish State, namely that the enormous contribution to the War of Independence made by many republican families compelled the nationalists when they came to power to ensure the practical and symbolic importance of the family in the nation (Coulter, 1993, 10). Julia O'Faolain's novel, *No Country for Young Men*, portrays the involvement of the members of one such family, the Clancys, in the struggle for independence and the consequent encroachment of politics into the domestic sphere:

> What bound the family together was their Republicanism. In the yard, behind the family pub, a coal pile and stacked porter barrels provided a ladder for quickly scaling the back wall in time of need. Unknown young men came and went unquestioned, sleeping on the kitchen settle or in the guest bedroom. Kathleen's *fiancé*, Owen, was active. Eamonn, their elder brother had been killed when Judith was fifteen. Seamus too was with the lads. (O'Faolain, 1980, 20)

The family had been the locus of resistance to the occupier and the transmitter of nationalist aspirations and therefore it was natural that it was around the family that the 1937 Constitution was based. However this had implications for women's lives. For the sake of the nation, woman's role was to be confined to the home where she was to ensure the stability of the state, the preservation of the family and the upholding of Catholic values. This is most clearly stated in Article 41.2 of the Constitution which reads:

---

[4] O'Dowd, 1987, 27.

In particular the State recognizes that by her life within the home, woman gives to the State a support without which the common good cannot be achieved.

The State shall therefore endeavour to ensure that mothers shall not be obliged by economic necessity to engage in labour to the neglect of their duties in the home.

There are, as Yvonne Scannell has pointed out (Hayes and Urquhart 2001, 71–8), two ways of looking at this article: it may be read as a tribute to mothers and as providing them with economic protection or it may be seen to imply that the natural vocation of all women is in the home (note the slippage between 'woman' and 'mothers', implying that the two are synonymous). In practice, it was the second, most restrictive, interpretation which held sway among Irish legislators for the next thirty years. Fixed constructs of gender thus played a central role in the building of the Irish nation. Politics and public life were regarded as masculine spheres and women were confined to a single identity, the domestic. Moreover, as Caitríona Beaumont points out, the Constitution's seeming endorsement of Irish motherhood did not translate into practical help for mothers such as family allowances or free health care (Beaumont, 1999, 102).

Women's groups at the time were well aware of the dangers to their citizenship posed by the Constitution. The National University Graduates' Association joined forces with the Joint Committee of Women's Societies and Social Workers and the National Council of Women to demand the removal of the offending articles from the Constitution. Although de Valera caved in to pressure and deleted reference to women's 'inadequate strength' from Article 45 dealing with work, he was nevertheless determined to safeguard the male role as breadwinner. Cumann na mBan remained silent on this important issue and Margaret Ward speculates that if they had mobilized they might have helped defeat de Valera (Ward, 1989, 240–5). As it was, the Constitution received lukewarm support in the referendum, being passed by 685,105 votes in favor and 526,945 against, with a 31 per cent abstention level. Margaret Ward's anthology, *In Their Own Voice*, provides extracts of protests by women of the period. Kate O'Callaghan, commenting on the offending articles dealing with women, is quoted as saying: 'These articles I regard as a betrayal of the 1916 promise of "Equal Rights and Equal Opportunities guaranteed to all citizens". They are a grave danger to the future position of women' (Ward, 1995, 166). Hanna Sheehy Skeffington remarked that in certain parts of the Constitution: 'Mr de Valera shows a mawkish distrust of women which has always coloured his outlook' (Ward, 1995, 165).

In 1938, the Women's Social and Progressive League published an *Open Letter to Women Voters of Ireland* urging them to vote only for candidates who would defend women's equal citizenship. In the course of the letter they detailed current injustices to women. These included the marriage bar for primary school teachers and compulsory retirement at 60, thus depriving them of full pension rights; the lower pay of female secondary school teachers; the lack of fixed rates of wages for women agricultural workers; inferior pay and opportunities for female civil servants; exemption from jury service.

Mary Leland's novel, *The Killeen*, published in 1985 but set in Cork in the 1930s, vividly conveys the repressive nature of Irish life at this time. The symbol of the 'killeen', a graveyard for unbaptized babies, is used to portray Ireland as a place where individual aspirations are stifled. In particular, girls' education is seen as unimportant: Margaret's mother refuses to countenance the suggestion that Margaret attend senior school. At this time secondary education was fee-paying and therefore largely for the middle classes. Until 1967, when secondary education became available to a majority of young people in Ireland, most girls only received primary education.[5] Margaret, coming from a small farm, is directed towards kitchen work in a convent where a kindly nun encourages her thirst for reading until she falls pregnant, when naturally all education for her ends.

Like *The Killeen*, Kate O'Brien's novel, *The Land of Spices*, published in 1941, demonstrates that education for girls could not be taken for granted in the period and had to be fought for. Anna Murphy, from a middle-class family, has been allowed to complete her secondary education but succeeds in following her brother to university only through the intervention of the Reverend Mother, who applies pressure to her reluctant family. Female students had been admitted to Trinity College, Dublin as early as 1904 but their presence was severely regulated, with the result that their position in the life of the university was marginal. The 1908 Universities Act had admitted women to the National University on an equal footing with men as regards teaching and examinations but in practice the university remained male-dominated in its teaching staff and governing authorities (Cullen, 1987).[6]

The period under consideration was a regressive one for Irish women. As Maryann Valiulis demonstrates in 'Neither Feminist nor Flapper: The Ecclesiastical Construction of the Ideal Irish Woman' (O'Dowd and Wichert, 1995, 168–78), both church and state contributed to the construct of Irish womanhood as pure and good and, above all, domestic. Though women did protest against the all-pervasive nature of this stereotype they failed to make much headway, perhaps because, as Margaret Ward suggests, these same women were often associated with the kind of radical republicanism which had by now fallen out of favor (Ward, 1995, 167–8). In addition, as Caitríona Beaumont points out, middle-class feminist groups attacking the government's gendered legislation failed to attract widespread support amongst women during the 1930s because their concerns seemed too remote from the everyday struggle of most Irish women to feed and clothe their families (Valiulis and O'Dowd, 1997, 185). Beaumont argues that non-feminist organizations like the Irish Countrywomen's Association, founded in 1910 to improve conditions for rural women and which concentrated on women in the home and health care issues, did more to help ordinary women in their daily lives. The situation is rather similar to that in England during the inter-war period where the New Feminist emphasis on women's roles as wives and mothers did succeed in bringing in some improvements in women's lives (Ingman 1998, 18–20). However, it can be argued that, as in England, the emphasis on women in the home during this period did little to advance the cause of women in professional and public life in Ireland. In Jennifer Johnston's novel, *Two Moons* (1998), eighty-year-old Mimi, looking back on this period, reflects:

---

[5] For an account of the gradual expansion of secondary education in Ireland, see Brown, 1981/2004, 239–44.

[6] There are many interesting first-hand accounts by women of life at UCD down the century in Macdona, 2001. For women at Trinity, see Parkes (ed.), 2004.

My expectations, like most of the women of my generation, were negligible; a family, a reasonable life, safety, with luck for ever. In return we ran good homes, were loyal wives, loving mothers, smiled at the right people; we saw our men right. It sounds pretty despicable now, but then it was the natural scheme of things. (Johnston, 1998, 192)

1940s and 1950s

The economic, political and cultural stagnation of the 1940s and 1950s is well-documented, and Ireland in these years has been memorably summed up by Terence Brown as: 'a mediocre, dishevelled, often neurotic and depressed petit-bourgeois society that atrophied for want of a liberating idea' (Brown, 1981/2004, 146). It was a period when the Roman Catholic Church held sway over the nation, when literary censorship was in operation and when the construct of women as wives and mothers was in full force. This is the background out of which many of Mary Lavin's short stories are written, and they vividly depict the social and material constraints on Irish people's lives at the time. In 'The Will', for example, a Lavin story dating from the 1940s, the Conroy siblings are thrown into turmoil by the unconventional behavior of their sister Lally. Lally has married a man of inferior social standing and now, to the Conroys' mortification, keeps lodgers and sends her children to free schools. At their mother's funeral, her siblings try unsuccessfully to bribe Lally into giving up her boarding house, arguing that she is bringing disgrace on their family. This is a picture of a society trapped by the minutiae of social convention, and in the end even Lally's imaginative spirit is crushed by the materialism around her.[7] Another Lavin story, 'A Gentle Soul', dating from the early 1950s, illustrates the searing effect of social convention on Rose Darker who has been prevented by class snobbery and her own timidity from marrying her father's farm laborer, despite their mutual love. Lavin's stories portray the Catholic middle class in this period as rigid, convention-bound and materialistic. Her analysis of the effect of contemporary constructs of femininity on women's lives in particular will be examined in a later chapter.

In this period, also, the pressures on a girl who wished to enter secondary school but whose family could not afford to send her remained. They are referred to in Evelyn Conlon's novel, *Stars in the Daytime* (1989). Growing up on a small farm in Monaghan in the 1950s Rose is encouraged by her mother to think of going on to secondary school but in order to do so she must win a scholarship. The stress this puts on Rose is enormous and when she arrives at secondary school she is conscious of bearing the weight of generations of education-starved women on her shoulders:

She was the daughter of Phyllis, of her grandmother, and of every dead great aunt who had wanted to learn to read. Starving ghosts of women stood friendlily behind her, peering into her Latin books, frowning with her when she couldn't understand something, nudging each other gleefully when they saw their country mentioned in

---

[7]   For a discussion of this story see J. Heaney, '"No Sanctuary from Hatred": A Reappraisal of Mary Lavin's Outsiders', *Irish University Review*, 28 (2), 294–307.

history books, never once wondering why they weren't there with their brothers. (Conlon, 1989, 53–4)

So Conlon pays tribute to the generations of Irish women who, before the days of free secondary education, longed for but never received schooling.

The day to day reality of women's lives in the period is outlined by Caitríona Clear in her study, *Women of the House: Women's Household Work in Ireland 1922–1961* (2000). Clear details the hard physical labor of the home maker whose work involved the household washing, preparation of food, lighting fires, baking bread, sewing, darning and knitting. Rural women added to these tasks milking, feeding livestock, making their own butter, helping with the hay or the potato picking. Like Rose's mother in *Stars in the Daytime*, many women, both rural and urban, lacked running water and electricity. Their tasks might also involve caring for elderly relatives as well as any number of children. Like Beaumont, Clear makes the point that middle-class feminists of this period were mostly out of touch with the realities of working-class women's lives and failed to help improve the lives of women bearing and rearing large numbers of children in poverty.

Not surprisingly, perhaps, there was large scale emigration of single women during the 1940s and 1950s caused not only by poverty and unemployment but, as Pauric Travers argues in 'Emigration and Gender: The Case of Ireland, 1922–60' (O'Dowd and Wichert, 1995, 187–99), by women's real dissatisfaction with their life and status in Ireland. Travers cites the evidence of the Irish Housewives' Association to the Commission on Emigration asserting that female emigration was not only a product of poor conditions on small farms, but of the marriage bar and of the inferior status of women generally in Irish society. Sharon Lambert gives the figures: between 1926 and 1951, 52,000 Irish women emigrated to the US and a further 180,000 went to Britain (Hayes and Urquhart, 2001, 181).

In her novel, *Florrie's Girls* (1989), Maeve Kelly portrays seventeen-year-old Caitlin Cosgrave (Cos) leaving Ireland in the late 1940s in order to train as a nurse in England. Cos' reasons for leaving are partly economic: 'There's no room for me at home. Jimmy is to get the place even though I'm better with the stock than he is' (Kelly, 1989, 15). The family farm in Kerry can only support one family; when the eldest son, Jimmy, marries, the other siblings have to leave. But Cos' reasons for emigrating are not simply economic. She has, after all, received an offer of marriage from Chris, a neighboring farmer. She refuses this because she desires a larger life than is available to her in Ireland: '"There's a big world out there," I said. "A world of ideas and music and other people"' (Kelly, 1989, 19).

During the 1940s and 1950s, then, the situation of women in Ireland remained largely unchanged. They were confined to domestic roles, restricted in their professional lives and forbidden access to contraception, abortion and divorce. '1940s Ireland was a living tomb for women', Nuala O'Faolain declares in her autobiographical memoir, *Are You Somebody?* (O'Faolain, 1996, 15) and she gives a heart-wrenching description of the mental and physical toll that bearing and raising nine children took on her mother's life. Recently, however, the picture of Ireland as insular and conservative during these years has been challenged. In *An Age of Innocence: Irish Culture 1930–1960* (1998), Brian Fallon argues that Ireland was less impoverished culturally and socially during this period than has been supposed and makes the point that many seeds were planted in these decades which came to fruition later. Though he is right to point to the danger of taking a monolithic view of the period, Fallon's arguments are not always entirely convincing and he has little to say specifically about women's lives.

For a re-evaluation of women's lives during the period we must turn to the work of Caitríona Beaumont, Carol Coulter, Caitríona Clear and Mary Daly which challenges the view that early twentieth-century feminism disappeared under the new Irish state and only re-emerged in the 1970s. In 'Women and the Politics of Equality: The Irish Women's Movement 1930–1943' (Valiulis and O'Dowd, 1997, 173–88), Caitríona Beaumont argues that these years were not such a low point for Irish women as they have traditionally been seen. She regards non-feminist organizations like the Irish Countrywomen's Association (ICA) and the Irish Housewives' Association (IHA) as providing a vital link between the suffrage campaign and the women's liberation movement of the 1970s. The ICA was concerned to alleviate some of the drudgery for rural women. As well as providing classes in domestic science, handicrafts, farming skills, music and drama, the ICA encouraged women to get involved in local government and campaigned for provision of running water and electricity, the introduction of school meals and nursing schemes. The Irish Housewives' Association, founded in 1942 by a group of Protestant women, some of whom had links back to the suffrage movement, also aimed to improve the quality of women's lives in the home and campaigned for price control, the provision of school meals and a general amelioration in the lives of the poor and unemployed.

Hilda Tweedy's account of the IHA, *A Link in the Chain: The Story of the Irish Housewives' Association 1942–1992*, makes clear that organizations like these provided an outlet for women who were now generally excluded from politics and the world of work. Tweedy, a founder-member of the IHA, describes how that organization drew on strategies used earlier in suffrage campaigns in order to intervene in state policy. By centering their work on women in the home, the place where ecclesiastical and state authorities wished them to be, they made it difficult for governments to attack them. Whether this was a clever ploy or a regressive step depends on your point of view. Hanna Sheehy Skeffington said she would not join any organization which had the word 'housewife' in it. Nevertheless organizations like the IHA allowed women to develop strategies for challenging the status quo despite being excluded from public life. A quotation from Rosaleen Mills in *The Irish Housewife* of 1949 underlines this point: 'To the Politician the Housewife is a haunting question mark. She shows signs of cynicism about political promises, and she cannot be trusted to accept party slogans with proper trust' (*The Field Day Anthology*, vol. V, 170). Hilda Tweedy sees the IHA as providing a vital link between the suffrage campaigns and the feminist movements of the 1970s.

There were some successes. In 1944 children's allowances were introduced for every third and subsequent child, and this was extended to every second child in 1952. However, feminist groups failed to ensure that the allowance would be paid directly to the mother. Noël Browne's Mother and Child Bill providing state care for babies and maternity services may have been defeated in 1951 due to the efforts of the Catholic hierarchy who argued that the Bill usurped the father's duty to provide for his family, but free health care for mothers and babies up to six weeks was introduced by 1953. There was a great improvement in maternal mortality in the period: in 1961 27 women died in childbirth as compared with 297 women in 1923 (Clear, 2000, 96).

In her essay '"Oh, Kathleen Ni Houlihan, Your Way's a Thorny Way!" The Condition of Women in Twentieth-Century Ireland' (Bradley and Valiulis, 1997, 102–26), Mary Daly argues that too much focus on equal rights feminism has obscured the good work done by non-feminist organizations during the 1940s and 1950s, but she also points out that the high level of marital fertility in Ireland until the 1960s meant that many women simply did not have the leisure to pursue political activity outside the home. A similar point is made by Carol Coulter in *The Hidden Tradition*. Women who did not join any organization might be involved in running the family farm single-handed while the men emigrated to find work. Even if the man worked the farm, the women often controlled the finances or were involved in autonomous farm production centered on poultry, eggs or pig-rearing. Coulter argues that an Anglo-American feminist analysis of the dependent urban housewife cannot be straightforwardly applied to Irish women's lives in this period (Coulter, 1993, 38). To do so would be to obscure the complexities of women's lives at this period and the real energies with which they managed their daily lives.

In *Women of the House* Caitríona Clear challenges the view that there was any consistent ideology during the period to relegate women to the domestic sphere. She argues that women in public life had their defenders as well as their attackers among male politicians, churchmen and journalists and reminds us that women sat in both houses of the Oireachtas. In addition for some occupations, such as white-collar secretarial and office work, the number of women working substantially increased during this period (Clear, 2000, 16–17). Her arguments are not entirely convincing; for instance while it is true that females competed in school-leaving examinations on equal terms with males, this bald fact fails to take into account the psychological disincentive to take their education seriously on girls conditioned into wife and mother roles. Nevertheless, Clear's study does provide a more nuanced view of these decades.

From a reading of these historians it is evident that evaluation of this period depends on one's definition of feminism. If the emphasis is on male-dominated political life, then clearly there were few gains for women; if feminism is extended to include women in the home then organizations like the ICA and the IHA may be regarded as carrying on the struggle to improve women's lives during these years. Tweedy's account provides a direct link with 1970s feminism by showing that the IHA was instrumental in persuading the government in 1970 to form the Council for the Status of Women, from which developed the influential Commission on the Status of Women.

1960s and 1970s

In 1959 Sean Lemass took over as Taoiseach from Eamon de Valera and implemented the program for economic development drafted by T. K. Whitaker to open up Ireland to foreign investors and give priority to export industries. There was a general air of renewal in the country and the tide of emigration turned. There was some progress for women also during the 1960s. Caitríona Clear has shown that by 1961 paid work had become more common for young and single women and was even encouraged (Clear, 2000, 22). Worries about the flow of female emigration led to the marriage bar coming under attack. Clear argues that during the 1960s life for women in the home was slightly ameliorated. Women's general health had improved from the 1940s, infant and maternal mortality fell, standards of housing and hygiene rose and men began to associate themselves with housework and childcare (Clear, 2000, 193–202).

Nevertheless, conditions for many women remained unchanged. For half a million Irish women, full-time education still ceased at fourteen and the 1966 Census showed that only .02 per cent of the female population had received a university education (Rose, 1975, 63). Even those who did attend university might devalue the experience, or have it devalued for them, in comparison with the business of finding a husband and having children. 'I don't really care if you get a degree or not,' Nuala O'Faolain's mother wrote to her. 'I'd far rather see you with a husband and a few kids' (O'Faolain, 1996, 89). This was despite her mother's own wretched unhappiness in marriage.

Catherine Shannon points out that the pressure in poor urban working-class families for children to secure a job as quickly as possible meant women often took on low-skilled, poorly paid factory or service jobs (Bradley and Valiulis, 1997, 260). In 1961 average female earnings were still only 53 per cent of male earnings. Small farmers' wives continued to struggle without running water in some cases and without benefit of such modern conveniences as refrigerators and washing machines. Male dominance in the home continued: a woman could not open a bank account or take out a loan without her husband's signature. Asked in an interview to sum up the 1950s and 1960s, Mary Dorcey described these years as follows:

> Silence. Repression. Censorship. Long dark winters. Poor food. Nuns and priests everywhere. Drab clothes. Censorship of books and films. Fear and suspicion surrounding anything to do with the body or the personal life. The near total repression of ideas and information. A Catholic state for a Catholic people. (O'Carroll and Collins, 1995, 25).

Edna O'Brien's first published work, *The Country Girls* (1960), underlines the drudgery and isolation of rural women's lives. Caithleen Brady and her mother live in fear of violence and abuse from the alcoholic and feckless Mr Brady. Since the family unit is inviolate, the abuse cannot be publicly acknowledged. Mr Brady is thought of in the neighborhood as 'a gentleman, a decent man who wouldn't hurt a fly' (O'Brien, 1987, 27). In her article, '"To Bounce a Boot Off Her Now and Then": Domestic Violence in Post-Famine Ireland' (Valiulis and O'Dowd, 1997, 125–43), Elizabeth Steiner-Scott reveals that such silence over domestic violence was widespread at the time:

> Following the foundation of the Irish Free State in 1922, reports of wife-beating declined in the press. The new State showed in many ways that it was reluctant to inquire too closely into what was considered to be the private domain of the family, largely taking its lead from the Catholic hierarchy who considered such intervention to be indicative of socialist, and even communist, social policy. (Valiulis and O'Dowd, 1997, 125)

Domestic violence features in Dorothy Nelson's novel, *In Night's City* (1982) which registers a protest, through the mouth of Esther Kavanagh, against Catholic idealization of motherhood. Fifty-three at the time of her husband's death in 1970, Esther recalls her life during the 1950s and 1960s married to a violent and abusive man:

> I thought how easy it was for the priests and nuns to preach about motherhood when they didn't have to pay for it. They didn't have to give their whole life to exalt the motherhood they worshipped from the altar of God.
> Then I had Sara. And then two more. And I thought how the same 'motherhood' cut through me like a knife as I lay in the dark waiting for them to exalt me while I listened for his footsteps on the stairs knowing how he'd beat me if I refused him. The people who preached that word didn't know the meaning of it. If they lived what they preached they would have found out that motherhood wasn't a thing to be welcomed with open arms but sleepless nights followed by thrashings and beatings that left no place for dignity or reverence or whatever it is they wanted you to believe 'motherhood' was. (Nelson, 1982, 64)

In her account of her involvement with the feminist movement, *Sisters: The Personal Story of an Irish Feminist* (1982), June Levine encapsulates the social climate in Ireland during the 1960s in her comment that having a baby outside marriage was regarded by some as more shameful than being tried for manslaughter (Levine, 1982, 91). Girls gave birth in secret away from their families and handed their babies over for adoption. Nuala O'Faolain's memoir about growing up in those times confirms this oppressive atmosphere: 'No matter how progressive the circle you moved in, you lost almost everything if you became pregnant outside marriage' (O'Faolain, 1996, 87). Levine concludes: 'Women may have been thinking in Ireland in those days, but they had not yet found a voice' (Levine, 1982, 85).

This was to change: under the influence of the international feminist movement, feminist activism re-emerged in Ireland in the following decade. In 1970, the Irish Women's Liberation Movement was launched, 'over cups of coffee in Bewley's café on Westmoreland Street, Dublin', according to June Levine (*The Field Day Anthology*, vol. V, 179). Founder members included Levine herself, Mary Maher, Mary Kenny, Mary Anderson, Nell McCafferty, Nuala Fennell and Mairin de Burca. Many of these women worked in journalism and indeed female journalists were to do a lot in the 1970s to highlight discrimination against women. They were middle class, articulate and knew how to use the media. The IWLM's manifesto, *Chains or Change? The Civil Wrongs of Irish Women*, made five demands: equal pay, equality in the law, equal educational and employment opportunities, access to contraception, and justice for single mothers, deserted wives and widows. The manifesto was delivered in an explosive edition of the Radio Telefis Éireann (RTÉ) television program, *The Late Late Show*, on 6 March 1971. Women's issues began to be discussed on Irish radio and television. Newspapers started feminist women's pages.

The first mass meeting of the IWLM, chaired by Nell McCafferty, was organized in the Mansion House in Dublin on 14 April 1971. Over a thousand women attended, exceeding all expectations. From this meeting it emerged that contraception was a major issue for women and hence was born the idea of a Contraceptive Train. On 22 May 1971 forty-seven women boarded a train to Belfast intending to buy contraceptives and declare them at Irish customs on their return as a way of protesting against the Republic's ban on contraception. They were greeted by cheering crowds and embarrassed Gardaí officers on their return to Connolly Station. Contraception had at last become an issue which could be discussed in public.

By September 1971, however, splits began to emerge in the IWLM. It had moved too quickly. Its alignment with left wing issues and its demand for legalized contraception upset the class and religious affiliations of some members. Nuala Fennell resigned in protest at the direction the movement was taking, particularly at what she perceived as its anti-men bias. She went on to found Action, Information, Motivation (AIM), composed of both women and men, and called for a revision in the laws regarding marriage and the family. Mary Kenny left Ireland to take up a post as features editor of the *Evening Standard*. Mary Anderson resigned and joined Sinn Féin. The IWLM splintered off into local associations and more specialized, single-issue groups and organizations (Connelly, 2003, 129).

However, the publication in December 1972 of the report of the National Commission on the Status of Women mobilized a wider spectrum of support amongst women for change. The report gave forty-nine recommendations for legislative reform and provided comprehensive evidence of the discrimination faced by women in employment, education and social policy. The Council for the Status of Women was set up in 1973 to monitor implementation of these recommendations. Hilda Tweedy was its first chairperson, thus providing a direct link with the IHA.

Ireland's accession to the EC in 1973 aided women in their legal battles and the right of appeal to the European Courts of Justice and Human Rights was used in a number of instances to alter existing Irish law. A series of legal challenges on the issue of contraception, initially filed by Mary Robinson in 1973 in the *Magee vs. the Attorney General* case, were presented to the European Court and eventually resulted in the Health and Family Planning Act of 1979. Married couples could now procure contraceptives provided they had a doctor's prescription.

Other progress in the 1970s included equal pay legislation introduced in 1977 and the appointment of the first woman to the Cabinet since Constance Markievicz, Máire Geoghegan-Quinn, Minister for the Gaeltacht. In 1977 the national election gave a demonstration of the emergence of women's political power. Twenty-five women ran in the Dáil elections and six won seats, doubling the number of female Teachta Dáls (TD)s. Nuala Fennell ran as an Independent on the grounds that women were being ignored by the mainstream political parties. She failed to get elected but her campaign did so well that it made her point for her. She subsequently entered the Dáil in 1981 as a Fine Gael TD. The late 1970s also saw the setting up in Dublin of the Well Woman Service and the Rape Crisis Centre.

Lesbians too, previously so invisible in the life of the Irish nation, began to organize. Joni Crone pinpoints 1978 as a crucial year for Irish lesbians when, inspired by a women's conference held at Trinity College, they came together to organize a specifically lesbian conference, the Women's Conference on Lesbianism (O'Carroll and Collins, 1995, 63–6).

There were limits, however, to Ireland's embrace of modernity as Grainne reflects in Julia O'Faolain's novel, *No Country for Young Men*:

> Laws here had not changed, nor people's attitudes underneath. Not for women. Like a group riding the last steps of an escalator, Ireland moved with the times but stayed in the rear. Women could now live openly with their lovers but legal protection lagged. There was no divorce. Alimony – if you obtained one abroad – was hard to collect. (O'Faolain, 1980, 101)

The scandal, which came to light only in 2003, of symphysiotomies performed on pregnant women in certain Irish hospitals from the 1950s to the 1980s would seem to confirm Grainne's view. The rationale behind these operations, which involved sawing through the pubic bones to aid labor, was a fear that cesarean sections would result in women being reluctant to become pregnant again and thus lead to an increased use of contraception or sterilization. This barbaric practice was inflicted on 343 women in Our Lady of Lourdes hospital in Drogheda alone. Women are only now beginning to come forward to talk about the appalling long-term after-effects of symphysiotomies (incontinence, lameness, chronic pain). Whether they will receive compensation from the State remains to be seen.

The 1980s to the present

In her chapter on 'The Women's Movement in the Republic of Ireland 1970–1990', Ailbhe Smyth describes the late 1970s and early 1980s as years of consolidation (Smyth, 1993, 250). The feminists had forced mainstream politicians to take notice of their demands and the gains continued. In 1980 Mella Carroll was appointed first female High Court judge. In 1982, Mary Harney, Mary Flaherty and Alice Glenn entered the Dáil under their own steam with no links to political families. In 1980 the mainstream national television program, *The Late Late Show*, featured an interview with Joni Crone who spoke openly about her lesbianism.

Then came the years of backlash, 1983 to 1990, aided by the economic recession of the mid-1980s and by the strengthening of conservative opinion following Pope John Paul's visit to Ireland in September 1979. Evelyn Conlon's short story, 'The Park', recalls the Pope's visit and explores what it felt like to be a dissenter on the day of his celebration of Mass in the Phoenix Park. She sums it up: 'Those who thought otherwise were, simply, invisible for the day' (Conlon, 1993, 67). As a result of this conservative backlash, in 1983 a national referendum brought in the so-called 'pro-life' amendment to Article 40 of the Constitution still in force in Ireland today. The amendment states that the right to life of an Irish mother is not superior to that of her unborn child. Another referendum in 1986 upheld the existing ban on divorce.

Various shocking events confirmed the problems still faced by Irish women around the issues of pregnancy and childbirth. In 1982, Eileen Flynn, a teacher in a Catholic convent school, lost her job for becoming pregnant while living with a married man. In 1984, the cases of Ann Lovett and Joanne Hayes horrified the nation. Fourteen-year-old Ann Lovett gave birth in secret and alone. Both mother and child died. In the same year Joanne Hayes gave birth secretly, the baby died and she was later charged with the murder of another baby. The charges were dropped for lack of evidence but the following year Hayes was obliged to endure a protracted public tribunal where her personal and sexual behavior was dissected.[8]

During these years of right wing backlash, there nevertheless developed, as Ailbhe Smyth has argued, a feminist counter-culture with a focus on education and the arts (Smyth, 1993, 265). Women writers and artists became more visible, feminist publishing houses started up and in the universities Women's Studies programs developed. As Smyth puts it: 'the tide was on the turn and Irish women were once again signalling their desire for change and their determination to bring it about' (Smyth, 1993, 266). The culmination of this quiet revolution was the election in 1990 of Mary Robinson, a feminist and civil rights lawyer, as Ireland's first female President. Her election was regarded as a triumph for those supporting a modernizing liberal agenda over those associated with nationalist and Catholic traditionalism. Her victory speech of 9 November acknowledged this:

> I was elected by men and women of all parties and none, by many with great moral courage, who stepped out from the faded flags of the Civil War and voted for a new Ireland, above all by the women of Ireland, mna na hEireann, who instead of rocking the cradle, rocked the system and who came out massively to make their mark on the ballot paper on a new Ireland.

In her inaugural speech, Robinson declared that: 'The Ireland I will be representing is a new Ireland, open, tolerant, inclusive.' She would represent the poor, Travellers, the disabled, emigrants and women. In December 1992 she invited representatives of the lesbian and gay community from both sides of the border to Áras an Uachtaráin and Kieran Rose, who was present, describes the general feeling that they had been welcomed symbolically into the Irish nation (Rose, 1994, 34). Fintan O'Toole, summing up the significance of Mary Robinson's Presidency, said simply: 'She has helped us to re-imagine Ireland' (*The Field Day Anthology*, vol. V, 287).[9]

Ireland in the 1990s displayed a growing national confidence, economic optimism and cultural sophistication as it entered the global economy. The so-called Celtic Tiger ushered in a period of rapid change: urbanization and secularization continued apace. The 1990s also led to an increase in materialism, individualism and general selfishness and not everyone benefited from the new prosperity.[10] The era is evoked in Kate O'Riordan's novel, *The Memory Stones* (2003), through the thoughts of Nell Hennessy who returns to Ireland after thirty years:

> Celtic Tiger, Riverdance, Bailey's Irish Cream, Guinness sexified, advertisements in French urging graduates *home* to work [...] Computer companies seeking support technicians, property developments in Dublin satellite towns. As far away as Leitrim is satellite now, Nell observes with astonishment. Celtic clothes, Celtic jewellery, Celtic glass, Celtic bars [...] Beautiful tinted photographs of islands off the west coast. Second

---

[8]　For documents on both these cases, see *The Field Day Anthology*, vol. V, 1435–44.

[9]　For more on the impact of Mary Robinson's election, see Ailbhe Smyth, 1992, 61–75.

[10]　For the downside of the Celtic Tiger see Kirby, Gibbons and Cronin (eds), 2002.

homes in Portugal. Offshore investment companies. A country proudly selling itself. A country for sale. (O'Riordan, 2003, 40)

With regard to women, in 1991 the government established the Second Commission on the Status of Women. Reporting to the government in 1993 it was highly critical of the absence of women from influential political positions and recommended the introduction of a quota system to encourage political parties to recruit more women. In 1993 also, the Irish Senate declared homosexuality legal. Lesbians and gays felt they could at last be, in the words of Kieran Rose, 'full and equal citizens of this Irish Republic' (Rose, 1994, 59). In 1995 the ban on divorce was removed.

The drift away from Catholic teaching accelerated during the 1990s as Irish people became disillusioned over the Church's rigid position on contraception, divorce and mixed marriage. The flood of revelations about the cruelty and abuse of children in church-run orphanages and children's homes added to the disenchantment, as did the bringing to light of the sexual abuse of children by Catholic priests. The Catholic hierarchy's apparent slowness to act on this problem only increased its unpopularity. In her novel, *Necessary Treasons* (1985), Maeve Kelly describes the disillusionment of her heroine, Eleanor, over the misogyny of the Catholic Church:

> Her life had once been regulated and encompassed by faith in this one Church and yet she had been forced by her very need for truth to abandon it [...] no woman with a shred of self-respect could be a member of a church which so obviously despised and feared her. (Kelly, 1985/1991, 117–18)

Eleanor's loss of trust in the Catholic Church is not presented as an isolated phenomenon: 'Her women patients had lost confidence in the wisdom of a celibate male clergy' (Kelly, 1985/1991, 120).

There remained the thorny problem of abortion. In 1992 a High Court order initially prevented fourteen-year-old Miss X, pregnant as the result of rape, from traveling to England for an abortion. In what became known as the 'X' Case, the Supreme Court subsequently reversed the High Court order and ruled that abortion is legal where there is a substantial threat to the life of the woman. The case aroused strong feelings on both sides of the argument and sparked large public demonstrations in Dublin. The implications of the 'X' Case for Irish women will be examined in more detail in our discussion of Edna O'Brien's novel, *Down by the River* (1996), which is based on the case. The 'X' Case led to a referendum on abortion in November 1992 when the public was asked to vote on three issues. Women's right to travel and their right to freedom of information were passed. The right of Irish women to have an abortion if the unborn child threatens the life of the mother was defeated.

The 'X' Case was followed in 1995 by the 'C' Case where a teenager in state care was involved in a court case over her right to travel to England for an abortion following rape. The case was resolved in her favor. In March 2002 the Irish public was asked to vote again to disallow abortion on the grounds of threatened suicide. The referendum was narrowly defeated. 50.42 per cent voted against removing suicide as grounds for abortion. 49.58 per cent voted in favor. The issue again aroused strong feelings on both sides but in the end only 42.9 per cent of the electorate turned out to vote. The entire debate illustrates the way in which the pregnant female body has been used to define the boundaries of the Irish nation, a point we shall come back to in our discussion of *Down by the River*.

The situation of women in Ireland has not been one of gradual change; rather it has been a series of sudden leaps forward followed by periods of regression. But by the end of the 1990s women had made too many gains for them to be taken away. Mary Robinson's highly successful term of office was followed by the election to the Presidency in 1997 of another feminist and human rights lawyer, Mary McAleese.

Much remains to be done. Women in Ireland continue to be under-represented in politics, in business, and in the churches. In the 1997 general election twenty women deputies replaced twenty-three outgoing female TDs. Frances Gardiner makes the following comment on the failure of the large political parties to recruit women candidates:

> Perhaps the difference between women's apparently easier access to the presidency than the Dáil lies in the caring Mother Ireland role (and with little real power) acceptable in a woman president; at the cutting edge of political power, by contrast, women's entry seems less welcome. (*The Field Day Anthology,* vol. V, 237)

Women hold few of the top posts in economics and business in the state and are debarred from becoming priests in the Catholic Church. The efforts of feminist theologians and philosophers to rework Catholic theology in order to provide a space for women have made little impact yet on the thinking of the Catholic hierarchy in Ireland.

Part of the reason for the continuing absence of women from posts of influence must be the woefully inadequate provision of childcare and other support services for working parents in Ireland. There is a lack of after school care, lack of provision of school meals and lack of support for parents of special needs children. In addition, the short school day, the random and unpredictable closure of schools for training days, staff meetings and parent teacher meetings, and the lengthy summer holidays (three months as opposed to six weeks in England), means that the Irish school system militates against working parents. Women continue to work in part time, poorly paid jobs and receive little help from male partners in the home. Female-headed households fall disproportionately below the poverty line. Abortion is still illegal and the ideology of the family remains firmly embedded in the Irish Constitution. The lives of rural women are still hard. The realities of their daily battle against 'a litany of disasters, storm damage, pests, disease, accidents' are accurately reflected in Maeve Kelly's short story, 'The Last Campaign' (Kelly 1990/1991, 77–87). 'It's no life for a woman' Joe tells his wife as the herd they have so painstakingly built up is revealed to be diseased and taken away to be slaughtered.

The final section of volume V of *The Field Day Anthology*, 'Ethnicities', highlights the increasing immigration into Ireland in recent times and reminds us of the particular problems faced by women who are refugees or asylum seekers or who belong to ethnic minorities which have existed in Ireland for a long time, such as Jews and Travellers. In recent years the use of the pregnant female body to define national identity has been extended to non-national pregnant women in Ireland, in particular Roma and Nigerian women, as the debate surrounding the citizenship referendum of June 2004 illustrated. The outcome of this referendum was that children born in the state are no longer automatically entitled to keep their non-national (usually Nigerian) parents here. This has led in some cases to the brutal rounding up and deportation of non-nationals who have been forced to leave their children behind in Ireland. Maternity continues to be the force through which the boundaries of the nation, now defined so as to exclude the threat of the pregnant immigrant body, are worked out. We need to hear more stories from immigrant women, for they too are helping to shape the Irish nation and to turn it into, in the words of Liam Harte and Michael Parker: 'the hybridized, globalized, multi-textured society that Ireland is fast becoming' (Harte and Parker, 2000, 4).

Conclusion

This brief survey of Irish women's history in the twentieth century supports Linda Anderson's claim that: 'women cannot simply be added on to history [...] without putting under pressure the conceptual limits that excluded them in the first place' (Anderson, 1990, 130). With this in mind, it may be argued that landmarks for Irish women in the twentieth century are different from those of men: 1916, certainly, but also 1908 when Hanna Sheehy Skeffington founded the IWFL, 1910 when the ICA was founded and 1922 when all Irish women over twenty-one received the vote. More positive landmarks for women than the 1937 Constitution are the founding in 1942 of the IHA which kept the feminist struggle alive during a bleak period for Irish women, the introduction of children's allowances in 1944 and free health care for nursing mothers and babies under six weeks in 1953. If the expansion of secondary schooling in 1967 was significant for boys, arguably it was even more crucial for girls whose parents might at a pinch be prepared to pay for secondary education for their sons but needed their daughters to help out the family at home or to supplement the family income by taking on a factory job. In 1970 the IWLM was founded and after this the landmarks for women come thick and fast: the setting up of the Council for the Status of Women in 1973, equal pay legislation in 1977, the Health and Family Planning Act of 1979, the election of Mary Robinson in 1990, the legalization of divorce in 1995.

If, then, Ireland's history in the twentieth century is looked at from women's point of view, significance shifts from the beginning of the century, when the state was established, to the end when conditions finally allowed Irish women to become equal citizens in fact as well as in theory. The nationalist struggle may have provided Irish women with a public platform and the founding of the Irish nation granted them freedom from the colonial oppressor, but whether an independent Irish state did much to improve the quality of Irish women's daily lives is debatable. It is ironic that, as we have seen, those women who were most committed to the cause of Irish freedom were the ones who became most disillusioned with the Irish state during the 1930s and 1940s.

Our brief survey has shown that, during a large part of the century, Irish women were on the margins of their nation's life. This, as was argued earlier, has particular relevance for Julia Kristeva's theories which position women on the boundaries of public discourse. However, Kristeva maintains that this position on the margins of the nation's life may not be a disadvantage: 'Women' she says, 'have the luck and the responsibility of being boundary-subjects' (Kristeva, 1993, 35). They may occupy a marginalized position in the nation but Kristeva explains how this may be turned to women's, and indeed the nation's, advantage as women use their voice on the margins to subvert entrenched nationalisms and open them up to more fluid identities. In the following chapters we will examine whether Irish women writers from their position on the borders do indeed succeed in opening up the nation to different voices. Specifically, in chapter three of this study, the topic of women speaking from the margins of the nation's life is addressed in the context of writing by Evelyn Conlon, Mary Leland, Jennifer Johnston and Mary Dorcey.

From its earliest period, Kristeva's work has emphasized the way in which identity is formed through the encounter with otherness, both internal and external. Her later work has extended this theme to the political context of the stranger within the nation. In chapter two of this study, the theme of reaching out to the other in the Irish nation is examined in novels by Elizabeth Bowen, Jennifer Johnston and Edna O'Brien. Chapter five focuses on the topic of the foreign other and the theme of the Irish woman abroad is looked at in the light of Kristeva's theory that women are particularly adept at translating between cultures. Novels by Deirdre Madden, Kate O'Brien and Elizabeth Bowen are discussed. Chapter four analyzes Kristeva's refiguration of the mother and examines its application to the Irish mother as portrayed in fiction by Edna O'Brien, Jennifer Johnston and Clairr O'Connor. Chapter six tackles a theme which has always been important in Kristeva's writing but which has, arguably, become more prominent recently, namely the relationship of women to the religious life of the nation and to the sacred in general. Writing by Mary Lavin, Kate O'Brien, Elizabeth Bowen and Éilís Ní Dhuibhne is looked at in this context. The final chapter examines these Kristevan themes of the other, the semiotic, the foreigner, the mother and the sacred in the context of women's writing from Northern Ireland.

If Kristevan theory is, as Kelly Oliver argues, 'a matter of embracing the return of the repressed other, the foreigner, the outcast, the unconscious, *jouissance* in all of its manifestations' (Oliver 1993b, 19), we might expect a reading of Irish women's fiction through a Kristevan lens to yield insights into the heterogeneity of Irish society in past decades. We might expect it in other words to support the contention of the new nationalists that there has always been more difference in Irish society than revisionist historians have supposed. However, it is not the intention of this study to become entangled in the polarizations of the nationalist/revisionist/new nationalist debates where the Irish nation often functions as a monolith leading in turn to the homogenization of Irish women. Instead our focus in all these chapters will be on the particularities of the Irish nation as it figures in the work of individual women writers.

Kristeva herself anticipates the usefulness of literature in promulgating a more flexible national identity. Quoting Ernst Curtius, she speaks of the role that literature might play in producing a discourse on French national identity more open to difference:

Literature plays a considerable part in the consciousness France acquires of itself and its civilization. No other nation grants it comparable place. Only in France does the entire nation consider literature to be the representative expression of its fate. (Kristeva, 1993, 43–4)

Pace Curtius, this statement could equally be applied to Ireland where national identity was formed during the cultural revival of the late nineteenth and early twentieth centuries. The idea of the nation has often been examined in relation to Irish male authors but what does the nation look like from the point of view of Irish women writers?

Chapter 2

Reaching Out to the Other in the Nation

Introduction

In *Nations without Nationalism* Kristeva describes the nation of the future as polyphonic, flexible and heterogeneous. In the past, she argues, nations have formed their identity on the basis of exclusion but in the modern world, with its shifting populations and global economy, the modern nation can no longer afford to be homogeneous. The demands of immigration necessitate that nation-states be flexible, polyphonic and welcoming of strangers, that they become what she terms: 'The nation as a series of differences' (Kristeva, 1993, 41). How will this heterogeneity be achieved? According to Kristeva, it will be achieved by learning to embrace the other. In *Strangers to Ourselves* (1991) she argues that all identity, whether individual or national, is formed on the basis of exclusion. To overcome this exclusion of the other, we must learn to live with others without erasing their difference or ostracizing them.

Kristeva's notion of embracing the other was first developed in her essay 'Stabat Mater' (1974), in the context of maternity. Prompted by her own experience of maternity, Kristeva sees pregnancy as providing the basis for a new ethics based on community rather than the individual since in her view maternity breaks down the boundaries between self and other. 'The child's arrival,' she argues, 'extracts woman out of her oneness and gives her the possibility [...] of reaching out to the other, the ethical' (Kristeva, 1997, 382). Kristeva calls this new ethic 'herethics' and describes it as an ethic of loving attentiveness to the other which operates outside the Law of the Father and is therefore something women are peculiarly equipped to do. Kristeva elaborates on this ethic in a moving passage in 'Women's Time' (1979):

> The arrival of the child [...] leads the mother into the labyrinths of an experience that, without the child, she would only rarely encounter: love for another. Not for herself, nor for an identical being, and still less for another person with whom 'I' fuse [...] But the slow, difficult and delightful apprenticeship in attentiveness, gentleness, forgetting oneself. (Kristeva, 1986, 206)

More recently, in the conclusion to the third volume of *Le génie féminin,* Kristeva has reiterated this notion of maternity as a time of reaching out to the other, linking it now with the Christian notion of *agape* which has featured so prominently in her work:

[...] lorsque le sujet femme parvient à accomplir le tourniquet complexe que lui imposent l'*OEdipe prime* et l'*OEdipe bis*, elle peut avoir la chance d'acquérir cette étrange maturité dont l'homme manque si souvent, ballotté qu'il est entre la pose phallique du 'macho' et la régression infantile de l' 'impossible M. Bébé'. Dotée de cette maturité, une mère peut accueillir son enfant non pas comme une prothèse phallique ou narcissique (ce qu'il est le plus souvent), mais comme la présence réelle de l'autre: peut-être la première, à moins que ce ne soit la seule possible, et avec laquelle commence la civilisation comme un ensemble de liens basés non plus sur Eros, mais sur sa sublimation en Agapè. (Kristeva, 2002a, 556)[1]

Herethics for Kristeva is a relational, dialogic practice of love in which recognition of alterity takes precedence over personal identity.

In *Strangers to Ourselves*, Kristeva applies this psychoanalytic insight to politics, drawing on Freud's notion of the Uncanny, that is, the uncanny sensations we experience in relation to certain objects or people stemming from the unconscious projection of our desires and anxieties onto the world around us.[2] So Kristeva argues that it is our own unconscious that is projected onto those whom we exclude from the nation: 'The foreigner is within us. And when we flee from or struggle against the foreigner, we are fighting our unconscious' (Kristeva, 1991, 191). She suggests that the way to overcome exclusion of the other is to first learn to embrace the other (strangeness, monstrosity) within ourselves for, by accepting the other in ourselves, our own radical strangeness, we will accept the other in the nation: 'The foreigner comes in when the consciousness of my difference arises, and he disappears when we all acknowledge ourselves as foreigners, unamenable to bonds and communities' (Kristeva, 1991, 1). When we become aware of how our values and beliefs do not entirely fit in with the national ethos – and whose ever do? – we will then become more tolerant of other outsiders in the nation and begin to work towards a more flexible national identity, 'promoting the togetherness of those foreigners that we all recognize ourselves to be' (Kristeva, 1991, 3). She repeats this insight in *Revolt, She Said*: '[...] by recognizing this strangeness intrinsic to each of us, we have more opportunities to tolerate the foreignness of others. And subsequently more opportunities to try to create less monolithic, more polyphonic communities' (Kristeva, 2002c, 64).

In *Nations without Nationalism*, Kristeva sees women as particularly equipped to negotiate the passage between self and the other, between the known and the strange, since they are frequently positioned as strangers and exiles within the public life of the nation. Just as, for Kristeva, women are never entirely at home in the symbolic order, so they are never entirely at home in the nation: because of their marginality in relation to power and discourse, women remain skeptical and

---

[1]   'When the female subject has succeeded in negotiating the complex manoeuvre imposed on her by the primary and secondary Oedipal complexes, she has the opportunity of acquiring this strange maturity that the male so often lacks, torn as he is between the macho phallic pose and regression to the infantile state. Equipped with this maturity, the mother can welcome the child, not as a phallic or narcissistic prothesis (as he so often is), but as the real presence of the Other: perhaps the first, or even the only possible, and which inaugurates civilization as a network of connections, based no longer on Eros but on its sublimation in Agape' (my translation).

[2]   See Freud, 'The "Uncanny"' in Freud, 1955, vol. 17, pp. 217–53.

ironic vis-à-vis the social order. In 'What of Tomorrow's Nation?' she argues that their marginality puts a special responsibility on women to welcome strangers into the nation:

> The maturity of the second sex will be judged in coming years according to its ability to modify the nation in the face of foreigners, to orient foreigners confronting the nation towards a still unforseeable conception of a polyvalent community. (Kristeva, 1993, 35)

In the light of Irish women's often marginal position in the nation, it seems appropriate to investigate Kristeva's view that women, because of their boundary position within the nation, are especially skilled in mediating between the self and the other, in the context of some twentieth-century fiction by Irish women.

The Last September (1929)

In Elizabeth Bowen's novel, *The Last September*, published in 1929, nineteen-year-old Lois may be read as precisely this sort of Kristevan woman as outsider, skeptical of the values of the Anglo-Irish class to which she belongs. Bowen's novel is set in 1920 during the War of Independence and Lois, seeing through the pretense of her aunt and uncle, the Anglo-Irish Naylors, that everything will carry on as it is, is well aware that the particular pattern into which she has been born is in the process of disintegrating. However, just as the new Irish state has not yet come into being, so Lois has not yet found her path in life. Like those fighting for the Irish nation, Lois is in the process of defining herself, and in this respect, Bowen's novel lends itself to being read in the light of Kristevan theory.

For Kristeva, the continual rethinking of identity is a process which she believes is vital both on an individual and a national level. In the life of the individual, the self in Kristevan theory is always provisional and 'in progress'. 'Le sujet en procès' is a term that appears frequently in Kristeva's writings and she explains it as follows: 'the *subject-in-process* [...] gives us a vision of the human venture as a venture of innovation, of reaction, of opening, of renewal' (Kristeva, 1996, 26). Similarly a nation must always be rethinking its values in order to avoid the rigidities inherent in political discourse which, in Kristeva's view, lead to totalitarianism. She has said: 'Rebellion is a condition necessary for the life of the mind and society' (Kristeva, 2002c, 85). In the opening pages of *The Sense and Non-sense of Revolt* she insists that permanent revolution is vital both in the life of an individual and in the life of a nation for, without it, values become frozen and humans are in danger of resembling automata (Kristeva, 2000b, 7). In Bowen's novel, the linked themes of a nation attempting to establish itself and a young girl trying to find her place in the world may be read in the light of these Kristevan notions of identity.

Lois is first presented to us as performing with accuracy the part expected of a young girl in an Anglo-Irish household while at the same time aware that it *is* a performance: 'Lois stood at the top of the steps looking cool and fresh; she knew how fresh she must look, like other young girls' (Bowen, 1929/1987, 7). This emphasis on Lois' performance of her role as niece of the Big House is repeated several times in the novel: 'her youth seemed to her also rather theatrical [...] she was only young in that way because people expected it. She had never refused a role' (Bowen, 1929/1987, 32). Her life in Danielstown strikes Lois as quite as vacant as this emphasis on performance suggests. Her vacancy is partly gendered: her cousin, Laurence, who is similarly *désoeuvré*, does at least have Oxford to look forward to. For Lois, aware that exciting developments are going on around her as the Irish wage their war against the British, her gender is a trap. When Gerald, the young English officer who hopes to marry Lois, mentions the recent burning of an army barracks by Irish nationalists, Lois explodes in frustration at the feminine role she is expected to play:

> Do you know that while that was going on, eight miles off, I was cutting a dress out, a voile that I didn't even need, and playing the gramophone? [...] How is it that in this country that ought to be full of such violent realness, there seems nothing for me but clothes and what people say? I might just as well be in some kind of cocoon. (Bowen, 1929/1987, 49)

Lois is a split subject from the beginning, in rebellion against the gendered role she is expected to perform. Her consciousness of the restrictions imposed by her gender induces in her a feeling of being an outsider to events in Ireland. However, that feeling of being an outsider arises not only from her gender, but also from her ambivalent position in the nation as a member of the Anglo-Irish caste, divided in loyalty between England and Ireland. In *Bowen's Court*, published in 1942, charting the rise and decline in the fortunes of the Bowen family and their Big House, Elizabeth Bowen describes how the Anglo-Irish, unsure of their status in Ireland, put their trust in style to protect themselves against an inner uncertainty. Their Big Houses, imposed on the colonized Irish countryside and reflecting not the native but the colonizers' architecture, resembled alien structures in the land. In *The Last September*, there is an evocative description of Danielstown as just such an alien in the Irish countryside:

> The house seemed to be pressing down low in apprehension, hiding its face, as though it had her vision of where it was. It seemed to gather its trees close in fright and amazement at the wide, light, lovely unloving country, the unwilling bosom whereon it was set. (Bowen, 1929/1987, 66)

No wonder that Lois, driving through this Irish countryside, feels her Anglo-Irish presence is no more than an 'illusion' (Bowen, 1929/1987, 65).

In *Bowen's Court*, Elizabeth Bowen contrasts the English squire's readiness to involve himself in the activities of his tenants with the huge walls the Anglo-Irish built around their demesnes cutting them off from Gaelic Ireland and its inhabitants. Lack of contact with the natives of Ireland exacerbated the unreality of the Anglo-Irish way of life. They had nothing to sustain them but a certain standard of behavior which living in the Big House imposed on them and which in turn developed into a performance and a belief that 'life ought to be lived in a certain way' (Bowen, 1984, 32). The Big House, Bowen wrote in an oft-quoted line from *Bowen's Court*, is 'like Flaubert's ideal book about nothing, it sustains itself on itself by the inner force of its style' (Bowen, 1984, 21). Life in Danielstown involves all of its inhabitants in a performance.[3] The vacancy Lois perceives in herself is matched by the vacancy she senses in Danielstown: 'after every return – or awakening, even, from sleep or preoccupation – she and those home surroundings still further penetrated each other mutually in the discovery of a lack' (Bowen, 1929/1987, 166). Unlike Lois, however, the class to which she belongs is unable or unwilling to question its identity.

Lois' class, the Anglo-Irish, suffers from the sort of rigidity Kristeva sees as inevitable in a group or a nation which neglects to rethink its identity. Lois' aunt and uncle can only preserve their identity by clinging to the past and ignoring the rise of the nationalists. But this is just what Lois cannot do. Though aware of the attractions of living in a pattern ('she could not try to explain the magnetism they all exerted by being static', Bowen, 1929/1987, 166), she also chafes against its constraints. In contrast to the rigidity of the Anglo-Irish, Lois is determined to keep her identity fluid and open-ended. When in her bedroom she overhears Lady Naylor and Francie Montmorency discussing her, she takes her water jug and bangs it down into the basin to get them to stop:

> But when Mrs Montmorency came to: 'Lois is very –' she was afraid suddenly. She had a panic. She didn't want to know what she was, she couldn't bear to: knowledge of this would stop, seal, finish one. Was she now to be clapped down under an adjective, to crawl round lifelong inside some quality like a fly in a tumbler? Mrs Montmorency should not! (Bowen, 1929/1987, 60)

The water jar makes a crack in her wash basin which becomes a permanent reminder to Lois of her uncertainty about her identity: 'Every time, before the water clouded, she would see the crack: every time she would wonder: what Lois *was* – She would never know' (Bowen, 1929/1987, 60). In his illuminating article, 'Discovery of a Lack: History and Ellipsis in Elizabeth Bowen's *The Last September*', Neil Corcoran interprets this crack as symbolic of Lois' uncertainty, over not only her personal, but also her cultural identity (Corcoran, 2001, 320).

Lois' awareness of the flaws in the role both her gender and her class require her to fulfill opens her to the possibility of difference and leads her to take an interest in the nationalists who haunt the Irish countryside and hide guns in the woods. In other words, Lois' awareness of her alterity within, that she is other to herself, prepares her to relate, as Kristeva has argued awareness of alterity always does, to the other as other. The similarities between Lois' situation in relation to the Anglo-Irish and that of the Anglo-Irish other, namely the Irish nationalists, in relation to the Anglo-Irish are made apparent in a series of parallels carefully drawn by Bowen but seldom remarked upon by critics.

One such parallel is that both Lois and the nationalists tend to be ignored by the older generation of Anglo-Irish unless circumstances force them upon their attention. None of the older generation in Danielstown takes any notice of Lois unless they have need of her services: 'Lois hesitated, went in after them and, as nobody noticed, came out again' (Bowen, 1929/1987, 8). She knows her invisibility is partly a consequence of her youth but also of her class and her

---

[3]   For more on the Anglo-Irish and style and, developing from this in connection with Bowen, the notion of the Anglo-Irish writer as dandy, see Kiberd, 1995/1996, 365–79.

gender. It is not proper for 'a lady' to attract attention: 'She was tired of being not noticed because she was a lady' (Bowen, 1929/1987, 99). Lady Naylor is ruthlessly determined not to notice the relationship that has formed between Lois and the unsuitable Gerald until remarks by her old friend, Francie Montmorency, force her opposition to the match into the open.

Similarly, the Naylors' response to the Troubles is to play them down as far as possible: 'Lady Naylor continued: "From all the talk, you might think almost anything was going to happen, but we never listen. I have made it a rule not to talk, either"' (Bowen, 1929/1987, 26). The Anglo-Irish, caught in their divided loyalty between their Irish tenants and the British army and fearful of their position in the Ireland of the future, adopt a self-protective policy of not acknowledging what is going on around them. Ambushes, arrests, raids are all played down. Laurence posits that even if Danielstown itself were to burn, they would all be 'so careful not to notice' (Bowen, 1929/1987, 44). For Kristeva, as we have seen, identity, whether personal or national, is formed on the basis of exclusion. In order to maintain their identity, the Anglo-Irish are forced to exclude the Irish nationalists from their line of vision. Just how much violent reality the Naylors are evading ('a kind of total war in miniature') has been pointed out by Neil Corcoran (Corcoran, 2001, 321).

As someone partially excluded herself, Lois naturally takes an interest in the excluded other. When, breaking away from the Big House one evening to wander in the darkness, she comes across a man in a trench-coat, she is eager to communicate with him. However, she realizes that it is pointless to tell the other inhabitants of the Big House about her exciting encounter with the rebel since they will not listen. Here, Lois' fate and that of the nationalists merge in the Naylors' determination 'not to know'. Lois' desire to find out what the rebels are like and whether there really are guns buried in Danielstown is swiftly squashed by Sir Richard.

Both Lois and the nationalists are portrayed as rushing to meet their uncertain futures. Knowing that marriage must be her destiny, Lois is 'anxious to love soon' (Bowen, 1929/1987, 82). Marda sums up Lois' eagerness to love using a typical Bowen simile: 'She is in such a hurry, so concentrated upon her hurry, so helpless. She is like someone being driven against time in a taxi to catch a train' (Bowen, 1929/1987, 82). A similar thing is said of the man in the trench-coat whom Lois spies rushing through the bushes: 'It must be because of Ireland he was in such a hurry' (Bowen, 1929/1987, 34).

Though this is not made explicit in the book, the nationalists have the memory of past rebellions, of 1798 and 1916, to sustain them. Lois has the memory of her dead mother, Laura, who features in the book as a woman who chafed against social restraints. Lois remembers Laura as being 'rather a bad hostess' (Bowen, 1929/1987, 11). Laurence recalls her as given to 'epic rages' (Bowen, 1929/1987, 107). In one of these fits of rebellion Laura, 'averting from the stare of the house an angry profile' (Bowen, 1929/1987, 107), fled North and married Mr Farquar, instead of the more socially acceptable Mr Montmorency. The marriage, it is suggested, did not turn out well. Hugo Montmorency, the rejected suitor, remembers Laura as restless: 'She never knew what she wanted' (Bowen, 1929/1987, 19). In much the same way, the rebels are depicted in the novel from the Anglo-Irish point of view as having no clear idea of the nation they are fighting to bring about. However, like Laura, the nationalists may in fact have a clearer idea than the Naylors and their friends give them credit for. As Laura scrawled her initials on the walls of the box-room in an endeavor to establish a sense of her individuality against her Anglo-Irish clan's desire to absorb her into a safe marriage, so the Irish nationalists are searching for an identity other than the one imposed upon them by the English colonizer.

Lois is a secret rebel against the constraints placed on her by life in the Big House where, like the nationalist rebels, she lacks power: Lady Naylor easily outmanoeuvres Gerald in his bid to marry Lois. Nevertheless, it is not Lois' short-lived engagement to Gerald which makes a social rebel of her, however much Lady Naylor may disapprove of it; it is the fact that Lois, whose engagement to Gerald is an attempt at self-definition ('it *is* something definite' she tells herself, Bowen, 1929/1987, 162), comes to realize that life with Gerald will be as constraining as life in Danielstown. This is underlined by the explicit link made between Gerald and Danielstown in the following passage:

> In his world affections were rare and square – four-square – occurring like houses in a landscape, unrelated and positive, though with sometimes a large bright looming – as of the sunned west face of Danielstown over the tennis court. (Bowen, 1929/1987, 40–1)

It is because marriage with Gerald would not be sufficiently different from her life at present and because she cannot in the end foreclose her future by marrying him that Lois rejects him. Later, Irish nationalists, probably tenants of the Naylors, shoot him. After his death, Lois yokes Gerald's love and his politics together: 'He loved me, he believed in the British Empire' (Bowen, 1929/1987, 203). Political domination is linked to gender divisions: Gerald's attitude to Lois and his attitude to the Irish are intertwined in his mind. He writes to Lois: 'What I am doing this morning [suppressing the rebels] seems so important – although it keeps me away from you – because I am doing it *for* you' (Bowen, 1929/1987, 162). His sense of chivalry impels him into a protective attitude towards both Lois and Ireland. Like the nationalists, Lois resists Gerald's colonizing efforts and draws a parallel between England's misplaced sense of chivalry in regard to Ireland (their refusal to declare outright war on the country) and male chivalry towards women: 'Can you wonder this country gets irritated? It's as bad for it as being a woman. I never can see why women shouldn't be hit' (Bowen, 1929/1987, 49).[4] Lois' moment of outrage only strengthens Gerald's feelings of protectiveness. As a woman, she cannot be expected to understand his point of view, just as the Irish nationalists cannot understand England's. The implication is that Gerald knows what is best for both Lois and Ireland. He is here to protect both of them. For both Lois and Ireland, though, the price of his protection – loss of freedom to act – is too high.

---

[4]   There is a later echo of this intertwining of nation and gender in Iris Murdoch's novel, *The Red and the Green* (1965), where young Frances Bellman resists stereotypical gender divisions which, while supposedly protecting women, turn them into the merely decorative: 'I think being a woman is like being Irish […] Everyone says you're important and nice, but you take second place all the same' (Murdoch, 1965, 32).

Gerald's kiss in the drawing-room at Danielstown seals his fate. Leaving Lois indifferent, the kiss makes her realize that she has no future either with Gerald or in Danielstown. His kiss prompts in her feelings of loneliness and homelessness, reminding her of the times when she has been seasick and 'locked in misery between Holyhead and Kingstown' (Bowen, 1929/1987, 89). In this scene Lois' sexual identity and her national identity combine to cause her confusion. As a member of the Anglo-Irish caste, her identity is forever hyphenated, torn between Ireland and England (Bowen notably remarked that her home was somewhere in the middle of the Irish Sea). As a woman, Lois' sexuality remains unaroused by Gerald's kiss. She longs to escape both gender and nationality. Nationality when she desires to be 'enclosed in nonentity, in some ideal no-place' (Bowen, 1929/1987, 89). Gender when she tells Marda: 'I hate women. But I can't think how to begin to be anything else' (Bowen, 1929/1987, 99).

In a gender divided society, such as that depicted in *The Last September*, it is older women who provide clues for her young heroines as to how to live. It is this, rather than the sexual ambivalence stressed by some critics, which in my view prompts Lois to look to the older Marda for a sense of her identity.[5] She tries on Marda's fur coat, experimenting with a different identity: 'a dark, rare, rather wistful woman, elusive with jasmine' (Bowen, 1929/1987, 76). She studies Marda and questions her as to how to go about beginning to be a woman. Through observing Hugo Montmorency's infatuation with Marda, Lois becomes aware of the nature of sexual passion. She learns that it is not the respectable indifference she feels for Gerald but something violent and unpredictable, like a bomb exploding. In the abandoned mill (itself a symbol of colonial exploitation) into which Marda has led her, Lois comes up against two realities simultaneously: the reality of violence in her nation as the IRA man's gun goes off, and the reality of sexual passion in the violence of Hugo's reaction to Marda's wounding. 'I had no idea – I was too damned innocent' she comments (Bowen, 1929/1987, 128). Lois' recognition of the nature of sexual passion and of her country's fight for freedom leaves her feeling 'quite ruled out' (Bowen, 1929/1987, 125).

Despite her longing to get to know the IRA men, as a member of the Anglo-Irish, Lois can have no part in her country's future. When she meets the IRA man in the shrubbery, he hurries past without noticing her. When she questions Michael Connor as to the whereabouts of his son, Peter, he clams up. Lois knows that, despite her wish to communicate with the rebels, as a member of the Anglo-Irish, she cannot share their feelings about Ireland. 'She could not conceive of her country emotionally' (Bowen, 1929/1987, 34). For the Anglo-Irish Lois, Ireland, so far from being a secure homeland, will always feel precarious, like 'an oblique frayed island, moored at the north but with an air of being detached and washed out west from the British coast' (Bowen, 1929/1987, 34). In the same way, the scene in the mill reveals to her that, as Gerald's wife, she will never know sexual passion. The scene of her awakening in the mill determines her future – away from Ireland and from Gerald.

---

5   For a balanced assessment of the lesbian undertones in Lois' relationship with Marda, see Patricia Coughlan's essay on 'Women and Desire in the Work of Elizabeth Bowen' (Walshe, 1997, 103–31).

Unlike Marda who will capitulate to her society's gender and class expectations by marrying Leslie Lawe and allowing herself to 'be moulded by his idea of her' (Bowen, 1929/1987, 129), Lois' future, like Ireland's, is left uncertain. After Gerald's death, she is packed off to France to perfect her language, an apparently random choice by her aunt which has little to do with Lois' own wishes or plans. Art school and Italy are what have been talked of for most of the novel. None of these options will provide a real future for Lois. She knows that she does not draw well. In the eyes of her Anglo-Irish family, she has in fact only one destiny – marriage to someone of her own class, but this is left as uncertain in the novel as Ireland's future. The burning down of Danielstown subsequent to her departure underlines the fact that there can be no return to the fixed patterns of the past for Lois. Whereas Lois' mother lingers on in the text like some kind of trapped ghostly presence, haunting Danielstown with her scratchings on the walls, her rotting trunks and the memory of her unappeased rages, by the end of the novel Lois has escaped the paralysis of the Anglo-Irish Big House and evolved into a Kristevan 'subject-in-process'. Her future is left open-ended, her identity perpetually in question: 'every time she would wonder: what Lois *was* – She would never know' (Bowen, 1929/1987, 60). By the act of burning down Danielstown but, even more, simply by what they represent (the other to the Anglo-Irish that Lois is seeking) the Irish nationalists have facilitated this opening out of Lois' life.

Questions of gender and nationality are never simple in Bowen's work. In *The Last September* Lois awakens to her place in society but also to an awareness that she is unable straightforwardly to accept the identity prepared for her by her class and her sex. As an outsider she becomes interested in the nationalists' struggle, an interest she cannot pursue very far because of the constraints of her gender and class. Not only do the Naylors discourage her interest in the rebels, but when she does attempt some approach to the republicans, the latter reject her on account of her class. Michael Connor refuses to trust her enough to give her news of his son's whereabouts. The IRA man in the mill warns her to stay in the Big House 'while y'have it' (Bowen, 1929/1987, 125). Nevertheless Lois' openness to the rebels' point of view helps her to question her upbringing and the value of the place she is expected to take in the Anglo-Irish scheme of things. Lois, like the rebels, constructs her identity in opposition to that offered by the Anglo-Irish and her future, like that of the Irish nationalists, remains uncertain at the end of the novel. The process of 'destructive genesis', to borrow Kristeva's term from *Revolt, She Said*, is only half complete. There has been destruction but no rebirth, neither for Lois nor, yet, for the Irish nation.

The Old Jest (1979)

Jennifer Johnston is a writer whose fiction has attracted much criticism, notably from Rüdiger Imhof in his study, *The Modern Irish Novel*, where he takes Johnston to task both for the implausibility of her plots and for deficiencies of narrative technique and style (Imhof, 2002, 101–21). In *The Contemporary Irish Novel*, Linden Peach argues that such criticisms arise from adopting naturalistic or historical approaches unsuited to her work. Instead he suggests regarding

Johnston's characters as 'sites of ideological conflict or embodiments of ideological positions' (Peach, 2004, 101). This is a fruitful approach for his reading of *The Railway Station Man* in particular but, in showing how Johnston's women characters struggle for an identity 'predicated on freeing the known from their stabilizing referents' (Peach, 2004, 105), Peach inevitably falls into an ahistorical and in the end apolitical reading of Johnston's novels. Reading Jennifer Johnston's novels through a Kristevan lens may provide a solution to this problem, as well as producing fresh insights into the ways in which her female characters struggle to establish a voice for themselves within the life of the Irish nation.

Jennifer Johnston's novel, *The Old Jest*, is a direct literary descendant of *The Last September*. *The Old Jest* is set in the same year (1920) as *The Last September* and, like Bowen's novel, deals with a nation and a young girl in the process of defining their identities. Nancy is coming of age just as her nation is on the brink of coming into being and, like Lois, Nancy, perplexed as to her future, turns to the other in her quest for answers.

Like Lois, Nancy Gulliver is the daughter of a Big House, albeit one which is in severe decline. Nancy's mother died giving birth to her and her father, whose identity she has never known and who may or may not be dead, haunts her thoughts. At present, Nancy lives with her Aunt Mary who, like the Naylors in Elizabeth Bowen's novel, survives by a policy of 'not noticing'. Neither Nancy's unknown father, nor the growing violence of the Black and Tans nor the family's steady slide into impoverishment may be mentioned at home. As in Bowen's novel, the Anglo-Irish are presented in a state of stasis, caught between their ties with England and their unwillingness to betray their Irish neighbors. The Misses Brabazons refuse to lend their car to the rebels, but neither will they inform on them to the police.

Like Lois, Nancy feels ambivalent about the world in which she finds herself. She chafes against the petty restraints imposed on her as daughter of a Big House. 'I lead a very sheltered life' she tells Joe. 'All my movements are catalogued' (Johnston, 1979/1984, 120). She loves her Aunt Mary but does not want to grow up to be like her. She confesses to Harry, the rather staid stockbroker on whom she has a crush, her desire to 'know and understand' (Johnston, 1979/1984, 27). In pursuit of this, she interrogates him about war and sex to the point where he feels persecuted: Harry, a literary descendant of Elizabeth Bowen's Gerald, shares that character's views on appropriate female behavior. Like Lois, Nancy is in rebellion both against her place in the nation and her gender; like Lois, her rebellion causes her a good deal of internal anguish and anxiety; like Lois, she is in a good position to relate to an other as other since she is already other to herself.

On her eighteenth birthday, Nancy signals her intention to examine the world around her and her place in it by commencing a diary. For Kristeva, as she has repeatedly stated (see, for example, *Intimate Revolt*, 2002b, 253–4), writing and creativity are impossible without the sort of exile, either physical or mental, which provides the necessary distance from the values of the culture in which one lives. The fact that Nancy has started to write down her thoughts may therefore indicate that she already feels some kind of inner exile from the life around her. Indeed, the opening paragraphs of her diary express her longing to be elsewhere as she describes how on a clear day it is possible to see Wales from the hill at the back of the house: 'It's not really very exciting, just a grey lump in the distance, but it's somewhere else. Somewhere new' (Johnston, 1979/1984, 9). When the view of that other country is cut off, she experiences life in Ireland as claustrophobic: 'For the last two weeks there has been no sign of Wales at all, just that pale haze steaming gently up into the sky, shutting this island off from the rest of the world' (Johnston, 1979/1984, 9).

Not only is Nancy dissatisfied with the constraints of life in Ireland, she is also, like Lois, on a quest to discover an identity larger than the one that has hitherto been forced on her. She has packed away her school clothes and books and 'the rules for living that for so many years they have tried to impose upon me' and intends 'to start to become a person' (Johnston, 1979/1984, 10). Like Lois, Nancy is a Kristevan 'subject-in-process' and, as in *The Last September*, the young heroine's quest for identity is set against the wider backdrop of her country's struggle for self-definition. Like Lois, Nancy has a maternal inheritance of rebellion on which to draw, though this is only lightly sketched in by Johnston. Nancy's father was a Bolshevist, her grandfather informs her, a Traveler with 'a lot of funny ideas' according to Bridie, the family servant (Johnston, 1979/1984, 131). The fact that she was willing to form a relationship with such a man indicates at least a questioning of her Anglo-Irish background on the part of Nancy's mother.

Nancy's project of writing a diary in order to enter, or at least to understand, the wider world around her, illustrates Kristeva's theories of women's writing as providing women with a space in which to reshape the social order to suit themselves.[6] In 'Women's Time', Kristeva argues that women's desire to write is a 'desire to lift the sacrificial weight of the social contract and to furnish our societies with a freer and more flexible discourse' (Kristeva, 1997, 365). Similarly, Nancy's diary reveals her secret rebellion against the values of the world in which she has been raised for in her diary Nancy is more knowing than she is allowed to be in her familial and social life where comments about her father or the republicans' activities are discouraged. One of the first things she mentions in the diary is the current violence in her country: 'Barney Carney was shot last week coming out of a dance hall in Bray, by the Black and Tans. They said it was a mistake' (Johnston, 1979/1984, 11). Forced to collude in the silence about her father, in her diary Nancy clings to the hope that one day he will arrive to rescue her. Kept on the margins of life, regarded as a young girl in need of protection by Aunt Mary and Harry, Nancy believes that it is her father who will help her into adulthood, as in Kristevan theory it is the imaginary father who provides the support necessary to allow the child to move into the symbolic order (Oliver, 1993a, 69–90).

Nancy's interrogation of her world is helped along by her meeting with a middle-aged nationalist on the run. Nancy names the nationalist Cassius and naturally, in view of her yearning for her lost father, converts him into a father

---

[6]   For a later example of this, see Una Woods' novel, *The Dark Hole Days*, where the teenage Colette attempts to clear a space for herself during the Troubles in Belfast by writing a diary: 'I knew there were possibilities. With writing this I feel they may be opening up. And if I never do anything, at least I'll have this. It's an extra me. I've created an extension' (Woods, 1984, 22).

figure. He is, in fact, as she later learns, an Anglo-Irishman who fought in the British army during the First World War but who is now involved in the struggle for Irish freedom. Cassius teaches Nancy to think for herself. Her Aunt Mary may not always be right: losing the family home, for instance, may not be a disaster but a removal of a constraint on her future.

Cassius encourages Nancy to re-think her views on the fight for freedom. He shows her his gun and warns her that life is not always polite and easy but 'full of violence, injustice and pain' (Johnston, 1979/1984, 59). Though Nancy is horrified, she decides not to inform on him but to try to understand his reasons for being a gunman. The parallels, largely implicit in Bowen's novel, between political rebels struggling to shape their nation's identity and a rebellious young girl's efforts to create a personal identity, become explicit here as, under the influence of her encounter with the other, Nancy finds herself drawn out of her sheltered life into involvement in the struggle for Ireland's independence.

It is this initiation into political action by the father figure which brings Nancy to adulthood. Although she loathes violence, she commits herself to the extent that she delivers a message from Cassius to Joe, another IRA member. The message leads directly to the assassination of twelve British soldiers. At the end of the novel, she refuses to betray Cassius to the British and runs to warn him that they are on his trail. She has outgrown her aunt's protection and become an adult responsible for her own decisions, in the process abandoning her aunt's stance of 'not noticing' in favor of direct involvement. 'I'm a republican' she tells Bridie, defining herself at last (Johnston, 1979/1984, 87). Nancy's personal development and her political development are thus intertwined: she crosses several religious and political boundaries in the friendship she strikes up with Joe, a working-class, Catholic republican.

However, in measure as Nancy's political activity takes off so her writing trails away. Her final entry begins: 'I think I'll stop writing in this book. I find it harder and harder to put down in words my direct thoughts about what happens day by day' (Johnston, 1979/1984, 136). By abandoning her diary, Nancy loses the writer's ability to interrogate the values of the struggle she has now joined. By initiating her into the symbolic, Nancy's surrogate father figure, Cassius, has induced her to abandon the boundary position which Kristeva sees as an advantage both to women and to the nation. She thus loses her woman's ability to question from the margins. Her diary becomes a symbol of the way in which a potentially subversive, female-centered version of events has become silenced by direct involvement in the national struggle, bearing out the foreboding of those who, like Hanna Sheehy Skeffington, claimed that feminism and nationalism were in conflict and feared that feminism would be subsumed by the nationalist conflict.

Critics have provided various readings of the ending of *The Old Jest*. In 'The Masculine World of Jennifer Johnston', Shari Benstock interprets Nancy's story, as I have done, as overtaken by the events of Cassius' life and death (Staly, 1982, 191–217). An opposite interpretation is given by Ann Owens Weekes, who reads the ending of the novel as illustrating Nancy's growth in freedom from gender and class constraints (Weekes, 1990, 202). Rachel Sealy Lynch, too, gives a more positive interpretation of Nancy's self-development than I have done. She points out that Nancy is due to study history at Trinity and as such she will become one of the early number of Irish women to benefit from higher education. Yet Lynch also puts *The Old Jest* with a group of Johnston's novels which she describes as demonstrating how: 'personal space is invaded and destroyed time after time by political reality' (Kirkpatrick, 2000, 252), an interpretation which is nearer my own.

In chapter one of this study we saw that Kristeva's argument in *Nations without Nationalism* that even political movements which have freedom as their goal risk becoming totalitarian if they substitute one form of absolute truth for another, has some applicability to the position of Irish women within the Irish state for much of the twentieth century. In a later work, *Intimate Revolt*, Kristeva reiterates her view that revolutions, rather than leading to further questioning, often install their own brand of totalitarianism (Kristeva, 2002b, 266). She positions women and artists as particularly well situated to combat totalitarianism, women because of their position as strangers and exiles within the public life of the nation, artists because they intervene on an individual level. By abandoning her Kristevan position on the margins in favor of political commitment, both Nancy's individual woman's voice and her voice as an artist become subsumed by the nationalist struggle. In that sense, her future is less fluid and open-ended than that of Lois at the end of *The Last September*.

The Country Girls (1960–1964)

In Edna O'Brien's trilogy, *The Country Girls* (1960–64, first edition), the Irish state has now come into being but it has not brought much happiness for Caithleen Brady. In the first book in the trilogy, *The Country Girls* (1960), Caithleen and her mother live in fear of violence and abuse from the alcoholic and feckless Mr Brady. Since the family unit is inviolate, the abuse cannot be talked about. As we saw in chapter one, such silence over domestic violence was widespread in Ireland at the time due to a reluctance on the part of the authorities to interfere in the family unit. The Brady family fits O'Brien's iconoclastic description in *Mother Ireland* of the typical Irish family as: 'the martyred Irish mother and the raving rollicking Irish father' (O'Brien, 1976/1978, 19). Her childhood environment predisposes Caithleen to grow up to become an outsider, resisting the values of her community and looking to other outsiders for empathy.

Caithleen's upbringing is a lesson in the vulnerability of females in Ireland during the 1950s. Her country's gender divisions discourage married women's employment outside the home, thereby rendering Caithleen's mother almost entirely dependent on her husband for money. Like most farmers' wives, Mrs Brady keeps hens and earns a little pin money by selling eggs, but she is powerless to prevent her husband from squandering the family income on drink. Moreover, Mrs Brady's vulnerability is not only financial but sexual: she is prey, like her daughter, to the random sexual attentions of various males in the neighborhood. Jack Holland, for example, fondles Mrs Brady's knee in exchange for presents of candied peel and chocolate. Fourteen-year-old Caithleen is expected to kiss their farm laborer, Hickey, Jack Holland and other assorted adult males. [7]

The convent school which Caithleen and her friend Baba attend after Mrs Brady's death continues their initiation into their nation's gendered behavior as the nuns stress the equation of Irish Catholic girlhood with modesty and chastity. The girls are made to dress and undress under the shelter of dressing gowns to prevent them from seeing themselves naked and Caithleen's abundant mop of hair is dismissed censoriously as something of which 'Our Lady would hardly approve' (O'Brien, 1987, 74). In this community the female body is severely censored.[8] Naturally Baba, looking for something that will get them expelled, alights precisely on this equation of Irish girlhood with chastity. At the age of seventeen, she and Caithleen are expelled from the convent for writing 'a dirty note'. They have become 'the abject', that which has to be expelled by the individual or community in order for identity to form: 'we were filthy and loathsome and no one could speak to us' says Caithleen (O'Brien, 1987, 106). They are what the symbolic must cover over and contain if its unity is not to be threatened. The young women's subsequent eager embrace of single life in the city, 'the giddy country girls brazening the big city' as Caithleen calls it (O'Brien, 1987, 121), shows Caithleen by her way of life beginning to provide a counter-narrative to the nationalist construct of Ireland as a family-centered, rural nation. Caithleen has become an outsider to her nation, a fact which is stressed when she and Baba lodge with a foreign landlady. Caithleen's unconsummated romance with Mr Gentleman, who attracts her precisely because he is a foreigner and an outsider, confirms her sense of otherness.

In the following book in the trilogy, *The Lonely Girl* (1962), Caithleen's growth to maturity further threatens the boundaries on which the Irish nation is constructed.[9] She is still looking for romance and constructs one around the mysterious and ascetic Eugene Gaillard, a successor to the foreign Mr Gentleman. Eugene, though in fact half-Irish, is perceived by the locals as foreign due to his way of living (he is separated from his American wife, he does not attend Mass). Like Mr Gentleman, Eugene is a good deal older than Caithleen and functions as a substitute for her unsatisfactory Irish father. When Caithleen's family and neighbors come after her, the debate is not simply about the 'immorality' of Caithleen's decision to live with Eugene, a married man; it is a tussle over the very notion of what constitutes Irish womanhood. In the homogeneous Irish state depicted in *The Lonely Girl*, Eugene is castigated for being a foreigner and enticing

---

[7]   For more on food and sexuality in Edna O'Brien's work, see Mary Burke, 'Famished: Alienation and Appetite in Edna O'Brien's Early Novels' in *Edna O'Brien: New Critical Perspectives*, eds. K. Laing, S. Mooney and M. O'Connor, Carysfort Press, Dublin, 2006, pp. 219–41. This volume was published too recently for me to be able to take it into account in this study.

[8]   See Cheryl Herr's article, 'The Erotics of Irishness', where she argues that the various ideologies which have held Ireland in their grip during the twentieth century have been responsible for a general suppression of the body in Irish society. 'Ireland has literally eroded, in the sphere of representations that constitute social identity, a comfortable sense of the body' (Herr, 1990, 6).

[9]   The title was changed to *Girl with Green Eyes* for American editions.

Caithleen away from her rightful place as an Irish Catholic girl who should be embodying the purity of her nation. The anonymous author of a note sent to Caithleen's father insists: 'I would not like to see a nice Catholic Irish girl ruined by a dirty foreigner' (O'Brien, 1987, 246). Caithleen's relationship with Eugene is judged to threaten the homogeneity of the Irish nation. They want her to marry one of her own nation and religion, but Caithleen has been an outsider to their brand of Irishness for too long, she knows now that she never will marry 'one of her own kind' (O'Brien, 1987, 252).

Ireland as defined by Mr Brady and his companions is narrowly Catholic. Having fought in the War of Independence they regard the nation as their property: '"We won our fight for freedom. It's our country now," Andy said' (O'Brien, 1987, 300). Since they, in their role as masculine defenders of the nation, now own it, they believe they have the right to extend this ownership to the women of their nation. They reject Eugene's repeated insistence that Caithleen is twenty-one and therefore legally an adult and declare their right to expel anyone who threatens their definition of Irishness: '"We can have her put away. She's not all there" my father said' (O'Brien, 1987, 300).

In this row with Caithleen's father and neighbors, Edna O'Brien presents their kind of nationalism as obliterating all dissent. When Eugene tells them that Caithleen is 'running away from you and your way of living', Jack Holland immediately turns this into a political point, presenting Ireland and Caithleen as victims of foreign interference: 'The tragic history of our fair land. Alien power sapped our will to resist' (O'Brien, 1987, 297). The integrity of the Irish nation is seen by these men as threatened by Caithleen's relationship, both because Eugene is a foreigner and because their idea of Ireland is bound up with a certain construct of female behavior to which Caithleen refuses to conform. Despite Caithleen's hope that she might escape and 'live my life the way I wanted to' (O'Brien, 1987, 267), her female body and the Irish nation are conflated so that it becomes her community's business, and in the end the bishop's, to try to get her away from Eugene. In doing so, they believe they are preserving one Catholic girl from foreign, atheistic ways and safeguarding the homogeneity of their nation.

Caithleen's gender has collided with her nation. She has become, to employ Kristevan terms, the abject. In *Powers of Horror* (1980), Kristeva describes the abject as that which: 'disturbs identity, system order. What does not respect borders, positions, rules' (Kristeva, 1997, 232). Since it does not respect boundaries, the abject threatens identity in both individuals and nations and requires expulsion. Caithleen must give up her relationship with the foreign other or be expelled from the nation whose uniform identity she threatens. In her village she is faced with 'staring disapproval' and school children shouting at her (O'Brien, 1987, 260). When she and Eugene go to a pub together they are ostracized and branded 'pagans' (O'Brien, 1987, 339). In the end Caithleen, who has not yet sufficiently matured to handle the sophistication of Eugene's way of life, decides to flee to England with Baba. Her choice of destination is ironic since in the eyes of her father and his cronies England is the Other, 'a pagan place' in contrast with Catholic Ireland, 'as if the morals of Ireland were any better' thinks Baba in *Girls in their Married Bliss* (O'Brien, 1987, 440). In *The Lonely Girl*, Caithleen's desire to reach out to the other is thwarted by her nation's rigidity.

The portrait of Ireland in *The Lonely Girl* is confirmed in Edna O'Brien's non-fiction work, *Mother Ireland*. There is the same recognition of the uniformity of national identity affecting Irish social mores: 'You feel they will pinion you down with their beliefs and their unyielding opinions' (O'Brien, 1976/1978, 23). There is the same highlighting of the all-pervasive Catholicism inculcated into Irish children: 'The spiritual food consisted of the crucified Christ. His Passion impinged on every thought, word, deed and omission' (O'Brien, 1976/1978, 28). Anyone outside the Catholic construct – Protestants, 'the black doctor' and 'the travelling Jew man' (O'Brien, 1976/1978, 37) – is rejected as foreign. The Irish person who wishes to adopt a different identity has no option but to leave Ireland: 'That is why we leave. Because we beg to differ. Because we dread the psychological choke' (O'Brien, 1976/1978, 87).

Though Caithleen's maturing process is not completed even in the final novel of the trilogy, nevertheless she has grown up enough by the end of *The Lonely Girl* to see through the hypocrisy of her community. When she is hauled back home by her father, she finds that previously sympathetic people like Baba's mother and Mr Gentleman who used to be outsiders in the community, have suddenly conformed and become insiders unwilling to help her return to Eugene. She senses the falseness of their position and wonders: 'Why did everybody hate a man they'd never met? All those unhappily married people wanted to be sure that I came home and had it happen to me?' (O'Brien, 1987, 259). She recognizes that a country whose national identity is centered on the family unit is nevertheless littered with unhappy family lives.

In the final book of the trilogy, *Girls in their Married Bliss* (1964), Caithleen, now Kate, continues her maturing process as she experiments with different identities. She is living in London and married to Eugene but conducting a tentative relationship with another married man. She is also a mother. It is Eugene now who keeps trying to pull Kate back into the 'simple' identity of Irish country girl which is the image he has constructed for her. Needing her to be this, Eugene rejects her when she turns out to be more complicated. For not conforming to a stable category of womanhood, Kate has been rejected three times – by her country, by her family, and now by her husband. This third rejection is the most painful for, by it, she loses her son. The trilogy ends with Kate having herself sterilized. We may see in this not only the elimination of the possibility of losing another child in the future, but also a radical refusal to conform to her nation's view that the natural vocation of Irish women is motherhood. Kate, in effect, refuses her nation's conflation of itself with her body. The affairs she and Baba embark on outside marriage provide a counter to idealization of the chastity of Irish Catholic womanhood, an idealization reinforced by Baba's Irish husband whose Madonna/whore way of thinking leads him to suppose that Baba should be perfectly happy without sex.

The trilogy originally ended with Kate's sterilization but for the 1987 collected edition, Edna O'Brien added an Epilogue narrated through Baba's voice twenty years later. Kate has committed suicide. In a conversation with Baba before her death, Kate puts her feelings of depression down to the failure of yet another romance. Baba, however, has another explanation, she blames Ireland:

Her son and I will have to take her ashes there and scatter them between the bogs and the bog lakes and the murmuring waters and every other fucking bit of depressingness that oozes from every hectometer and every furlong of the place and that imbued her with the old Dido desperado predilections. (O'Brien, 1987, 523)

Baba's hope for vengeance on their native country is that Kate 'rises up nightly like the banshee and does battle with her progenitors' (O'Brien, 1987, 523). In this final volume of the trilogy, Baba's astringent views on Ireland and romance provide a skeptical counterpoint to Kate's romantic notions both about men and about Ireland.

Faced with an outcry over her trilogy in her native land, Edna O'Brien insisted she was not attacking the Irish nation. In an interview given in 1971, she said: 'Nobody outside this country considers that I write a condemnation of Irish life; they just take it for granted that I am writing about a set of people in Ireland' (Eckley, 1974, 24). O'Brien was surely being disingenuous: her choice of subject matter in *The Country Girls*, namely the growth to maturity of two young Irish girls in the 1950s, allows her to give a detailed critique of nationalist pieties about family life and the construct of Irish womanhood. This critique becomes overt in the final volume of the trilogy through the use of Baba's voice. In O'Brien's depiction of Ireland there is no room in the life of the nation for the other, whether in the form of a foreigner, Eugene Gaillard, or of a woman who does not conform to Ireland's construct of femininity.

The Christmas Tree (1981)

The Last September, *The Old Jest* and *The Country Girls* are all accounts of young girls rebelling against the constraints of nation and gender. Lois' attempt to reach out to the other is thwarted by her class. Nancy's encounter with the other does have repercussions for the wider life of her country, though in the process her individual woman's voice is silenced. Caithleen's relationship with the foreign other causes outrage among her fellow countrymen who are wedded to the homogeneity of the Irish nation. In none of these novels therefore is the attempt to reach out to the other really successful. Elements in Irish national life always defeat it. For a more successful working out of the theme of reaching out to the other we must turn to another novel by Jennifer Johnston, *The Christmas Tree*.

Unlike our earlier three heroines, the heroine of *The Christmas Tree*, Constance, is a mature woman who has chosen a marginalized position as a way of critiquing her society and has evolved her own set of values and way of living. Perhaps for this reason, her attempt to reach out to the other in the form of Jacob Weinberg, a Polish Jew, is more successful.

Constance has long been in rebellion against the values of the Dublin 4 society in which she was brought up. When she first encounters Jacob, her consciousness of 'their mutual foreignness' (Johnston, 1981/1982, 35), is prompted by more than just the fact that in Italy they are both in a foreign country. Jacob, a survivor of a German concentration camp, rejects the kind of militant Israeli nationalism he might have been expected, because of his experiences, to adopt: 'I have no love for politics of that kind' he tells Constance. 'It appalls me. No matter what different names it gives itself, flags it waves, it is the same' (Johnston, 1981/1982, 128). Constance too feels foreign to the ethos of the middle-class Protestant world in which she was brought up. Her reaching out to the other, 'some deadbeat foreign Jew' as her sister, Bibi, calls him (Johnston, 1981/1982, 88), results in a daughter whose otherness to the kind of upbringing Constance's sister envisages for her is clear:

> She will be brought up nicely. She will be taught to be truthful, charitable and responsible. To be a lady. She will go to the Convent of the Holy Child in Killiney, and no one will have the bad taste to mention her nose or her deep-set black foreign eyes. (Johnston, 1981/1982, 5)

Like the mother in Kristeva's 'Stabat Mater', Constance literally embraces strangeness within herself, her maternal body becoming the embodiment of alterity within. It is important to note, though, that unlike Kristeva's stress on maternity as initiating openness to the other, Constance's reaching out to the other does not begin with pregnancy but with her meeting with Jacob, which starts the movement of breaking down the boundaries she has erected between self and other. Constance is not able to enjoy her motherhood for long as, shortly after giving birth, she discovers that she has leukemia. She lives long enough, however, to ensure that her daughter will be brought up by Jacob in an international setting rather than in the bourgeois Irish environment her sister envisages.

Johnston's novel is constructed around forty-five-year-old Constance's last dying days. Under the influence of alcohol and pain-killing drugs, she moves in and out of time, recalling fragments from her past life, while the linear progress of her illness is marked out by the church bells which punctuate her narrative. From one point of view, Constance's life may be regarded as a failure. Too easily discouraged, she early on gave up hope of publishing a novel, repeating the pattern of her father's failure to commit himself to the life of an artist. Afraid of the pain of involvement until she met Jacob, Constance protected herself against forming relationships by remaining a virgin. Bibi accuses her of immaturity: 'You are like a child, some Peter Pan character, who had never bothered to grow up' (Johnston, 1981/1982, 125). Constance herself feels: 'Here I am, eyeball to eyeball with death, and I haven't moved the world in any way. I haven't even left a footprint on its surface' (Johnston, 1981/1982, 140). As Tamsin Hargreaves has pointed out, Constance realizes that avoidance of life has led to lack of pain but also to lack of commitment to her own life (Kenneally, 1988, 302).

Defeated by the symbolic order, the dying Constance feels the pull back to the semiotic:

> Coils of mermaids' hair twisting round my legs pulled me deeper into the boiling sea. She smiled and raised her hand in some kind of benediction. Hot salty water washed over my head and ran down my face. The salt stung my eyes, clung to the corners of my mouth. Finish good lady, Shakespeare himself calling from under the water, the bright day is done, a sonorous voice, my head was filled with sound of it, and we are for the dark. Mother, I called. She smiled. Mother, the bright day is done. More weed grasped at my arms. Mother. (Johnston, 1981/1982, 156)

The mother in this passage is not Constance's actual mother, a woman with whom she had a chilly relationship stemming from her mother's disappointment that Constance was not a boy and from Constance's failure to espouse Dublin 4 values. Like those female writers – Woolf, Plath, Tsvetaeva – cited at the end of 'About Chinese Women', Constance in her dying delirium experiences 'the call of the mother' described by Kristeva as 'a call from beyond time, or beyond the socio-political battle. With family and history at an impasse, this call troubles the word: it generates hallucinations, voices, "madness"' (Kristeva, 1986, 156–7).

Yet Constance's life does not end in failure. In her relationship with Jacob, Constance literally embraces the other, a passionate man, passionately involved in life and consequently one who, unlike herself, has pursued his vocation and become a published writer. By ensuring that her daughter will go with him, Constance opens her child up to a future in a world larger and more liberal than Bibi's Ballsbridge. Moreover, as she lies dying, Constance is finishing the novel that will become, after her death, *The Christmas Tree*. Unlike Nancy's meeting with Cassius, this encounter with the other does not foreclose Constance's writing but provides the impetus for it. Her previous lack of involvement with others was an evasion of life which gradually, she now realizes, led to her writing drying up: 'I hate to lose my equilibrium. I look after my self very well. I think that's why I can't write with any success. I have the right instincts, but I have no courage' (Johnston, 1981/1982, 84). Both through her postmortem novel and through her daughter, Constance has finally been able to leave her mark on the world with the result that Jacob believes she will now rest in peace. This is one reaching out to the other which has been successful, not only in terms of Constance's private experience but perhaps also in the life of her nation, in the impact Constance's postmortem novel about her encounter with the other may have on her readers.

The Kristevan theme of women, the other and the nation as presented in *The Last September*, *The Old Jest*, *The Country Girls Trilogy* and *The Christmas Tree* may almost be said to mirror the course of Irish women's history in the twentieth century. In the opening years of the century, as reflected in *The Last September*, the identity of both the Irish nation and Irish women was fluid and open-ended; 'in process', to use Kristeva's term. By the time of the publication of Edna O'Brien's trilogy, the identity of the Irish nation has become homogenized and ideas of appropriate female behavior have congealed to such an extent that girls like Caithleen and her friend, Baba, have very little room to express divergent views with the result that they have in the end to leave Ireland, mirroring the fate of those many Irish women who emigrated in the middle decades of the century out of a fundamental dissatisfaction with the quality of life on offer to women in Ireland. By the 1980s, Jennifer Johnston's heroine, Constance, has a little more room for manoeuvre, although she too has established her life as a professional single woman outside Ireland. Taken as a whole, then, these novels reflect both the process by which the identity of the Irish nation narrowed into rigidity and the way in which some Irish women remained Kristevan subjects-in-process by rebelling against the constricting views of femininity prevalent in their nation, a rebellion which included reaching out to the other in protest at the homogeneity of their nation or, in the case of Lois and Nancy, their class.

Chapter 3

Dialog from the Margins

Introduction

In chapter one of this study we saw that Kristeva's argument, in *Nations without Nationalism*, that women are often particularly well situated to combat totalitarianism since they are frequently positioned as strangers and exiles within the public life of the nation, was relevant for much of the twentieth century to the situation of Irish women, prevented as they were from shaping the discourse of their nation. In an interview given in 1985, Kristeva envisages that, from their position on the boundaries, women will make raids on the notion of a homogeneous nation. By becoming unsettling presences in the text of the nation's life, women will, she argues, contribute to the flexible, heterogeneous and polyphonic nation states which she sees as the states of the future:

> That is to say, a sort of separate vigilance that keeps groups from closing up, from becoming homogeneous and so oppressive. That is, I see the role of women as a sort of vigilance, a strangeness, as always to be on guard and contestatory. (Gubermann, 1996, 45)

Applying Kristeva's analysis to Irish women it follows that, from their position on the margins of the nation, Irish women have the opportunity to use their voices to subvert entrenched Irish nationalism and open it up to a more fluid identity. In this way Irish women may avoid on the one hand complete identification with a nationalism which may be oppressive for them and, on the other, total ostracism from the life of their nation.

This chapter begins by looking at two Irish novels, *Stars in the Daytime* by Evelyn Conlon and *Approaching Priests* by Mary Leland, which illustrate just this point by portraying women on the margins of their nation's life, skeptical about much that goes on in their nation, yet wishing to remain in dialog with it.

Stars in the Daytime (1989)

The position of belonging and yet not belonging to the Irish nation is one which Rose, the rebellious heroine of Evelyn Conlon's novel, *Stars in the Daytime* (1989), ultimately evolves for herself as she adheres to the margins of her society while remaining in dialog with it.

Rose, a young girl growing up in rural Ireland in the 1950s and 1960s, chafes against the restrictions of her life. Hers is a harsh, judgmental, hypocritical society which treats people like Johnny, brought up in a children's home in Artane, as outsiders. Johnny eventually commits suicide as a result of this ostracism. Observing the social and sexual repression of women's lives, Rose is determined to live her life in a different way from her mother and grandmother: 'her grandmother belonged to a mass of Irish women who had not one choice available to them about anything in their lives' (Conlon, 1989, 35). Rose is portrayed as a skeptical observer of this world, occupying a Kristevan position on the margins.

Education seems likely to provide a route out. Rose wins the scholarship which enables her to go to secondary school but after a few years she yearns for more knowledge than the school can teach her and when she arrives at university she realizes that this is not the place to learn the kind of knowledge about life she is seeking. In an effort at self-education she takes on various menial jobs, experiments with sex, marries briefly, has a miscarriage and goes traveling in an effort to free herself from the last lingering constraints of her upbringing. Yet even abroad she does not entirely break the dialog with her nation: 'Rose felt the need [...] to do something about her own country. Let it do something for her' (Conlon, 1989, 148).

In an encounter with a stranger on a train she becomes pregnant. Her family's horrified reaction is predictable. Faced with their anger, Rose retreats to one room from where her only communication with others is through a half door. By this means, Rose adopts the Kristevan model of opening up a way to articulate her views without either on the one hand relinquishing her difference or on the other cutting herself off from dialog altogether:

> The idea wouldn't go away, it dared her. So they've hurt you, they don't want to know of you and your creation, their laws are not yours, shut them out. That means closing yourself in. The half door spoke of talking to people without letting them in. (Conlon, 1989, 155)

Through the half door Rose communicates to the world outside, represented by her parents, a doctor and finally her feminist friend, Dymphna.

Rose closes herself away in order 'to think about Ireland' (Conlon, 1989, 156) and determine whether her country, whose morals are 'those of a sneaky bunch of men who had always been old' (Conlon, 1989, 130), will have a place for herself and her baby. She is eventually persuaded to emerge having re-negotiated her relationship with her family and rethought her relationship with her country. Rose's time in her room has helped clear a space for her to re-enter family and national life on her own terms:

> Rose herself, during what she would in future call The Five Days, had put her fingers in the eyes of Ireland. She had ground them in mercilessly drawing some dubious tears. She had thumped the country in the stomach to see what would come up. And felt the better of it. She didn't do this for the crack, it would have been easier not to know what she found out but at least now she knew where she stood and that had always been the first principle for Rose. (Conlon, 1989, 161)

The epilogue reveals Rose now living in Ireland as a single mother, raising her child and working her way towards discovering her own truths. Her position as a single mother living in Ireland is in itself a sign of resistance to a narrowly Roman

Catholic version of the Irish nation: 'she was outside, where she had always been most comfortable' (Conlon, 1989, 166). At the same time, like the poet Eavan Boland, Rose is reluctant to give up all connection with the life of her nation. She will continue working to bring about change in the life of the nation, to discover 'some sort of woman's truth that could be stitched together with what was already there to make a whole truth' (Conlon, 1989, 171). From her marginal position Rose works, as Kristeva has argued women should do, to open her nation up to other voices, most notably here that of the single mother.

Approaching Priests (1991)

Like Rose in *Stars in the Daytime*, Claire Mackey, the protagonist of Mary Leland's complex and subtle novel, *Approaching Priests* (1991), contests narrow definitions of Irishness and works from the margins to open up her nation to other voices. As a lapsed Catholic and a journalist, Claire stands slightly apart from her society, an observer of its political, cultural and spiritual life. She finds authority for her stance in the following lines from a novel by Somerville and Ross, *Mount Music*: '[...] but she had discovered her soul, and had discovered also that it had been born on the farther side of the river of life from the souls of her brethren' (Leland, 1991, 49). From the beginning, Claire is positioned as an outsider who interrogates the political and spiritual assumptions of her community. The position Claire ultimately evolves for herself is a Kristevan one, contestatory and vigilant, on the borders of her nation yet still in dialog with it.

Approaching Priests is an account of Claire's spiritual and political growth over a span of twenty years set against the background of a nation split between people who welcome Ireland's opening up to outside influences and those who wish to preserve the homogeneity of Catholic Ireland. Claire learns to negotiate her way between these opposing factions while remaining in dialog with both sides. Part One of *Approaching Priests* is set in the 1960s at the moment when the reforms of Vatican II are being introduced to dubious Irish Catholics. Claire is positioned as an outsider in this debate since, although she comes from a staunchly Catholic family, she has renounced her faith. Nevertheless she remains friendly with Damien Sebright, a Catholic priest, and through him she involves herself in the debate over the recent reforms in the Catholic liturgy and criticizes the Pope's encyclical, *Humanae Vitae*, prohibiting the use of contraception.

Like the Kristevan outsider, Claire, because of her position on the margins, is able to maintain dialog with those who have opposing visions for the Irish nation. While preserving her friendship with Damien, she has a socialist boyfriend, Leon, who campaigns against Ireland's entry into the EC on the grounds that Ireland's unique sense of identity as a nation, its language and its commitment to neutrality will be lost, not to mention putting in jeopardy Ireland's unfinished struggle for national unity. For Claire the question of Irish identity is more complex than Leon allows. Her family connections emphasize that Irish identity is not homogeneous. Her sister, Angela, has married an Irish Protestant whose relatives fought in the British Army. The girls' own grandfather served in the British Army in India thus becoming, as Leon points out, part of the British colonizing effort. The sense that the Irish nation is more polyphonic than Leon allows for is underlined during Claire's visit to Fota with her mother. Although of 'Catholic commonality' (Leland, 1991, 79), Claire loves the old Anglo-Irish estate. She resists the exclusive identification of Ireland with Catholic nationalism by claiming the estate as part of Ireland's heritage:

> With each visit she asked herself the question, and although the visits were few the question came again and again – was there never to be a way of claiming its perfection as part of Irishness? Even if the model was foreign, and if to be English was to be foreign, surely this reality lying innocently under the sky could only be Irish? (Leland, 1991, 82)

Claire stands for an inclusive nation, one that will not reject old Anglo-Irish estates like Fota as irrelevant but will cherish them as 'part of what we are' (Leland, 1991, 275) and she questions the simplicities on which Leon's rhetoric about the Irish nation is founded.

From her position on the margins of her nation's life, Claire works to subvert narrow forms of nationalism and open up her nation to a more fluid identity. Her journey down to the south-west in the company of members of Sinn Féin who are campaigning against Ireland's entry into the EC shows Claire resisting narrowly defined political ideologies which threaten to divide the Irish nation. The men are from different parts of the republican movement and have different agendas but have been brought into a temporary alliance by their opposition to the EC. They are committed to the Irish language as an expression of the nation's soul. Though in sympathy to a certain extent – she has tried and failed to keep her Irish up to scratch – Claire knows that in the mouths of these men, 'Irish was a code for something else' (Leland, 1991, 148). She senses the element of 'compulsion' in Father Anselm Daunt's words that: 'we know where the real truth of Irish nationhood lies' (Leland, 1991, 145) and she is aware that the speaking of Irish can carry 'a licence to hate':

> [...] below its creamy luxury of consonant on consonant ran that stream molten with vengeance, as if all future excess must now be forgiven, understood, accepted, everything absolved for ever, because of those eight hundred years of domination by another race, another culture, another creed. (Leland, 1991, 145)

These men's ownership of the Irish language ties it to the past and to a version of Irish identity which resists the modern, pluralistic world.

In the same way as these men claim ownership of the Irish language and the Irish nation, they also lay claim to possession of the Irish countryside, particularly to that land beyond Glengarrif, the historic heartland of resistance to the British:

> It was theirs in the same way the language was theirs, as if they alone identified the symbolism of the territory they surveyed, as if, although it belonged to other people, those smallholders of some ancient lease would recognise, without argument, a superior spiritual right [...] It was a heartland, to be shared only with those who had proven their claim in vengeance, or in victimisation. (Leland, 1991, 149)

During the journey, the men's talk of nationalism with its implications of bloodshed is counter-pointed by Claire's experience of female embodiment in the form of her menstruation. In describing Claire's consciousness of 'the hot pulse of blood against the pad between her legs' (Leland, 1991, 147), Leland juxtaposes the female body to the abstractions of violent nationalism. Claire's submission to a natural process over which she has no control contrasts with the men's determination to wrest control of the land. Claire rejects the men's certainties of ownership of the land and the nation. She resists Anselm Daunt's taunts about her lack of commitment to their struggle, evading his attempts to pin her down and thus control her.

In Part Two, set in the 1980s, the Troubles have started up and Anselm Daunt has become the public mouthpiece of the IRA. Listening to Daunt expound his concept of 'a just war', Claire questions his simplistic certainties about fighting for Irish freedom and the right to establish a 'Catholic republic' (Leland, 1991, 217). She leaves his presence with a feeling of 'creeping revulsion' (Leland, 1991, 220). Claire remains unaligned, on the borders of nationalist discourse, hating the violence in Northern Ireland, hating those in the Republic who give it tacit support, yet feeling compassion for the hunger strikers while refusing to go along with the nationalistic fervor surrounding them.

When her gentle sister Angela is murdered by paramilitaries, Claire momentarily loses faith in her country. To the priest, Damien, Claire cites planning decisions, court judgments, corrupt politicians and 'the extradition shambles' as 'shaming indictments of a shallow, vainglorious and fragile national consciousness' (Leland, 1991, 262). Damien argues that Ireland is still such a young state that it is too soon to judge how it will turn out. He urges her not to lose faith in the Irish nation. And indeed, though she points out to Damien that living in Ireland involves effort, Claire decides she will stay in Ireland and test her conviction that it is possible to live there and evade the traps set by nationalism and Catholicism. Unlike the poet, Jarleth Tattin, whose faith in the Irish language is destroyed by the political uses to which violent nationalists in the North are putting it, Claire does not, ultimately, lose faith in her country. Unaligned, she maintains her dialog with it.

As a result of her decision to stay and try to make a space for herself within the life of her nation, Claire has become, she realizes, 'one of the stories that make up this country' (Leland, 1991, 290–91). The novel ends with Claire's acknowledgment that the stories which form the life of her nation are multiple and open-ended. She knows, for instance, that the stories she invents for foreign magazines about the beauty of the Irish landscape, are only one part of the truth. There is another side of the story to the 'comely maidens and beauteous mountains of dear old Erin' (Leland, 1991, 210), as she puts it, and that is the rapid destruction of the Irish countryside as documented in many passages in Part Two of the novel. Likewise, Claire resists the homogeneous, ideologically closed version of Irish nationalism represented by Anselm Daunt with his 'old slogans, shaken like tattered flags in the face of modern life, modern progress' (Leland, 1991, 154). In contrast to Daunt's rigidities, Claire remains a Kristevan 'subject-in-process', flexible and open to change. As a Kristevan 'subject-in-process', Claire is committed to the polyphonic and heterogeneous Irish nation of the future.

Oscillating between the semiotic and the symbolic

In a development to her argument that women, because of their position on the margins of their nation's life are potentially ideally qualified to disrupt received truths, Kristeva argues that women's subversive tendencies are enhanced because of their general estrangement from language and culture. In Kristevan theory women, because of their imperfect separation from the world of the mother, can never feel at home in the symbolic order; they remain on the boundary between the semiotic and the symbolic. This is an insight repeated many times in Kristeva's work, most recently in *The Feminine and the Sacred*:

> That osmosis with the primal mother, which Freud compares to the Minoan-Mycenaean civilization at the foundation of ancient Greece, might be the source of woman's splitting in two. I also see it as the reason why women cling more firmly to the sensible, to prelanguage, to 'perfumed paradises' – so many imponderables that make women seem a little absent, not really in their place in the phallic order, not at ease in its stilted language. (Clément and Kristeva, 2001, 59)

The association here with the archaic mother does not imply that the semiotic is to be identified with the feminine or the maternal. For Kristeva the semiotic transcends gender, as Marilyn Edelstein points out: 'the semiotic need not be identified with the maternal or the feminine, since the pre-Oedipal archaic mother with which it is associated includes or transcends both masculine and feminine' (Edelstein, 1993, 204). Nevertheless, on occasions, as in the passage quoted above, Kristeva does suggest that women are particularly close to the semiotic.

It is Kristeva's theory of the way the semiotic functions in the symbolic which differentiates her work from that of Jacques Lacan on which she draws. In Kristevan theory, unlike Lacanian theory, pre-oedipal drives are never completely repressed, traces of the semiotic surface in gaps in language and this allows for oscillation between the semiotic and the symbolic which makes signification possible, whereas for Lacan femininity cannot be represented in the language. Ultimately, the semiotic and the symbolic are dependent upon one another in Kristevan theory, which is why, in *Intimate Revolt: The Powers and Limits of Psychoanalysis*, she defines the semiotic as transverbal rather than solely pre-verbal: 'the semiotic is not independent of language; it interferes with language and, under its domination, articulates other arrangements of meaning, which are not significations, but rhythmic, melodic articulations' (Kristeva, 2002b, 259). The semiotic breaks down rigidities in thought and language. It undermines meaning, disrupts structures and hints at a new kind of truth. As Anne-Marie Smith puts it:

> The semiotic can be seen as an articulation of unconscious processes which fracture the common idealisation of those images and signs which secure the status quo, and guarantee the establishment. It is a constant and subversive threat to the symbolic order of things. (Smith, 1998, 16)

It is the semiotic which possesses the potential for inaugurating change.

In 'About Chinese Women', Kristeva extends this psychoanalytic insight about the semiotic to politics. She argues that women: 'cannot gain access to the temporal scene, that is, to the political and historical affairs of our society, except by identifying with the values considered to be masculine' (Kristeva, 1986, 155). On the other hand, she says, if women refuse identification with the father's world they will remain marginalized and ineffective: 'we will forever remain in a sulk in the face of history, politics and social affairs' (Kristeva, 1986, 156). Kristeva advocates a middle way, neither identifying with the symbolic order nor remaining excluded from it. She calls this process:

> A constant alternation between time and its 'truth', identity and its loss, history and that which produces it: that which remains extraphenomenal, outside the sign, beyond time. An impossible dialectic of two terms, a permanent alternation: never the one without the other. (Kristeva, 1986, 156)

Kristeva adds:

> It is not certain that anyone here and now is capable of this. An analyst conscious of history and politics? A politician tuned into the unconscious? Or, perhaps, a woman ... (Kristeva, 1986, 156)

In her essay, 'The Body Politics of Julia Kristeva', Judith Butler argues that the semiotic cannot be as subversive as Kristeva claims because it is always subservient to the symbolic:

> Although she effectively exposes the limits of Lacan's efforts to universalize the paternal law in language, she nevertheless concedes that the semiotic is invariably subordinate to the symbolic, that it assumes its specificity within the terms of a hierarchy which is immune to challenge. If the semiotic promotes the possibility of the subversion, displacement, or disruption of the paternal law, what meanings can those terms have if the symbolic always reasserts its hegemony? (Butler, 1993, 164–5)

However, as Kelly Oliver points out, the potential for effective political practice in Kristeva lies precisely in this movement of oscillation between the semiotic and the symbolic rather than in, as Butler has argued, 'a full-scale refusal of the symbolic'. This latter, according to Kristevan theory, can only lead to psychosis and refusal of language itself which would be in nobody's interests (Oliver, 1993a, 9). Nor, as we have seen, is 'a full-scale refusal of the symbolic' applicable to Irish women who, in the main, have wished to reform the idea of the nation rather than to destroy it. In the rest of this chapter I seek to apply Kristeva's theory that women are especially adept at moving between the symbolic and the semiotic to writing by Irish women which deals specifically with the marginal position of women in relation to the life of the Irish nation.

Fool's Sanctuary (1987)

In Jennifer Johnston's novel, *Fool's Sanctuary*, published in 1987, Miranda in her dying, fragmented ramblings interspersed with songs and quotations, attempts a Kristevan oscillation between 'truth' and time. Miranda is the daughter of an Anglo-Irish Big House, Termon, and her narrative, centering around the War of

Independence, begins by emphasizing her exclusion both on grounds of gender and class from the political events in Ireland: 'I felt briefly at one time a longing to fight for freedom, but I merely cried for freedom; an inadequate contribution to the struggles of a nation' (Johnston, 1987/1988, 3). Unlike the Anglo-Irish Naylors in *The Last September*, Miranda's father is a landowner who takes a responsible interest in the future of his country. He regards himself merely as steward of the land for future generations and wishes to hand it over in good order to the new Irish nation. To that end, he works on projects of tree plantation and land reclamation with his Catholic tenant, Mr Dillon, and he has sponsored Mr Dillon's son, Cathal, to study at the National University. But while her father's work on land reclamation will remain to benefit the new Irish nation, Miranda has made no such contribution: 'I walked like King Wencelas's page, in his footsteps leaving no trace of my own' (Johnston, 1987/1988, 6). In the Anglo-Irish Martin household, women are written out of the narrative. Miranda's brother, Andrew, remarks that their father was 'the first Martin for three hundred years not to serve King and country' (Johnston, 1987/1988, 30), thereby discounting all the female Martins who have not fought. Portraits of these fighting male Martins hang in the dining room at Termon but there is no portrait of Miranda's grandmother who ran the estate for years in her husband's absence.

Excluded from the symbolic order, Miranda places her narrative outside time: 'There is no day, no night, here' (Johnston, 1987/1988, 1). Her tale is that of a young woman of eighteen, a story of Nanny and haircuts, piano playing, horse riding and swimming. Made up of memory, fragments and dreams, it is set against the linear male narrative of war. At times Miranda's criticism of fighters on both sides of the war becomes overt. Remembering the IRA men who came at dawn to shoot Cathal as punishment for allowing Andrew and Harry to escape, she reflects bitterly: 'I looked for heroes then. Those men were the heroes that I got' (Johnston, 1987/1988, 7). At the same time she condemns her brother's accompaniment of his British Army regiment to Ireland to quell the rebellion: 'He shouldn't have come. He should have refused point blank. That's what I'd have done. No, I'd have said no' (Johnston, 1987/1988, 12).

Miranda, like other Anglo-Irish heroines, is trapped in her hyphenated identity. She accuses her brother of making no effort to understand the nationalists' point of view, yet she also wishes Cathal would give up fighting. The meeting between Cathal and her brother makes her aware that though she is, like her father, a republican sympathizer, she is also, like him, a pacifist. She tells Harry: 'There is some obscure morality inside me that stops me from going out with a gun and fighting' (Johnston, 1987/1988, 46). To Cathal's accusation that she does not live in 'the real world' she counters by affirming the reality of her world against his: 'There are so many different worlds. How can you say that one is more real than the other?' (Johnston, 1987/1988, 18).

When Cathal is killed, Miranda's story stops. Looking back over her life, she realizes that the eruption of violence into her life has stunted her development: 'I never reached maturity. I never allowed myself that luxury' (Johnston, 1987/1988, 35). Her stasis is willed, a protest against a world that robbed her of her chance of love. Instead of confronting the 'brave new world' like her Shakespearean namesake, instead of taking her place in the new Irish nation, she chose to remain isolated from the life of her nation in Termon (an Anglicization of the Gaelic word for sanctuary). She hopes God will forgive her 'for the willful destruction of myself' (Johnston, 1987/1988, 132).

Just as in *The Old Jest* Nancy's diary came to an end with her participation in the nationalist struggle, so *Fool's Sanctuary* is a portrait of female development cut off by an act of nationalist violence and as such it provides a telling comment on the stunting of women's lives in a country where nationalist narratives have celebrated male violence as male heroism. The novel, both in tone and content, becomes an elegy for female lives omitted from the narrative of Irish history. But, though Miranda remains excluded from the history of her nation and without a history of her own, her semiotic narrative pulsing against the symbolic order becomes her way of repossessing history and countering the heroic myths which have grown up around male violence.

The Railway Station Man (1984)

The Railway Station Man, published in 1984, opens with Helen Cuffe having already found the courage to renew her life after years of emotional paralysis. Helen is an artist intent on creating her own space, a room of her own outside the competing ideologies of her nation, where she can develop her creativity unimpeded. However, Johnston's novel does not simply proclaim the virtues of withdrawal. The position Helen ultimately evolves for herself is a Kristevan one, on the margins of her society yet in dialog with it.

It has taken Helen a long time to find her voice. Helen stands for flexibility, for change, for receptiveness to life but for a lot of her life she has been surrounded by people who believe in order and rules. Her art teacher blocked her development as a painter for many years by insisting she draw 'inside confining lines' (Johnston, 1984/1989, 5). Helen likes her lines blurred. For her, art, politics, personality, are more flexible than society assumes. She enjoyed the view from her former home in Dublin precisely because, though it was an urban landscape, it was always changing:

> There were seldom strongly defined lines, for the most part roofs merged into the sky, walls seemed to grow from the earth; the sea, the sky, the hill of Howth all seemed to be part of each other, shading and shadow, no hard edges. (Johnston, 1984/1989, 6)

It is revealing that Helen's most significant memory of her married life in Dublin focuses on aesthetics rather than emotion, for her marriage has not been a happy one. Like her art teacher, Helen's husband, Daniel, believes life should be lived within certain confines:

> He had been a neat, well ordered man. He believed in tradition, in keeping up appearances. 'Within the structures,' he used to say to her, 'you can be vague, careless, introspective, anything you like, Helen, but you must keep within the structures. Otherwise things fall apart.' (Johnston, 1984/1989, 13)

Committed to an ordered, hierarchical world, Daniel fears 'some destructive demon that he could see inside her' (Johnston, 1984/1989, 13). He exemplifies masculinist fear of women as representing the chaos and darkness of the Kristevan wilderness outside the parameters of society. He tries to turn Helen into someone orderly who will not walk bare-headed in the rain and who will fulfill her proper female role of keeping his house tidy. His belief in structures and hierarchies inculcates in Helen a feeling of inadequacy as she fails to live up to his standards. She continues for years in an unsatisfactory marriage in a state of paralysis akin to that of Miranda.

Only when Daniel is murdered by the IRA in Derry is Helen jolted out of the lethargy induced in her by living life according to other people's rules. Just as the polarized thinking of the paramilitaries has brought violence to the society in which she lives, so Daniel's linear patterns of thought have wreaked emotional violence on Helen. In fact they have caused her to all but disappear in her marriage, much as the paramilitaries' violence makes people disappear in the nation. 'He believed in the hierarchy of power' Helen tells her son. 'He believed that it was possible to impose, to keep peace by the use of violence' (Johnston, 1984/1989, 56). In her essay, 'From Cathleen to Anorexia: The Breakdown of Irelands' (1990), Edna Longley attributes the seeming inability of both sides in Northern Ireland to countenance 'grey areas' to a masculinist mentality (Longley, 1994, *passim*). Johnston's novel would seem to endorse this view, at least in the portrayal of Helen, who is presented as a woman attempting to think her way out of the patriarchal, linear structures that weigh on her life. She leaves Northern Ireland and moves to a remote part of Donegal intending to start living life on her own terms.

Helen's son, Jack, who shares his father's desire for order, resents this move. For Jack, as for Daniel, Helen fails to fulfill her proper female role, in this case her mothering task. He finds her slovenly and unpredictable and derives more comfort from his grandmother. In Helen's view, old Mrs Cuffe is a woman who colludes with the patriarchy, raising her daughters to be 'slaves' and her son to regard himself as 'some sort of superior being' (Johnston, 1984/1989, 34). Having escaped the role of dutiful wife, Helen chooses now to reject the role of dutiful daughter-in-law. She embraces her marginality, telling Roger: 'I like to live on the edge of things' (Johnston, 1984/1989, 113).

Helen's self-imposed isolation and her commitment to painting are not understood by her son. This is made evident by Johnston's juxtaposition of Helen's female narrative with Jack's male one. Whereas Jack regards the nationalist violence in Northern Ireland as a fight for freedom in which all Irish people should be involved, Helen rejects violence and feels 'there has to be some other way' (Johnston, 1984/1989, 151). All through the novel militarism is linked to a definition of masculinity that includes the duty to fight for one's country. Roger's description to Jack of how the expectations of his family and country compelled him to fight in World War II is ironically reinforced by pictures of the gun battle from the film *High Noon* showing on the television. In 1952 when the film came out, *High Noon*, which portrays a lone Marshal's battle against the murderous Miller gang, was billed as 'the story of a man who was too proud to run'. In the film the Marshal's Quaker wife, Amy, a part played by Grace Kelly, protests against her husband's involvement in the gun battle: 'There's got to be some better way for people to live.' In Johnston's novel, echoing Amy's words, Helen rejects the terms in which the nationalist conflict is described and seeks other ways of defining it: 'When you've something new to say ... oh God, when anyone has something new to say I will listen' (Johnston, 1984/1989, 33). What these other terms might be is gradually suggested in the novel.

Helen isolates herself in order to disentangle herself from the social constructs of her environment and cultivate her own voice. When she paints she enters a kind of semiotic trance:

> She spoke words to herself as she worked, meaningless jumbles of sound, and sang snatches of songs that had become embedded in her head for no reason. (Johnston, 1984/1989, 109)

As Anne-Marie Smith has pointed out, in Kristeva's work, the figures of the artist, the mother and the psychoanalyst are associated in that all three are in contact with the chaos of semiotic drives and involved in the need to order them: 'the mother who must educate the infant driven by bodily needs', 'the psychoanalyst who provides a structure for the patient's regression' and the artist who strives to give form to the semiotic drives (Smith, 1998, 19). This latter process is what Helen is engaged upon here: in touch with the chaos of the semiotic, yet seeking to impose some sort of artistic form on it.

In her isolation, one of the ways Helen resists death-dealing ideology is by valuing the human body and its connection, not to the technology of war, but to nature. There are parallels here with Claire's valuing of nature and the body as a way of resisting the paramilitaries in *Approaching Priests*. In Johnston's novel, Helen's delight in nature and her care for life are juxtaposed throughout with images of violence. Interspersed with references to her husband's death, Roger's maiming in the Second World War, and the struggle against the British, both past and present, are the many hours Helen spends observing nature on the beach or from her porch. Her paintings celebrate both the landscape and the human body. Even her manner of painting is physical for she puts her entire body into the act: 'She painted that way, crouching down beside the canvas, leaning and stretching' (Johnston, 1984/1989, 52). In contrast to her dreams, prompted by Roger's memories of war, of 'young men falling from the sky' (Johnston, 1984/1989, 159) and in contrast to the violent ending of the novel where dismembered male bodies litter the Irish countryside, Helen's sequence of four paintings of Damian, 'Man on the Beach, 1 2, 3, and 4', celebrates the beauty of the young male body against a background of nature.

Clearing a space for her painting has allowed Helen to focus on different values from those proclaimed by the nationalists. Her delight in the sea and in matching the rhythms of her body to those of the waves, provides a counterpoint to Irish nationalism's insistence on ownership of the land. The family unit for her has been a failure and she resists nationalist ideology which requires women to fulfill the domestic role while men lay down their lives for their country. One of the reasons why she rejects Roger's proposal of marriage is that she refuses to be drawn into any of her society's institutions which might impose limits on her independence and creativity. The scraps of English poetry, American songs and other intertextual references which run through Helen's mind point to a jumble of cultural influences which transcends national boundaries.

But Helen is not content merely to create a private space. In accordance with Kristeva's notion of women's dialectic movement between the public and the private, Helen regards her paintings as a way of communicating her vision to society. Helen wants society to 'recognize' her existence; otherwise she fears she will come to resemble some mad woman locked into an ivory tower. Preparing her first pictures for sale, she thinks: 'I must move now, somehow announce my presence' (Johnston, 1984/1989, 52). Through her painting she is determined her voice will come in from the margins and be heard. Roger's check is the first indication to her that she may succeed. 'The de-insulation programme' has begun (Johnston, 1984/1989, 78). She is filled with *jouissance* :

> When she woke up the next morning and looked at the moving shadows on the ceiling, she was filled with a joy that she had never experienced before, and likely never would again. Everything seemed so simple, so right. She lay and looked at the shadows and understood the meaning of ecstasy. (Johnston, 1984/1989, 79)

The text makes it clear that this *jouissance* would not have been available to Helen if her painting had remained a private pastime. Helen's retreat to the margins is not a withdrawal from society as some critics have claimed; it is a strategy enabling her better to disturb that society.[1] That her vision may be subversive and threatening to society is hinted at in the not altogether joking comment by the republican activist, Manus, that artists may have to be sacrificed in the interests of a homogeneous society: 'The people must speak with one voice. I believe it is possible to achieve the perfect society. Perhaps the artists may have to be sacrificed' (Johnston, 1984/1989, 123). Unlike Marshal Kane in *High Noon*, Manus is revealed at the end of the novel as someone who will have to run and run for the rest of his life.

After the explosion which kills Roger and Jack, Helen has to rebuild her life. Her private space is not immune to the outside world, nor will it be defeated by it. To rebuild it and go on with her vision is her response. The opening of the book makes it clear that she has held her first exhibition and that it has been successful. She will continue in her isolation to create works which will have the potential to disturb her society's settled certainties. She may have created a room of her own but out of that room come paintings which she hopes will initiate dialogue with the world outside: 'On canvas I belong to the world' she asserts (Johnston, 1984/1989, 186). We may recall the statement made by another Irish writer, Elizabeth Bowen, that writing provided her with a way of establishing herself in the world: 'My writing, I am prepared to think, may be a substitute for something I have been born without – a so-called normal relation to society. My books *are* my relation to society' (Bowen, 1986/1999, 223).

---

[1]   The accusation that Johnston's novels are female, closed and inward-turning is a perennial one see, for example, Shari Benstock's essay, 'The Masculine World of Jennifer Johnston' (Staley, 1982, 191–217). It has been successfully countered by Christine St Peter in 'Jennifer Johnston's Irish Troubles: A materialist-feminist reading' (T. O'Brien Johnson and D. Cairns, 1991, 112–27).

Born into a gender-divided society, alienated by the death-dealing ideologies of her nation, Helen uses her art to re-establish a dialog with her society, one that will be on her terms. Her determination not to adhere to the socially determined constructs of her environment but to remain on 'the edge of things' curiously echoes Kristeva's assertion that a marginal position within the French nation is the most comfortable one for her personally: 'I have since clung to the space of margin and rebellion, which at any rate is where I feel most at home' (Gubermann, 1996, 258).

In her depiction, in *Fool's Sanctuary* and *The Railway Station Man*, of women oscillating between the public and private world, Johnston exemplifies Kristeva's dictum in *Revolt, She Said* that: 'The role of the writer is precisely to complicate the notion of belonging: one has to belong and not belong' (Kristeva, 2002c, 131). In much the same way, Johnston's women both belong and do not belong to the Irish nation. They withdraw from society in order to attempt to think beyond its polarizing structures, yet by the very act of this rethinking they may have much to contribute to the life of their nation.

A Noise from the Woodshed (1989)

As she explained in an interview, Mary Dorcey's return to Ireland from Paris in the early 1970s was a political act, a deliberate intervention in her nation's life in order to prevent the term Irish being defined solely by conservative ideologies.

> We like to export our troublemakers, our dissidents, our critics. I have a dream of Ireland in which all the troublemakers have come home to roost. But for that to happen some of us have to refuse to leave. To make a roost for others to return to. (O'Carroll and Collins, 1995, 43)

Her short stories in *A Noise from the Woodshed* are designed to give a voice to those previously defined as marginal in the life of the Irish nation: the elderly, battered wives and above all in this collection, lesbians. Dorcey's stories thus play their part in what Kristeva envisages in *New Maladies of the Soul* as the therapeutic role of art and literature, namely providing a space in order to bring to the surface what society and culture has suppressed (Kristeva, 1995, 220–23). *A Noise from the Woodshed* challenges the old rigid ways of thinking, often in the process employing prose which, through its semiotic rhythms, hints at a new kind of truth.

The lesbian narrator of the title story, 'A Noise from the Woodshed', appears to be firmly rooted in the semiotic yet it is made clear that her tale will have repercussions for the life of the Irish nation. 'A Noise from the Woodshed' is narrated in a style which recalls Kristeva's revolutionary language, treading a thin line between sense and nonsense as the 'sense' of the world is wiped out through nonsense and laughter. The pulsing, hypnotic rhythms of the prose indicate women living close to the maternal *chora*:

> Once gotten going this getting it together was hard to stop, this departing from the norm and who's trying, because it was fun and fine and feeling good, and it brought on days, weeks of self-indulgence and knowing pleasure, wallowing in blissful know-how,

revelling in abandon, shared secrets and shames and delight and work and wanting and terror and protest and cooking and cleaning and getting the children to bed, and starting all over again and phoning a friend and saying so it isn't just me, it's the same for you and why did nobody tell us? (Dorcey, 1989, 11)

This is the voice of the repressed other, the lesbian, so long excluded from Ireland's definition of itself and from visibility in the life of the nation. Dorcey's use of the second person throughout suggests the breaking down of boundaries between the self and the other as the reader is compelled to become involved in this story of lesbian love.

As in Kristeva, Dorcey's language aims to bring about a revolution. The women in Dorcey's story not only relax together, laugh together, make love together, they are committed to political work:

And she told you some of the other things that were going on: unearthing imperialism, saving the whale and the beaches, reclaiming the fields and the night, cleaning the rivers and disturbing the minds, redistributing the capital, housing the homeless, whispering the forbidden addresses for women in distress, making refuges for the refugees: victims of the happy homes. (Dorcey, 1989, 6)

Dorcey's story suggests that the semiotic world inhabited by these lesbian lovers has the potential to disrupt and change the symbolic. Moreover the narrator and her lover are not the only women indulging in iconoclastic love:

[...] more and more women are having them – these days of languor and insurrection, armed to the teeth and dressed to kill, riding about backstreets and country lanes rescuing each other from race, class and creed. (Dorcey, 1989, 10)

Women are beginning to speak out about 'their departures from the norm' (Dorcey, 1989, 10). They are starting to experience the delights of lesbian love and in the process there may be a revolution in the life of the nation. The noise from the woodshed turns out to be the sound of lovemaking between two women and Dorcey's story suggests that this 'startling and disturbing noise' (Dorcey, 1989, 15) is spreading out from the woodshed to be heard across the whole nation. As in Kristeva, the semiotic does not operate in a vacuum; it has a destabilizing effect on the symbolic, disturbing settled habits of thought and threatening conventional discourse, here specifically the dominant heterosexual discourse, with collapse.

As Kristeva has resisted feminism because of its totalizing effect, so Dorcey's stories suggest there is not a homogeneous lesbian viewpoint.[2] Indeed her stories are careful to present lesbians in various stages of liberation from patriarchal ways of thinking: Anna in 'Introducing Nessa' is amazed to learn that her ex-husband is gay and even the lesbians in 'A Noise from the Woodshed' initially find the sound of two women making love 'startling'. In keeping with Kristeva's idea of a subject-in-process, Dorcey's lesbianism is open, fluid and various: 'The rules every day

---

[2]   Anne Fogarty, coming from a different theoretical viewpoint, makes a similar comment in her discussion of *A Noise from the Woodshed* in her article 'The Ear of the Other: Dissident Voices in Kate O'Brien's *As Music and Splendour* and Mary Dorcey's *A Noise from the Woodshed*' (Walshe, 1997, 170–99).

self-made. The definitions re-drawn' (Dorcey, 1989, 173). In an interview, Dorcey stated that she regards the lesbian as 'a pioneer, a woman who has escaped from the controlling grasp of masculine heterosexuality, a visionary, a free spirit, an adventurer, a self-creator' (O'Carroll and Collins, 1995, 30). So in 'A Noise from the Woodshed', the lesbian lovers dream of 'the possible world in the making' (Dorcey, 1989, 9).

Another story from this collection, 'Sweet, Practised, Endings' is equally celebratory of lesbian love. It describes a chance encounter and subsequent love making between two women abroad. As in 'A Noise from the Woodshed', the use of the second person compels the reader to become involved in the lesbian love-affair. The story recounts the joyous few days the two women spend making love and sharing with each other details of their lives. This is, however, a moment 'loosed from time' (Dorcey, 1989, 161). In the end, the two women must return home to their 'separate nations' (Dorcey, 1989, 179). Linear time reasserts itself:

> Without doubt you wept and made telephone calls at dawn and promises. But at last and maybe not so very much later after all, life, as we name it: daily existence, the necessary or at least repeated goings on of mornings, afternoons and nighttimes ensnared you, drew your flickering attention into their clutter and oblivion [...] (Dorcey, 1989, 179)

Yet amidst the many demands of linear time, some trace of this moment out of time lingers on, 'there still, hidden deep in the interstices of the flesh' (Dorcey, 1989, 180), a reminder that linear time is not all there is. It has been transcended by the narrator once and the story leaves open the possibility that it will be again.

'A Noise from the Woodshed' and 'Sweet, Practised, Endings' allow us direct access to the world of lesbians. By contrast, in 'The Husband', Martina's joyous discovery of lesbian love is recounted through her husband's voice. Barely suppressed anger and contempt are the dominant notes of his narrative. Martina's story pulses beneath her husband's one-sided commentary suggesting, to the attentive reader, both joy in her new-found sensuality and guilt over the ending of her marriage. Her point of view remains to some extent elusive though, reflecting the elusiveness of the lesbian in a heterosexual world: Martina's story is perceived only through gaps and fractures in her husband's narrative.

Other stories suggest the difficulty and even danger Irish lesbians experience in getting their world recognized. In 'A Country Dance' the narrator and her friend are threatened with male violence as their sexuality is seen to usurp territory marked out by men. In the disco they are surrounded by predatory and threatening males. They make their escape by running down a dark country lane but even then they are pursued by a car full of men chanting abuse. In 'Introducing Nessa', the narrator, Anna, is prevented by social convention from acknowledging Nessa as her lover. She is afraid of the reaction of her eleven-year-old daughter, Sally, and fearful of losing custody to her ex husband, Harry, in Canada. If she comes out as a lesbian at work (she teaches in a Catholic school) she is likely to lose her job. She fears her mother's reaction and indeed envisages that her mother might testify against her if Harry tries to get custody of Sally. When her old friends, Karen and Ben, visit from Canada, Anna alters the room she and Nessa share in order to hide the fact they are sleeping together. This subtle and sensitive story vividly depicts a woman trapped by social convention into camouflaging her life: 'it was not in the light we lived, but in the spaces between – in the darkness' (Dorcey, 1989, 133).

In both stories, the heterosexual prejudice which threatens the lesbians is cancelled out at the end, by love-making in 'A Country Dance', by liberating laughter in 'Introducing Nessa':

> And so there they were, no more than five miles apart, in the early hours of the city; holding tight to their receivers and carried over the distance; bouncing, gushing like water, unstoppable, laughter ran along the wires that joined them. (Dorcey, 1989, 158–9)

The semiotic world 'beyond the grasp of speech' (Dorcey, 1989, 63) is re-established, but the warning that it is always under threat from the Law of the Father remains.

A Noise from the Woodshed is not solely about the marginal experience of lesbians; it reveals that other sorts of stories are often passed over in the life of the Irish nation. 'Miss Callaghan's Day Out' is recounted through the voice of an elderly woman driven mad by the circumstances of her life. Miss Callaghan is a single woman who has been left by her married sisters to cope with her bullying, unloving mother. The sense that she is being cheated out of life eventually drives her to matricide and insanity. Like the narrative of Jennifer Johnston's heroine, Miranda, Miss Callaghan's semiotic ramblings about life in the home where she is now confined represent a protest against the circumstances of her life. They affirm the reality of her experience against the patronizing and dismissive attitudes of the nuns who care for her: '"We are not quite ourself, this morning, are we Miss Callaghan?" Sister Josephine said, taking my tray. But today we are more ourselves than ever' (Dorcey, 1989, 81). Miss Callaghan's narrative affirms her subjectivity against the idealized images of women in the songs her father used to sing to her. Even as a child, she realized that his songs of yearning for the Dark Rosaleen were not about her: 'His treasure he called me – mo stór. But Rosaleen was Ireland and I knew that' (Dorcey, 1989, 81). From an early age Miss Callaghan has had to come to terms with the exclusions on which Irish nationalism has been based.[3]

The voices of battered wives were rarely heard in Ireland until the second wave feminism of the 1970s. In 'A Sense of Humour', Kate has been forced to return to her parents' farm with her two daughters because of her husband's violence. No one in this rural society understands Kate's experience, nor do they wish to discuss it. Women themselves collude in this silence. Kate's mother makes it impossible for her to speak of her husband's violence, in the same way as in the past she forbade all mention of Kate's unmarried sister Breda and the pregnancy which forced her to go to England for an abortion. Kate observes to herself that:

---

[3]   Mary Dorcey continues her exploration of the life of the elderly in her volume of poems commemorating her mother's life and death, *Like Joy in Season, Like Sorrow*, published in 2001.

Reality [...] was made up of the things men did, what could be spoken of in public without lowering the voice. And the rest – all that concerned women only was veiled; a secret, so that even sisters lied to each other. (Dorcey, 1989, 31)

Dorcey's story carefully traces a connection between this public silence about women's lives and women's low self-esteem. Kate's mother, a woman who automatically puts her husband's need for food above her own, believes that women's suffering is simply not important enough to be aired in public. She argues women should endure their troubles (even rape) in secret; or at most confide them to their parish priest, in itself more evidence of her collusion with the patriarchy. These learned habits of silence and low self-esteem are what have held Kate in an abusive marriage for so long: 'She had told no one [...] She knew she deserved it. He would not beat her and abuse her unless she did; unless she was all the things he called her' (Dorcey, 1989, 38).

Confronted by a 'net of silence' (Dorcey, 1989, 31), Kate finds solace in listening to battered women speak of their experiences on the radio. Stories previously concealed in the life of the nation begin to emerge as these women insist on being heard: 'ordinary women, housewives and mothers like herself' (Dorcey, 1989, 35). The women speak of their bodies, of the pain of being beaten and Kate responds to the language 'as if it had been cut from her own flesh' (Dorcey, 1989, 37). Now that the truth about women's bodies is beginning to be heard in public, Kate glimpses the possibility of escape from the confines of her present life, constrained as it is by silence and by her mother's censoring gaze.

Yet when her would-be lover, Robbie, relates an account of his male friends' pornographic antics with an inflatable woman, Kate despairs:

She saw the blank face of the doll, without eyes or mouth; a thing to be used, to be pushed and mauled, their pleasure beaten from her. A woman's face, dumb and blind as hers had been, a body passive and unresisting as her own. (Dorcey, 1989, 41)

At this moment, the symbolic order, the Law of the Father which suppresses women's experience, seems to Kate unbreakable. She runs out into the night. Looking up at the vast sky, she glimpses a world beyond place and time:

A wave of exultation rose in her, a burst of consciousness so swift and sudden that she almost jumped from the ground where she stood and heard herself in the same instant cry aloud for joy. She opened her eyes and gazed about her, marvelling. What a little thing had held her captive – what a small, insignificant, scarcely visible thing had kept her prisoner! She had believed in place. She had believed in circumstance, she had allowed herself to be bound by the trappings of situation: this sky, these patched stony fields she could hardly now discern, a circle of hills, a house, a voice, a pair of hands. (Dorcey, 1989, 42)

Kate's sense of otherness to this narrow, rural setting opens out in the end into a moment of *jouissance* as she experiences a vision of possible freedom. Less radical in style and structure than 'A Noise from the Woodshed', 'A Sense of Humour' demonstrates nevertheless that even in this repressive setting of rural Ireland, the semiotic is present, pulsing against the symbolic order, challenging accepted pieties about women's place.

Mary Dorcey's marginal characters come in from the boundaries to which they have been relegated for so long and demand that the Irish nation heeds their voices and be changed by them. Her stories insist that, however muted their voices may be, lesbians, the elderly, battered women, are part of the fabric of the Irish nation. Her writing creates a space for what public discourse has silenced and exposes, as Kristeva argued literature should, 'the uncanny nature of that which remains unsaid' (Kristeva, 1995, 220). In the most radical of these stories, 'A Noise from the Woodshed', Dorcey's revolutionary language heralds the passage from a former signifying system to a second; it embodies the eruption into a different way of being and a different truth. 'A Noise in the Woodshed' is perhaps the most successful of our texts for marking the therapeutic eruption of the semiotic into the symbolic and the political consequences of that eruption for the life of the Irish nation.

Chapter 4

Reclaiming the Mother in the Mother-Daughter Story

Introduction: Abjection of the Mother

In her early linguistic work, centering on the semiotic and the symbolic, Kristeva's maternal is not biological. However, as she began to focus on psychoanalysis in her works, she turned her attention from the non-biological maternal to engagement with biological mothers. Anne-Marie Smith pinpoints *Powers of Horror* (1980) as the turning point when Kristeva moved from linguistic categories to 'a more concrete clinical and critical engagement with real women' (Smith, 1998, 30).

According to Kristevan theory, every society is founded on the abject, that which has to be suppressed in order for national identity to emerge. In *Powers of Horror*, Kristeva describes the abject as that which: 'disturbs identity, system order. What does not respect borders, positions, rules' (Kristeva, 1982, 4). Abjection is the underside of the symbolic, what society must reject, cover over and contain, usually involving repudiation of our link with animality, sexuality and mortality. Defilement is present when the border between two identities becomes blurred. Abjection, then, is ambiguity: the corpse, which is both human and non-human and thus points up the fragility of identity, is an example of the abject, as are filth, waste, excrement, blood (especially menstrual blood), nail clippings, and hair, all of which blur the body's boundary and for that reason may figure in ritual acts of purity, as Kristeva explains in *The Sense and Non-sense of Revolt*:

> If one examines the food taboos or the desires for purification in various religions, it seems at first that purification is recommended or imposed when the border between two elements or two identities has not held and thus these elements or identities blur. (Kristeva, 2000b, 20)

In contemporary society it is not religion but art, literature and psychoanalysis which for Kristeva embody the therapeutic possibility of speaking the abject. A text like Dorothy Nelson's highly experimental novel, *In Night's City* (1982), is one which, I would argue, 'speaks' the abject. Through the voice of Sara, *In Night's City* recounts a daughter's sexual abuse by her father: 'He was looking down on me and then he pulled the blankets off me an' touched me funny' (Nelson, 1982, 8). Through the voice of Sara's mother, Esther, the novel tells a tale of wife-beating: 'When he beats me I see violet reflections in the window and the shadows flitting by, armies of shadows of things not coming to pass' (Nelson, 1982, 63).

As we saw in chapter one of this study, for a long time silence surrounded domestic violence in Ireland and it was only towards the end of the twentieth century that the sexual abuse of children entered into the nation's discourse. Rather like the work of the French writer, Céline, analyzed by Kristeva in *Powers of Horror*, Nelson's novel shows us what we do not want to see, namely the underside of Irish family life which she portrays in such a way as to arouse, like the abject, fascination and horror in the reader. Even Nelson's style, like Céline's, challenges the symbolic, particularly in the sections recounted by Sara with their stream-of-consciousness, broken syntax, slang and onomatopoeia:

> To sing a lullaby, hush now, hush now. It's not the words that flow from mouths. It's not the eyes that smile, or the hands that touch. Touch lightly now, touch lightly now. These people. I have yet to hear one of them scream. Will someone please scrrrrrrrrrream? (Nelson, 1982, 16).

'The writer,' Kristeva remarks, 'fascinated by the abject, imagines its logic, projects himself into it, introjects it, and as a consequence perverts language – style and content' (Kristeva, 1982, 16).

As in Mary Dorcey's short story, 'A Noise from the Woodshed', Nelson's novel puts the reader in touch with the semiotic, but not, this time, in joyous celebration. Rather her novel with its litany of incest, cannibalism, blood, urine and excrement, could be defined, as Kristeva defined Céline's writing, as 'an unveiling of the abject' (Kristeva, 1982, 208). There is no outside perspective in the narrative; through Sara's voice we are taken directly inside the horror. Only at the end does the novel return to the symbolic order as Sara tries to claim that they were in fact a happy family:

> My Ma was a good woman. Da beat us sometimes but that's because we were bad. He loved us all the same. And my Ma loved me. My Ma LOVED ME. Someday I'll get married and have children just like she did. Everything will be all right. I don't hate being a woman. I don't. I don't. (Nelson, 1982, 113–14)

The insistent repetitions here tell their own story. In a novel which has so clearly revealed the abject, the blurring of boundaries in the breaching of the incest taboo, the symbolic order cannot so easily be reinstated. Nelson's novel achieves that which Kristeva argues we should all struggle for, namely a confrontation with the abject in order to understand the underside of our religious, moral and cultural codes; for it is only by confronting the horror, the abject, Kristeva maintains, that we can begin to understand and to cope with it. In that sense, Nelson's novel is a therapeutic warning to the Irish nation.

In Kristevan theory, abjection also functions as a necessary part of the acquisition of language and the setting up of a stable sexual and psychical identity in the life of an individual. Thus the first object of abjection is the pre-oedipal mother:

> The abject confronts us, on the other hand, and this time within our personal archeology, with our earliest attempts to release the hold of *maternal* entity even before existing outside of her, thanks to the autonomy of language. (Kristeva, 1982, 13)

For Kristeva, individual identity is constructed through the exclusion of the maternal body which the infant must learn to abject in order to achieve the separation necessary for individual identity. Before abjection, the infant is immersed in the *chora*, a non-spatial, non-temporal receptacle of drives where being is undifferentiated. Abjection precipitates the process by which subject and object are produced. Abjection is the rejection by which 'I' becomes. I give birth to myself through the exclusion of not-I. Fear of dependence on the mother, of our materiality and inevitable death remains nevertheless, forever threatening the subject with dissolution and engulfment: 'It is a violent, clumsy breaking away, with the constant risk of falling back under the sway of a power as securing as it is stifling' (Kristeva, 1982, 13). There is a perpetual risk of being drawn back into the undifferentiated *chora*. In *The Sense and Non-sense of Revolt*, Kristeva explains it thus:

> [...] the speaking being's relationship with maternal space is precisely an 'archaic' relationship in which borders are nonexistent or unstable, a relationship of osmosis in which separation, if it is under way, is never absolutely clear. This is the realm of narcissism and the instability of borders between mother and child, in the preoedipal mode of the psyche. (Kristeva, 2000b, 21)

The abjection process is obviously easier for males than for females since the female infant cannot abject the maternal body without, to some extent, abjecting herself. In order to identify as women, females must identify with the abject maternal body. This leads in Kristevan theory to a weak, or melancholy, sexuality. In Dorothy Nelson's novel, where mother and daughter might have been expected to form a bond against the abusive father/husband, the abuse sets them at odds with one another. Sara blames her mother for failing to prevent the abuse, while Esther's main concern is whether the neighbors will find out.

Kristeva's theory of maternal abjection and the obstacle it poses to women in their search for a strong and secure female identity may be used to illuminate a reading of the many Irish mother-daughter stories, especially from the early part of the twentieth century, where the mother-daughter bond is presented not as a source of strength for the daughter but as a source of anguish and disempowerment. Elizabeth Bowen's heroines, for example, are often motherless young girls whose memories of their dead mother are no help to them in their search for a place in the grown-up society in which they have to live. In *The Last September* Lois' dead mother, Laura, features as a sort of madwoman in the attic, her rage evidenced by an insulting drawing on the walls of the box room and scratchings on a window pane. Her trunks rotting away in the box room give off an air of mustiness so that her presence haunts Danielstown and creates an atmosphere of oppression which Laurence, for one, finds suffocating (Bowen, 1929/1987, 107).

Laura's name, as several critics have noted, connects her with the laurels that recur through the novel.[1] Hurrying through the shrubbery, Lois associates these laurels with pre-oedipal sensations of fear:

---

[1]   Bennett and Royle, 1995, 17; Corcoran, 2001, 323–5.

Laurels breathed coldly and close: on her bare arms the tips of leaves were timid and dank, like tongues of dead animals. Her fear of the shrubberies tugged at its chain, fear behind reason, fear before her birth; fear like the earliest germ of her life that had stirred in Laura. (Bowen, 1929/1987, 33)

The fact that the Danielstown laurels are not, as C.L. Innes has noted, deep-rooted and flourishing in the Yeatsian sense, but 'carefully trimmed to grow as dank and oppressive shrubs' (Innes, 1993, 169), may shed further light on Laura's feelings of claustrophobia. Her life has been 'trimmed' by the constraints of being a daughter of a Big House. Her feelings of entrapment linger on in a ghostly way through the association with laurels and affect the House's inhabitants: the laurels sicken the tennis party with their overpowering scent.[2]

The reader is provided with very little information about Laura apart from the fact that her wish to escape the constraints of the Big House led her to flee North into a disastrous marriage. Her example thus signals to Lois the threat marriage poses to a woman's freedom. Kissed by Gerald in the shrubbery, Lois experiences a moment of panic and confusion which she explains by saying: 'I don't like the smell of the laurels' (Bowen, 1929/1987, 172). This scene reinforces the association of laurels (Laura) with oppression and emphasizes the importance of Lois resisting her mother's entrapment if she is to secure her own identity.

However, although her rage against her entrapment warns Lois of the dangers inherent in the female role, Laura's example is of no practical help to her daughter who, as we saw in chapter two, is in search of an identity and a role to play. In her pioneering study of the mother-daughter relationship, *Of Woman Born: Motherhood as Experience and Institution*, Adrienne Rich famously stated that: 'The nurture of daughters in the patriarchy calls for a strong sense of *self*-nurture in the mother' (Rich, 1976/1977, 245). Where this is lacking, Rich argues, the daughter will grow up without pride in her femaleness, ambivalent about her mother and needing to reject her in order to avoid duplicating her subjugated life. It is perhaps this lack of a strong mother figure which leads Lois to exclaim: 'I hate women. But I can't think how to begin to be anything else' (Bowen, 1929/1987, 99). Despite Lois' lack of a positive mother-figure, her resistance to marriage with Gerald, together with the burning down of Danielstown, suggests that Lois may escape the paralysis of her mother's life.

In Bowen's later novel, *The Death of the Heart* (1938), another orphan, sixteen-year-old Portia, faces a similar problem to Lois. Portia's memory of the childish intimacy she shared with her mother, Irene, is of no help to her as she tries to negotiate her way in the worldly, sophisticated atmosphere of her sister-in-law's home. The intense, symbiotic relationship Portia experienced with Irene, a social outsider, has left her unable to cope with the complexities of upper middle-class life in Anna's house:

---

[2]   In Molly Keane's novel, *Good Behaviour*, laurels are also associated with the mother, but this time explicitly with female sexuality. 'A tide of musky, womanly scent from the wet Portugal laurels' makes the young Aroon dimly aware of the nature of the bond between her father and her mother (Keane, 1981, 15).

Untaught, they had walked arm-in-arm along city pavements, and at nights had pulled their beds closer together or slept in the same bed – overcoming, as far as might be, the separation of birth. Seldom had they faced up to society – when they did, Irene did the wrong thing, then cried. (Bowen, 1938/1989, 56)

Yet Portia has been bequeathed by her father to the Quaynes. Their world is 'the world in which she had to live' (Bowen, 1938/1989, 29). In Lacanian terms, Portia has to leave behind her symbiotic relationship with the pre-oedipal mother and enter the father's world of language and civilization. At Windsor Terrace, Portia substitutes for the absent mother, writing (her diary). It provides a more satisfactory guide to the world in which she has to learn to live than those around her: in their various ways Anna, Thomas, Mrs Heccomb, Matchett, Eddie all let her down, Anna, in particular, resisting the mothering role into which Portia tries to thrust her.[3] *The Last September* and *The Death of the Heart* both reveal the difficulty faced by daughters in establishing a secure sense of self in the face of weak or absent mothers, bearing out Adrienne Rich's claim that a mother's strong self-image is an essential legacy to her daughter:

As daughters we need mothers who want their own freedom and ours. We need not to be the vessels of another woman's self-denial and frustration. The quality of a mother's life [...] is her primary bequest to her daughter, because a woman who can believe in herself, who is a fighter, and who continues to struggle to create livable space around her, is demonstrating to her daughter that these possibilities exist. (Rich, 1976/1977, 247)

In *Eva Trout* (1968), where Eva's sole memory of her mother is a shriek (Bowen, 1968/1982, 39–40), Eva has difficulty establishing herself as a person at all.

Reduced to a shriek or scratchings on a windowpane, Bowen's mothers illustrate Luce Irigaray's statement that our culture is 'based upon the murder of the mother' ('Women-Mothers, the Silent Substratum of the Social Order', Irigaray, 1991, 47). In 'The Bodily Encounter with the Mother' (1981), Irigaray elaborates on this statement by pointing to the lack of linguistic, social, cultural, iconic and religious representations of the mother-daughter relationship in our culture as opposed, for instance, to the mother-son relationship. In classical myths, daughters such as Antigone have a choice between identifying with the patriarchy's laws and obliterating the mother, or identifying with the mother at the cost of exclusion and self-destruction. Irigaray concludes: 'Desire for her, her desire, that is what is forbidden by the law of the father' (Irigaray, 1991, 36).

This type of conflict is played out in Maeve Brennan's novella, *The Visitor*, published posthumously in 2001 but completed some time in the 1940s. Anastasia has chosen to follow her timid and sorrowful mother to Paris rather than stay behind in Dublin with her father and grandmother. When Anastasia returns to the family home in Ranelagh after her mother's death, she is punished for this choice by her patriarchal grandmother, Mrs King. Mrs King gives her granddaughter a chilly welcome and replicates with Anastasia the campaign of cruelty she waged against Anastasia's mother. Anastasia spends a lot of time outside the

---

[3] For more on the mother-daughter relationship in Bowen's novels, see chapter 4 in my *Women's Fiction Between the Wars* (Ingman, 1998).

unwelcoming house, repeating her mother's pattern of aimless wandering. She finds her greatest comfort in looking out of her bedroom window at the garden which she associates with her mother's solitary rambles.[4]

In the final scene of the novella, Anastasia is left standing outside the family home singing, as if in a dream, a scrap of a once-remembered song, symbolic of the lost world of the mother. Anastasia's song tells of a happy land 'Where we have eggs and ham/Three times a day' (Brennan, 2001, 80). As so often in Irish women's writing, food is a replacement for the absent mother's nurturing.[5] Anastasia has been punished for choosing her mother over her father by exclusion from the family home, bearing out Irigaray's argument that, by identifying with the mother and her world, a daughter risks exclusion from the patriarchy.

In her writings on the suppression of the mother, Irigaray draws on the earlier work of anthropologists like Jane Harrison who in *Mythology* (1924) and her earlier *Prolegomena to the Study of Greek Religion* (1903) argued that in the Homeric Olympus the Maid (Kore) became split from the Mother (Demeter). As a consequence, the power of the Great Goddess was weakened and her attributes scattered amongst various maiden goddesses. Harrison comments: 'Zeus the Father will have no great Earth-goddess, Mother and Maid in one, in his man-fashioned Olympus' (Harrison, 1903/1922, 285). The decline of the power of the Mother Goddess is linked by Harrison to the thwarting of women's creativity in the patriarchy. For Harrison, the buried Great Goddess is a symbol of the buried artist in all women. Retrieving her, she argues, would lead to a freeing of women's strength and creative power. Harrison's account clearly locates the power of the patriarchy in this initial separation of the daughter from the mother and the consequent suppression of the mother. In this, she anticipates by several decades the work of Irigaray and Kristeva. For Kristeva, too, in *Powers of Horror*, extends the theory of the abject from the individual to cultural, religious and national identity constructed against the exclusion of maternity and the feminine: 'That other sex, the feminine, becomes synonymous with a radical evil that is to be suppressed' (Kristeva, 1982, 70).

In *The Sense and Non-sense of Revolt*, Kristeva reiterates the point:

> [...] the constitution of the sacred therefore requires separation from the physiological and its framework, the maternal and the carnal, which in fundamental monotheism are connoted negatively and sometimes even considered pagan or diabolical. (Kristeva, 2000b, 21)

---

4   Brennan's own mother was a talented gardener (Bourke, 2004, 72) and mothers in Brennan's stories are frequently associated with gardens; see, for example, Rose Derdon in 'A Young Girl Can Spoil Her Chances'. The autobiographical resonances of this novella are even more marked if we take into account that Anastasia was the given name of Brennan's mother, before she changed it to the more nationalist-sounding Una (Bourke, 2004, 31).
5   Compare chapter 8 of *The Country Girls* where the girls in the convent school spend their first night 'eating and crying for their mothers' (O'Brien, 1960/1987, 70). On this connection between food and the loss of the nurturing mother, see Graham, 1996, 16–20.

She returns to the subject in *The Feminine and the Sacred* where she argues in her correspondence with Catherine Clément, that 'what is fundamentally warded off is maternal power' (Clément and Kristeva, 2001, 95). Thus, in *Powers of Horror*, Kristeva argues that Jewish purity rituals evolved out of a desire to separate from the mother's body:

> The body must bear no trace of its debt to nature: it must be clean and proper in order to be fully symbolic. In order to confirm that, it should endure no gash other than that of circumcision, equivalent to sexual separation and/or separation from the mother. Any other mark would be the sign of belonging to the impure, the non-separate, the non-symbolic, the non-holy. (Kristeva, 1982, 102)

Cooking a young goat in its mother's milk becomes prohibited under Jewish dietary laws since this mingles two identities which ought to be kept separate. Kristeva interprets this prohibition as a metaphor for the prohibition on incest (Kristeva, 1982, 105).

According to Kristevan theory, in both the life of the nation and of individuals, the abject is never fully obliterated but hovers at the borders of a subject's or a nation's identity, simultaneously fascinating and terrifying, a constant threat to stable identity. Since the abject does not respect boundaries and because it threatens identity in both individuals and nations, it requires expulsion. Kelly Oliver puts it succinctly:

> Although every society is founded on the abject – constructing boundaries and jettisoning the antisocial – every society may have its own abject. In all cases, the abject threatens the unity/identity of both society and the subject. It calls into question the boundaries upon which they are constructed. (Oliver, 1993, 56)

In Kristeva's argument what has to be expelled from national life is the maternal abject, as she makes clear in *The Sense and Non-sense of Revolt*:

> [...] if we look at the question in religious terms, we see that the social and symbolic pact [...] is a transversal link that is constituted by the evacuation of the maternal: in order to establish the symbolic pact, one has to get rid of the domestic, corporal, maternal container. (Kristeva, 2000b, 21)

In 'Stabat Mater' Kristeva suggests that Catholic societies contain the threat from the maternal body and its *jouissance* through the cult of the Virgin Mary. She argues that in the formulation of the doctrine of the Virgin Birth, all disturbing notions of the mother's *jouissance* are done away with and the mother's power is brought under paternal control. Drawing on Marina Warner's book, *Alone of All Her Sex*, Kristeva traces the way in which a 'compelling imaginary construct' (Kristeva, 1997, 311) began to be elaborated by the Catholic Church on the basis of a handful of references to Mary in the bible. A biography of Mary was invented along the lines thought appropriate for the mother of Christ. The young unmarried woman of the New Testament becomes a virgin, a queen, subject neither to the ordinary human processes of birth (the doctrine of the Immaculate Conception) nor of death (the Assumption). In such a construct Kristeva comments dryly: 'the humanity of the Virgin mother is not always obvious' (Kristeva, 1997, 309).

The patriarchal construct of the Virgin is used to control and defuse the threat posed by the maternal semiotic to the symbolic order. Women identify with the Virgin because such identification is a way both of identifying with the mother and of entering the symbolic order. In this way women's desire for the mother is both appeased and defused. The semiotic is incorporated into the figure of the Virgin, without opening up the possibility of subversion, in a way which both 'gratifies' the male and 'satisfies' women, Kristeva argues in 'Stabat Mater' (Kristeva, 1997, 310). Catholicism is thus able to maintain 'a certain balance between the two sexes' (Kristeva, 1997, 315).

Kristeva develops the arguments of this earlier essay in her later work, *The Feminine and the Sacred*, where she explains that the cult of Mary both appeases male anxiety about the maternal and flatters women with images of Mary the queen and Mary the mother of God: 'Those Maries confirm our participation in the order of the powerful, and encourage our latent paranoia. Who would deny herself that?' (Clément and Kristeva, 2001, 61). However she insists that entering the symbolic order through identification with the Virgin is dangerous for women, involving as it does a certain amount of masochism, a repudiation of the maternal semiotic body, as well as a repudiation of other women, rejected in favor of the unique Virgin. In 'Stabat Mater', by juxtaposing her personal experience of pregnancy and childbirth in columns alongside her discussion of the Virgin Mary, Kristeva attempts to bring into language what has been repressed in the Catholic construct of maternity, namely the semiotic maternal body.

Kristeva's reflections on her own bodily experience of motherhood break up her analysis of the historical development of the cult of the Virgin Mary in 'Stabat Mater' by emphasizing what that cult has suppressed or ignored, namely the pain, tears, sweat of childbirth, the sleeplessness, the milk, the eroticism of motherhood. In other words, Kristeva makes her point about the silencing of mothers in our society by using the semiotic maternal body, 'the immeasurable, unconfinable maternal body' (Kristeva, 1997, 322), to disrupt her analysis of the symbolic construct of motherhood in Western culture. In order to get rid of archaic idealizations about motherhood which amount to no more than 'a masculine appropriation of the Maternal' (Kristeva, 1997, 310) and which on that account have led some feminists to reject motherhood altogether, Kristeva urges women both to explore their own experiences of motherhood and to attend to what other women have to say about motherhood:

> There might doubtless be a way to approach the dark area that motherhood constitutes for a woman; one needs to listen, more carefully than ever, to what mothers are saying today, through their economic difficulties and [...] their discomforts, insomnias, desires, pains, and pleasures. (Kristeva, 1997, 326)

This kind of dialogic listening, Kristeva believes, should allow us to reject the repudiation of other women involved in the cult of the Virgin Mary and opens the way to relationships with mothers based not on idealization but on recognition of their individuality.

Kristeva's analysis of the Virgin Mary, a figure who was crucial to definitions of Irish womanhood for a large part of the twentieth century, is very relevant to Irish women's writing. In the same way as Jewish purity rituals arose from a desire to distinguish Judaism from the maternal cults by which Judaism was surrounded so, it has been argued, in Ireland hypermasculinized nationalism evolved as a reaction against the feminisation of Ireland in colonial discourse.[6] In this hypermasculinized Irish nationalism, maternal subjectivity featured as the abject, that which had to be suppressed in order for identity to form.

There has in fact been a lengthy silencing of the mother in Irish writing. The identification of Irish women with suffering Mother Ireland, reinforced by Catholic doctrine on the Virgin Mary, and later by the 1937 Constitution making womanhood synonymous with motherhood and placing women firmly back in the home, has weighed heavily on Irish women's lives. As we saw in chapter one, Catholic and nationalist ideologies idealized the mother figure with little emphasis on the physical realities of maternity and little practical help for the mother. In fiction and in poetry, the myth of Mother Ireland, sentimentalized portraits of idealized mother figures or, alternatively, martyred mothers, usurped the space which could have been occupied by attention to the realities of Irish mothers' lives. In addition, until very recently, lack of access to contraception meant that a mother's energies were likely to be consumed by the demands of childrearing. Consequently few Irish women spoke as mothers in popular culture, the church or the state.

An exception are some of Mary Lavin's short stories, which will be examined below, and her novel, *Mary O'Grady* (1950) where the portrayal of the mother figure is, however, very reminiscent of idealized Irish Roman Catholic motherhood. Anne Fogarty argues persuasively that the narrative of the various disasters undergone by Mary O'Grady's children undermines Mary's attempt to present her story of self-denying motherhood as a triumph (Giorgio, 2002, 90–91). Indeed, towards the end of her story Mary O'Grady herself reveals doubts as to whether her self-sacrificing mothering has been successful or stifling for her children, finally injecting a much-needed note of realism into the novel (Lavin, 1950/1986, 344). Despite this example, it remains largely true that maternal subjectivity is still a silence in writing by Irish women, though Anne Enright's recently published autobiographical memoir, *Making Babies* (2004), on the physical, psychological and social aspects of childbirth and motherhood, goes some way to filling that gap.

The Abject Mother in Irish Women's Fiction

Positive mother-daughter stories came late to Irish fiction. The iconization of the mother-son relationship in both Irish Catholicism and Irish nationalism ensured that for a long time the mother-daughter story remained unwritten in Irish literature. The consequences for Irish women's sense of self can only be imagined. As Adrienne Rich has said: 'the loss of the daughter to the mother, the mother to the daughter, is the essential female tragedy' (Rich, 1976/1977, 237). When the mother does make her presence felt in Irish women's fiction more centrally than in the texts by Bowen and Brennan discussed above, her relationship with her

---

[6] For the hypermasculinity of Irish nationalism see, for example, Cairns and Richards, 1988, 42–57.

daughter is often portrayed as one of mutual hostility and conflict. Some of the most dramatic examples of this are the novels of Molly Keane where fraught mother-daughter relationships are treated as the subject for black comedy.

In novel after novel by Keane, some of them written in the early part of the century while she was still using the pseudonym M.J. Farrell (*The Rising Tide* (1937), *Loving without Tears* (1951)), others written later under her own name (*Good Behaviour* (1981), *Loving and Giving* (1988)), phallic, castrating mothers are engaged in a power struggle with their daughters and, in the case of *Rising Tide* and *Loving without Tears*, with their daughters-in-law as well. While it could be argued that these cruel, self-absorbed and amoral mothers at least resist the stereotype of the self-sacrificing Irish mother, perhaps because they are Anglo-Irish and Protestant rather than Roman Catholic, the relationships portrayed in Keane's novels are anything but affirmative of the mother-daughter relationship. The novels as a whole endorse the view of mother as abject, someone who is best grown out of. 'Life starts when mother stops' says Oliver, one of the more attractive characters in *Loving without Tears* (Keane, 1951/1988, 8). Too often, as in *Good Behaviour*, the daughter grows up, not to redeem the past but to repeat it by exercising power brutally over others. This type of behavior is presented as the logical consequence of an Anglo-Irish world where horses and dogs were more valued than children and where there was a steady stream of nannies available to take over the mothering role. Keane's novels remind us that mothering is not an abstract or universal concept but always molded by the particular social environment in which the mothering takes place.

In *Good Behaviour*, the mother-daughter story may be interpreted more precisely in Kristevan terms. One of Aroon's earliest memories is that of isolation and abjection. The crust on her mug invokes a sense of disgust: 'Why do I hate the word "crusted"? Because I feel with my lips the boiled milk, crusted since the night before, round the rim of the mug out of which I must finish my breakfast milk' (Keane, 1981, 12–13). Crusted milk is in fact one of Kristeva's examples of the abject in *Powers of Horror*:

> Food loathing is perhaps the most elementary and most archaic form of abjection. When the eyes see or the lips touch that skin on the surface of milk – harmless, thin as a sheet of cigarette paper, pitiful as a nail paring – I experience a gagging sensation and, still farther down, spasms in the stomach, the belly. (Kristeva, 1982, 2–3)

In Keane's novel, Aroon's experience of abjection is followed directly by a description of the grim nursery where her mother is a significant absence:

> I am again in the darkness of the nursery, the curtains drawn against the winter morning outside. Nannie is dragging on her corsets under her great nightdress. Baby Hubert is walking up and down his cot in a dirty nightdress. The nursery maid is pouring paraffin on a sulky nursery fire. I fix my eyes on the strip of morning light where wooden rings join curtains to curtain pole and think about my bantams [...] Even then I knew how to ignore things. I knew how to behave. (Keane, 1981, 13)

In this bleak passage lies the source of Aroon's detachment and isolation and her later self-centered bullying behavior. She has experienced abjection and through this she has come into being: 'I give birth to myself amid the violence of sobs, of vomit' (Kristeva, 1982, 3). The mother's absence and cruelty are what Aroon must conceal from herself if she is to survive: 'I don't blame Mummie for all this' (Keane, 1981, 13). At the same time she learns from her mother's behavior how to bully and manipulate others. When Mr Kiely, the family solicitor, proposes marriage, Aroon adopts her mother's voice to put him back in his (socially inferior) place: 'One of Mummie's phrases came to me and I spoke it in her voice: "You must be out of your mind," I said, and I knocked his hand away' (Keane, 1981, 211). The novel ends in matricide as Aroon feeds her mother the food (rabbit) which most disgusts her, aptly punishing her mother for that moment of abjection in the nursery.

In Keane's hostile mother-daughter stories, clumsy, oversize daughters become victims of mothers who are perfectly adapted to their society's view of females as delicate, passive and pretty. Daughters' efforts to fend off their mothers' attempts to make them conform to constructions of femininity is a recurring theme in the conflict between mothers and daughters in Irish women's writing and it is a theme which features on both sides of the religious divide. Clare Boylan's novel, *Holy Pictures* (1983), depicts a selfish and self-protectively weak mother who tries to mold her daughter to fit in with the middle-class values of 1920s Catholic Ireland. Nan's mother is financially dependent on her husband and when he dies her one idea is to find another male protector for herself, even if it means virtually selling her daughter to do so. Nan's mother colludes in her society's equation of femininity with marriageability and is no help to Nan who wishes to resist this equation by opting instead for university. In Jennifer Johnston's novel, *The Christmas Tree*, Constance resists her Protestant mother's efforts to get her to conform to the standards of Dublin 4 and, as we saw in chapter 2, this conflict is carried on into the next generation as the dying Constance combats her sister's arrangements for mothering her daughter after her death.

In Johnston's novel, Constance has to resist her mother's influence in order to become a successful mother herself. In Maeve Brennan's series of stories about the Derdon family published in her collection, *The Springs of Affection*, Rose Derdon has been left so psychologically scarred by her mother's persistent denigration of her abilities that she allows herself to be bullied by her husband, Hubert. Rose's 'lifelong denial of herself, bolstered and fed as it was by fear' (Brennan, 1999, 155) enrages her husband: 'she would go on forever giving in and make no move to assert herself' (Brennan, 1999, 67). Her mother's cruelty has an impact on Rose's own mothering: Rose pours all her neediness into her relationship with her son, John, for whom her mothering eventually becomes so suffocating that he has to leave; see particularly the stories 'The Poor Men and Women' and 'An Attack of Hunger' (Brennan, 1999, 116–99). Hubert's rage against his wife's timidity as depicted, for example, in 'A Young Girl Can Spoil Her Chances' and 'Family Walls' is, it has been suggested, an expression of Maeve Brennan's own rage against her mother's weak and cringing behavior (see Bourke, 2004, 144–5). In other words, these stories express a daughter's rage against a mother who failed to provide an empowering role model. In a letter, Brennan described her mother as a 'pale patient and suffering cipher' (Bourke, 2004, 197).[7]

In Edna O'Brien's novels, too, mothers are often portrayed as joyless, self-denying victims of male violence. Lacking a secure identity of their own, they fail to empower their daughters with a sense of confidence and this has a catastrophic impact on the daughters' ability to mother. In *The Country Girls*, Caithleen loses her son to Eugene and then has herself sterilized to 'eliminate the risk of making the same mistake again' (O'Brien, 1987/1988, 160). In a later O'Brien novel, *Johnny I Hardly Knew You* (1977), Nora is uncertain at first how to care for her new baby son and eventually loses him to her domineering husband. In *Time and Tide* (1992) Nell, whose insecurity is revealed in her fear of being devoured by her mother from whom she has been unable to separate herself, finds herself replicating her mother's brand of suffocating, martyred mothering in her relationship with her sons.

These daughter figures also learn from their mothers' negative attitudes to sexuality. In *The Country Girls* trilogy, Caithleen's problems with sex are directly linked to her knowledge of her mother's dislike of the sexual side of marriage: 'I had been brought up to think of it as something unmentionable, which a woman had to pretend to like, to please a husband' (O'Brien, 1987/1988, 226). In *Holy Pictures*, Nan's mother refuses to discuss menstruation with her daughter:

> 'Ordinary women do not speak of such things.'
> She could feel herself freezing again, her limbs hinged to rusting metal. 'But mother...'
> 'If your father had come in! If your father should hear you speak of such things!'
> (Boylan, 1983/1998, 103)

Nan's mother is a woman who constantly censors her daughter and her daughter's body in the name of the father.

Given the pressure on Irish women to mother, it is perhaps no surprise that Edna O'Brien sets her stories of women's problematic mothering abroad, in England. Resistance to mothering is also a feature of some of Julia O'Faolain's short stories and, as in O'Brien, the resistance is displaced to a foreign setting, this time Italy. In 'Death Duties' Celia, 'the youngest of a fertile Irish family of nine' (O'Faolain, 1968, 142), is open about her dislike of children, despite the fact that her Italian in-laws are desperate for her to produce an heir. Finding herself pregnant by her brother-in-law, Celia procures an illegal abortion. In 'An Afternoon on Elba', the mother is so distanced from the care of her young son that mother and son speak different languages. While her language is English, he speaks only Italian learned from his nanny. The placing of these stories abroad raises the question as to whether O'Faolain at this date (the late 1960s) felt

---

[7]   This lack of a positive role model must have been all the more galling for Brennan since, as Angela Bourke points out, her mother started out as a rebel and a feminist, active in the 1916 Rising and in the Anglo-Irish War and the Civil War: 'but then in motherhood and middle age [she] becomes reduced to silences and domesticities, her individuality occluded by her relationships and her roles' (Bourke, 2004, 4). Una Brennan's life mirrors the fate of feminism in the middle decades of the century in Ireland.

prevented by Ireland's idealization of motherhood from giving these stories of resistance to motherhood an Irish setting.

Irish women's novels of the 1960s, 1970s, and 1980s frequently feature daughters who flee their mothers and often their mother country in order to escape repeating their mothers' thwarted lives. In Johnston's novels, *The Christmas Tree* and *The Illusionist*, her heroines move to London in order to lead the life they wish: 'At that time I was preferring London to Dublin. It was to do with my mother' Stella explains in *The Illusionist* (Johnston, 1995/1996, 7). However, in England Stella remains homesick for Ireland, and her mother's influence is not easily shaken off: 'I heard her voice constantly in my head' (Johnston, 1995/1996, 89). After many years and an abusive marriage, Stella returns to Ireland reconciled to her mother whom she now sees as 'benign' and 'comfortable' (Johnston, 1995/1996, 212). She wishes nothing more for her parents than that they will 'move quietly to their deaths still full of the certainties for which I used to despise them' (Johnston, 1995/1996, 90).

More often, though, removal to a new environment exacerbates the conflict between mothers and daughters as the daughters embrace the culture of their new country, while their mothers remain locked in old ways of thinking. This conflict is particularly apparent in Edna O'Brien's short story, 'Cords', where the narrator, Claire, who has lived in London for several years and mixed with people holding very different views from the people back home in Ireland, receives a visit from her mother: 'she tried to tell her mother that the world was a big place and contained many people, all of whom held various views about various things' (O'Brien, 1968, 143). Her mother remains unconvinced and indeed, faced with her mother's disapproval, Claire herself begins to wonder whether her present life is satisfactory: 'There was no one she trusted, no one she could produce for her mother and feel happy about it' (O'Brien, 1968, 142). In Kate O'Riordan's novel, *The Memory Stones*, it is not until Nell's return to Ireland after her mother's death that she is able to resolve her feelings about their relationship and understand that her mother did after all love her. With that understanding comes an opening out of her own emotional life. Nell will give up 'loving at a distance' (O'Riordan, 2003, 325) and take the risk of welcoming her lover into her flat, along with his daughter and her baby.

Perhaps because of its negative portrayal in Irish women's fiction, the Irish mother-daughter story has been largely neglected by literary critics. An exception is Ann Owens Weekes' article, 'Figuring the Mother in Contemporary Irish Fiction' (Harte and Parker, 2000, 100–123), where Weekes comes to similar conclusions as mine, namely that negative mother-daughter stories predominate in Irish women's fiction from the 1960s, 1970s and 1980s with mothers being either absent, or weak and uncertain in their mothering. Weekes' description of the 'concerned, uncertain, unsupported mother figures' who feature in Irish women's fiction (Harte and Parker, 2000, 121) is particularly illuminating in the context of the mother-daughter relationships in Mary Lavin's short stories, where the mother is not demonized as in the work of Molly Keane and Edna O'Brien, but shown to be hampered in her own mothering by the social constraints of the environment in which she mothers. In 'The Nun's Mother', for example, where Mrs Latimer genuinely wishes to dissuade her daughter Angela from entering a convent, her culture prohibits her from talking frankly to her daughter about the sexual pleasure to be found in marriage.

Another Lavin short story, 'A Cup of Tea', portrays a mother whose world has been centered in domesticity and who, as a consequence, is unable to empathize with her university-educated daughter. Again, as in *Good Behaviour*, the abject features when Sophy rejects with disgust the boiled milk in the cup of tea her mother offers her. The mother lifts off the offending skin which has formed on the milk, declaring: 'There's nothing disgusting about it at all. In fact, it's full of calcium and good for you' (Lavin, 1999, 95). She adds that at home they always boiled the milk. However Sophy refuses to be reconciled to the tea, as she refuses to be reconciled to her mother's view of life: 'You did a lot of things in your home that sound queer to me, if it comes to that' (Lavin, 1999, 96). Sophy resists her mother's efforts to pull her back into a world of domesticity, identifying instead with her scholarly father.

The widowed mothers who figure prominently in Lavin's stories expose the vulnerability of the widow in the Ireland of the 1940s, 1950s and 1960s and of mothers who attempted to raise their children without a male presence. 'In the Middle of the Fields' portrays the widowed mother's vulnerability both to physical attack and to being taken advantage of in business transactions with men. 'Villa Violetta' conveys the panic of a widow abroad for the first time with her young daughters. Her panic is increased by the presence of the frosty tourist agent, Carlotta, who expects foreign women to have husbands to help them find accommodation.

Rather than the open hostility displayed between mothers and daughters in the work of Molly Keane and Edna O'Brien, the conflict between mothers and daughters in Mary Lavin's short stories is often presented as the result of generational misunderstandings. Mothers and daughters make well-intentioned efforts to understand one another but these efforts usually fail due to mutual suspicion and insecurities which have built up between them over the years. As Ann Owens Weekes points out: 'Not only do the women read and misread each other, they also fall into inherited patterns of behaviour [...] Having once caused conflict, these patterns are likely to do so again' (Harte and Parker, 2000, 113). This is most clearly seen in a story such as 'A Family Likeness' where the misunderstandings between Ada and her mother are replicated in the misunderstandings between Ada and her daughter, Laura. Ada and Laura almost willfully misread one another, their sensitivity to one another's remarks heightened by their mutual fatigue which in Ada's case is the result of old age, in Laura's the result of mothering a young child.

What Lavin leaves us with, Weekes suggests, are brief moments of intimacy between mother and daughter before the misunderstandings begin again. In 'Senility', Laura's tactlessness at first seems like a deliberate attempt to undermine her elderly mother's dignity. Later it becomes apparent that her concern over Ada's incontinence arises out of love, as she says: 'I couldn't bear it if anything happened to you. It would break my heart' (Lavin, 1977, 122). In turn, Ada shows her love and concern for her daughter when she amends her prayer about old age from 'Don't make it too hard on me' to 'on Laura, I mean' (Lavin, 1977, 137). In 'A Walk on the Cliff', the misunderstandings and tensions caused by the mother's sensitivity and the daughter's eagerness to be the perfect hostess for her mother in her new married home dissolve in a moment of laughter as they hurry to rescue the dinner from burning. This does not, however, prevent the tensions from resurfacing later. In the end, Lavin's mothers and daughters never succeed in disentangling themselves from the social constraints of their environment, particularly the pressure to conform to notions of self-sacrificing femininity, and these pressures and constraints have an invidious effect on their relationship.

Reclaiming the Mother in Irish Women's Fiction

In her chapter on Irish mothers and daughters in *Writing Mothers and Daughters: Renegotiating the Mother in Western European Narratives by Women* (ed. Adalgisa Giorgio, 2002, 85–118), Anne Fogarty, like Weekes, demonstrates that the mother-daughter relationship in Irish women's fiction has usually been portrayed as a hostile and disempowering one for the daughter. Towards the end of her analysis, however, Fogarty suggests that there are signs that the mother-daughter story, based on conflict and repudiation of the mother, may be changing as daughters seek to recover the history of the mother in order to help them in their own quest for identity and self-knowledge. In the rest of this chapter I would like to build on Anne Fogarty's statement in order to explore ways in which Irish women writers have sought to reclaim the mother's voice.

Maeve Brennan's writings provide an early example of this. As we have seen, in her stories of the Derdon family, Brennan portrays her mother, in the guise of Rose Derdon, as a down-trodden figure. Rose's passivity enrages her husband who becomes in these stories the mouthpiece for Brennan's own anger against her mother and perhaps, from the vantage point of Brennan's life in the States, a means of expressing her general disillusionment at what Irish womanhood had become after Independence (Bourke, 2004, 173). However, after her mother's death in 1958 Brennan, in some confusion as to her own identity, began to desire to understand her mother's life: 'Since Una's death, Maeve's writing had been bound up with trying to find her and understand her: "I must know what she was," she wrote to Maxwell' (Bourke, 2004, 220). In a letter dated 1963, Brennan describes her efforts to retrieve her mother's voice: 'the voice you can say anything in [...] infinite, always changing, endlessly responsive, and capable of containing anything, and everything' (Bourke, 2004, 232).

To this end, Brennan embarked on a series of stories about the Bagot family which were published between 1964 and 1968 in *The New Yorker*. Delia Bagot shares Rose Derdon's anxiety and passivity which so annoys her husband Martin, but her relationship with her two small daughters is portrayed in a much more positive light than Rose's relationship with her son John. The Lily and Margaret who feature in these stories are portraits of Maeve and her younger sister, Derry. In 'The Sofa', mother and daughters delight in the carefree look of the front room which has been cleared of furniture in anticipation of the arrival of a new sofa. Waiting for the sofa, Delia experiences a moment outside time: 'the clock, which had been so domineering all these years, had no power over her today' (Brennan, 1999, 248). In the light of 'About Chinese Women' where Kristeva associates clock time with the father ('there is no time without the Father', Kristeva, 1986, 153), it may be argued that what Delia is experiencing here in her moment out of time is women's time. Ceasing to be bullied by the clock, Delia recovers some of the confidence that had been hers before marriage:

> She was in touch then with a spirit she did not know she possessed, and when she smiled, her face was lighted by the faint and faraway glimmer of an assurance that was truly hers, but truly buried, buried deep down under the sound, useful earth of her thirty-five years of unquestioning, obedient life. (Brennan, 1999, 249)

It is as if in this story Brennan is peeling away the layers of years of socialization and marriage in an effort to reclaim her mother's voice, 'the voice you can say anything in' (Bourke, 2004, 232).

What Brennan seems to be trying to do in these stories is to bring to the surface the submerged world of the mother and to affirm the strength of the mother-daughter bond. In another short story in this series, 'A Shadow of Kindness', Delia is rescued from loneliness over her daughters' absence by retrieving a moment of kinship with her own mother whose shadow she sees reflected on the wall. In a story published slightly earlier than these Bagot stories, 'The Beginning of a Long Story' published in *The New Yorker* in 1961, the mother remains unnamed but shares a family likeness with the anxious figures of Rose Derdon and Delia Bagot. Again, though the relationship between the mother and her husband is strained and tense, her relationship with her daughters is close: 'She was always unsure of herself except when she was dealing with her children' (Brennan, 2000, 210). She also deals confidently with the poor men and women who come begging at her door and the story ends with an affirmation of the mother-daughter bond as the eldest daughter, Ellen, dreams of replicating her mother's nurturing role with the poor men and women.

Nonetheless, despite Brennan's attempts to retrieve the mother's voice, her mother figures remain trapped in domesticity. After the freedom of a moment outside time, 'The Sofa' ends with mother and daughters eating dinner in the kitchen 'as usual' (Brennan, 1999, 251). In 'The Carpet with the Big Pink Roses on It', Delia is too conscious of what the neighbors will say to be able to yield to the temptation to lie down on the carpet laid out on the lawn during spring cleaning:

> The carpet looked so inviting down there on the grass. It would be just right, to lie there in the open air, and dream, not sleep. She envied people who felt free to do as they liked, without feeling self-conscious or ashamed of themselves. There were a lot of women who would lie down on that grass, or that carpet, and never think the less of themselves, and never wonder what other people thought of them. Mrs Bagot wished she could be like that. They were lucky, those people. (Brennan, 1999, 224)

It is Delia's daughter, Lily, who defies the neighbors' opinions and climbs onto the carpet. Lily imagines flying away to foreign cities, as Brennan herself escaped her mother's life of domesticity in Dublin to live the cosmopolitan life of a writer: 'Down in the garden Lily sat on the carpet and traveled without delay to Paris' (Brennan, 1999, 227).

Brennan's Bagot stories are an early example of a daughter trying, and perhaps in the end failing, to present the mother's world in a way that might be empowering for a daughter's sense of identity. A more successful presentation of a positive mother-daughter relationship may be found in Kate Cruise O'Brien's humorous and insightful novel, *The Homesick Garden*, published in 1991. There is little sentimentality about motherhood in *The Homesick Garden*: when Liz's sister Grace becomes pregnant, Liz and Grace agree that having a baby is 'a most unreal thing to do' (O'Brien, 1991, 3). The mother-daughter story in the novel is presented through the eyes of Liz's fifteen-year-old daughter, Antonia, and O'Brien beautifully conveys both the daughter's recognition of her mother's vulnerability and her awareness that her mother is doing the best job that she can. Antonia is wryly observant of the pressures her father exerts on her mother, monitoring her weight, her drinking and standards of cleanliness about the house, while never himself offering to lend a hand.

Antonia's recognition of her mother a person separate from herself and with her own history would seem to confirm Jessica Benjamin's argument in *The Bonds of Love* (1988) that recognition of the mother's subjectivity is as important a developmental goal as separation from the mother. In *The Bonds of Love*, Benjamin investigates the notion of intersubjectivity and posits the mother-child relationship as one between two mutually loving but autonomous beings, both of whom grow and change through the course of the relationship:

> The idea of mutual recognition is crucial to the intersubjective view [...] it implies that we actually have a need to recognise the other as a separate person who is like us yet distinct. This means that the child has a need to see the mother, too, as an independent subject, not simply as the 'external world' or an object of his ego. (Benjamin, 1990, 23)

Benjamin's insistence that the predisposition to separation and individuation is present in the mother-child dyad and that mutual recognition is as significant a developmental goal as separation frees us from the classic Freudian paradigm whereby the child is initially fused with the mother and only achieves selfhood by overthrowing her with the help of the father. It also, as Benjamin argues, frees us from the insistence of object-relations theorists such as Donald Winnicott on the mother as maternal mirror:

> Self psychology is misleading when it understands the mother's recognition of the child's feelings and accomplishments as maternal mirroring. The mother cannot (and should not) be a mirror [...] she must be an independent other who responds in her different way. Indeed, as the child increasingly establishes his own independent centre of existence, her recognition will be meaningful only to the extent that it reflects her own equally separate subjectivity. (Benjamin, 1990, 24)

In Kate Cruise O'Brien's novel, Liz recognizes her daughter's independent existence from the start: "'When I was a girl like you," she said once with a smile. "Only I never was a girl like you. I was something between a coward and a goody-goody'" (O'Brien, 1991, 1). Antonia, too, recognizes her mother as a person separate from her daughter's need of her. She acknowledges that Liz is a loving mother who nevertheless does not always behave like a mother. The Liz Antonia observes is often unreliable, cross and uncertain. She can be reduced to a quivering wreck by her own mother, Antonia's grandmother. Like one of Molly Keane's mothers, Antonia's grandmother plays the feminine role to the hilt, strapping herself into a corset, pretending helplessness, eating 'like a bird', while waging a continuing battle to denigrate Liz.

The Homesick Garden is not a Molly Keane novel, however. In relegating the castrating phallic mother to an earlier generation, O'Brien suggests that the old days of mothers and daughters as hostile rivals in a phallocentric society may be coming to an end. In contrast to *The Visitor* by Maeve Brennan where both Anastasia and her mother are defeated by the powerful and selfish Mrs King, in *The Homesick Garden* Liz eventually finds the strength to stand up to her mother and to protect her daughter from the bullying patriarchal grandmother. There is no sign in O'Brien's novel that the power struggle will be carried on into the next generation. By portraying a close and loving relationship between a mother and her, almost grown, daughter, *The Homesick Garden* heralds a new era in the Irish mother-daughter relationship.

Anne Fogarty's statement that there are signs that the Irish mother-daughter story, based on conflict and repudiation of the mother, may be changing is borne out by the above examples. One may go further and argue that in the 1990s, mirroring changes in Irish society, the mother-daughter story begins to be presented in Irish women's fiction in a way which now lends itself to being read specifically in the light of Kristeva's writings on the mother. The remainder of this chapter will be devoted to a Kristevan reading of three novels of the 1990s, *Down by the River*, *The Invisible Worm* and *Belonging*, looking particularly at ways in which Irish women writers portray the attempt by daughters to bring the maternal body into language. In 'Julia Kristeva: Take Two', Jacqueline Rose argues that Kristeva's concept of the semiotic, especially where it is related to the mother and placed beyond language, is 'the least useful aspect of Kristeva's work' (Oliver, 1993b, 50). It is the contention of this chapter, however, that Kristeva's theory of the semiotic is particularly illuminating in the context of the mother, the abject and the nation.

Down by the River

In Edna O'Brien's novel, *Down by the River*, published in 1996, the fact that maternal subjectivity features as the abject of the Irish nation is evident when fourteen-year-old Mary McNamara, pregnant as a result of rape by her father, becomes silenced in the ensuing national debate over whether she should be allowed to travel to England for an abortion. As different political groups air their views it becomes clear that Mary's body has become the boundary by which the Irish nation is defined. The debate does not entirely fall along gender lines. One of O'Brien's most interesting achievements in this novel is the polyphonic range she grants to her male characters. Some of the most virulent anti-abortionists are women. Some of the most sympathetic characters are men: Mary's headmaster, Luke, the Buddhist musician who gives her shelter, Cathal, her understanding lawyer, L'Estrange, her barrister, Frank, the judge who is prepared to listen to his daughter.

Down by the River is loosely based on the 1992 'X' case, mentioned in chapter one of this study, where fourteen-year-old Miss X, pregnant as the result of rape by the father of a school friend, was initially prevented by a High Court order from traveling to England for an abortion. The Irish Supreme Court subsequently reversed the High Court order and ruled that abortion is legal where there is a substantial threat to the life of the woman (Miss X had threatened suicide). In her analysis of the 'X' case, in 'Death of a Nation: Transnationalism, bodies and abortion in late twentieth-century Ireland', Angela Martin argues that:

> Miss X's experience exposes Irish anti-abortion rhetoric as a violent form of nationalist identity politics in which a coherence is established between the materiality of the nation (as it is manifested in the state juridical structure) and the materiality of women's bodies. (Mayer, 2000, 66)

In the novel, as various groups discuss what becomes known as 'Magdalene versus the nation' (echoing the Catholic ideology that hangs over the debate), it is clear that Mary's desire for an abortion threatens the very category of Irish woman as constructed by nationalist ideology. Anti-abortionists argue that if the abortion is permitted, Ireland's alterity will be abolished and her moral integrity threatened. 'We're a Christian country [...] We're a model for the whole world' declares one of the judges deciding Mary's case (O'Brien, 1996/1997, 285). The Irish state, and the nationalist ideology which underpins it, do not regard Mary's pregnant body as autonomous. 'It's not your child' a leading pro-lifer tells Mary (O'Brien, 1996/1997, 175). Mary's maternal subjectivity is denied. She is condemned, to quote Kristeva in 'About Chinese Women', to 'childbearing and procreation in the name of the father' (Kristeva, 1986, 146).

The connection between Ireland's masculinist nationalism and control of women's bodies is clearly demonstrated in the opening scene of the novel where Mary's father measures out his property before proceeding to rape his daughter, showing he has both land and female bodies under his control. The narrative then switches to Mary's bedroom which is dominated by a statue of the Virgin Mary, another agent of suppression in Mary's world. The Virgin-Mother, image of purity, can be no help to Mary who feels so unclean that she has been washing her private parts daily in the river. This bears out Kristeva's analysis of the Catholic construct of the Virgin Mary in 'Stabat Mater' where, following Marina Warner, she argues that the cult of the Virgin Mary has been used to silence and control women by setting before them an impossible ideal of virgin and mother: 'that ideal totality that no individual woman could possibly embody' (Kristeva, 1997, 317). Mary cannot tell her experience to anyone, least of all to the Virgin-Mother. Her rape is, literally, unspeakable.

Nor can Mary tell her mother, Bridget. Bridget, subject to beatings from her husband, does not see the abuse, or perhaps, since the servant, Lizzie, is aware of it, does not want to see it. Bridget has her own secret about her body that she cannot tell: she is dying, significantly in view of her failed motherhood, of ovarian cancer. Like Mary, Bridget has failed to speak out about her suffering:

Her mother had died, struggling, struggling to get something out, something that mattered and even when her tongue and her speech had failed her she had tried to convey it with her gums, her spittle. (O'Brien, 1996/1997, 60).

In 'The Bodily Encounter with the Mother' (1981), Luce Irigaray analyzes the silencing of the mother in the patriarchy and argues that daughters must work to recover the mother's story or else risk being silenced themselves:

We must refuse to let her desire be annihilated by the law of the father. We must give her the right to pleasure, to *jouissance*, to passion, restore her right to speech, and sometimes to cries and anger.
    We must also find, find anew, invent the words, the sentences that speak the most archaic and most contemporary relationship with the body of the mother, with our bodies, the sentences that translate the bond between her body, ours, and that of our daughters. We have to discover a language which does not replace the bodily encounter, as paternal language attempts to do, but which can go along with it, words which do not bar the corporeal, but which speak corporeal. (Irigaray, 1991, 43)

As in O'Brien's novel, Irigaray directly links women's silence with suppression of women's bodies in a patriarchy. The sense that her mother died with 'unfinished words' on her lips, silences Mary also: 'she now would not be able to say that which she had come to say' (O'Brien, 1996/1997, 64). Bridget's silence is no help to Mary who has come to ask her mother's permission to renege on her promise to stay at home with her father. The silencing of the mother in the patriarchy, as Irigaray warns, silences the daughter too and places her in danger from the father.

But there is more to the mother-daughter story in *Down by the River* than silence and defeat. On her deathbed, Bridget finally makes her voice heard in song and her suppressed body erupts in a vast gush of water. Similarly, Mary's body provides her with a way out of her predicament, through a spontaneous miscarriage.[8] Her tears – according to Kristeva in 'Stabat Mater', tears are 'the metaphors of nonspeech, of a "semiotics" that linguistic communication does not account for' (Kristeva, 1997, 320) – tell her lawyer what she cannot speak out loud, the name of her baby's father. Thus by the end of the novel, Mary's body has broken through the controls nationalist and Catholic ideology have tried to impose on it.

In 'About Chinese Women', Kristeva defines women's *jouissance* as that 'which breaks the symbolic chain, the taboo, the mastery' (Kristeva, 1986, 154). *Down by the River* ends with such a moment of *jouissance* as Mary, after her miscarriage, finally breaks her silence and, echoing her mother on her deathbed, raises her voice in song:

---

[8]   Although this mirrors the actual situation of Miss X who apparently suffered a miscarriage (Brown, 1981/2004, 366), the novel leaves room for an added feminist reading. O'Brien lays a trail of hints that Mary's miscarriage may have been induced with the help of Mrs B who gives her a hand mirror (O'Brien, 1996/1997, 283). The reference to 'wires in her, prongs' (O'Brien, 1996/1997, 289) also suggests Mary is an active agent. I am grateful to Ashgate's anonymous reader for this point.

Her voice was low and tremulous at first, then it rose and caught, it soared and dipped and soared, a great crimson quiver of sound going up, up to the skies and they were silent then, plunged into a sudden and melting silence because what they were hearing was in answer to their own souls' innermost cries. (O'Brien, 1996/1997, 297–8).

Mary finds her voice, breaking through the various patriarchies that have sought to silence her and, the last line suggests, her nation responds.

In his analysis of *Down by the River*, Rüdiger Imhof finds this final scene 'unconvincing' (Imhof, 2002, 95). In fact Edna O'Brien prefigures quite remarkably something that happened in an English courtroom in 2003. After the inquest into the death of her child, Victoria, following prolonged abuse and torture by relatives, her mother, Berthe Climbié, broke into song. The scene was described by Libby Purves in *The Times*:

Hampered by the language barrier, unwilling merely to weep and read a statement, this woman from a simpler and poorer society went straight to the point. She sang.

Undeterred by the cameras and microphones and the reporters impatient to do their piece-to-camera, she brought time to a standstill and in a strong, natural voice, without self-consciousness, she sang in French Victoria's favourite song about there being 'no frontiers between the children of God'.

It was an elegant tribute to a real child, but something else too: a lesson out of Africa for the bustling, self-important West. It reminded us that we all have music as another language within us, that song can say what speech cannot, and that in grief and horror a woman can still sing about hope. (*The Times*, February 1, 2003, 3)

Like Victoria's mother, like her own mother, Mary cuts through the obfuscation of legal procedure with a song from the heart. The abject has finally found a voice and may, it is suggested, alter the way the Irish nation looks at itself.

The Invisible Worm

Jennifer Johnston's novel, *The Invisible Worm*, published in 1991, takes a similar theme to that of *Down by the River*, namely sexual abuse of a daughter at the hands of her father which her mother is powerless to prevent. Johnston sets Laura's rape within a specific political context: Laura's father is a former IRA man turned Senator and modern Ireland is presented as run by men like him. Laura's mother, Harriet, is Anglo-Irish and Protestant and therefore on the losing side in the new Irish nation. Like Mary in *Down by the River*, Laura has difficulty finding the words to articulate her experience of abuse. She hates talking, she is afraid of using the wrong words, she can barely find the words to tell her mother she has been raped by her father. When she does speak out, her words lead directly to Harriet's suicide. Small wonder then that Laura is afraid of speech. Like Mary she has been silenced. She lives in a semiotic haze of dreams, memory, fragments of speech.

However Laura's lack of speech is not simply passive withdrawal, but in a more positive sense, a refusal to be cut off from the mother's world and the mother's language. Indeed she hopes, against all common-sense, that one day her mother will return: 'Maybe my mother will sail around the corner in that little boat. The dog will bark. We will all begin again' (Johnston, 1991/1992, 95). If language arises in the absence of the mother, Laura's failure to master language may be seen as a refusal to be separated from her mother despite her father's violence which has torn them apart in life as, in 'The Bodily Encounter with the Mother', Irigaray argues that historically in patriarchal Western civilization the father has intervened to separate mother and daughter.[9]

In disappearing from the narrative, Laura's mother functions somewhat similarly to Kristeva's notion of the abject, that which must be expelled in order to gain a stable identity for the self or the nation. However, the abject never entirely vanishes and just as the abject hovers at the border of the self or nation, disintegrating boundaries and threatening identity, so Laura's mother never entirely disappears from the narrative, her voice and her laughter surfacing at odd moments in Laura's memory. Laura's refusal to be separated from the abject maternal body threatens her stable self in the form of mental breakdowns. Laura's periodic depressions are a return to the safety of the womb where she can lie, fetus-like, lapped by the maternal waters:

> It's as if there were a stopper somewhere in my body, and when it is pulled out I become slowly drained of hope, love, confidence, even the ability to feel pain; I become an empty skin; I do not even have the energy to kill myself. I long for the safe, lapping waters of the womb, darkness. (Johnston, 1991/1992, 125)

Yet Laura's adherence to her mother also gives her power to oppose her father's world. Laura lives outside linear time: 'I am not sure in which tense I live, the present or the past. Both seem irreconcilably intermingled in my mind' (Johnston, 1991/1992, 83). In 'About Chinese Women' Kristeva equates linear time with the time of the father and argues that both speech and time belong to the father: 'There is no time without speech. Therefore, there is no time without the father' (Kristeva, 1986, 153). In rejecting both speech and time, Laura affirms her adherence to the mother's world.

Kristeva goes on to say:

> It is understandable, then, that what the father doesn't say about the unconscious, what sign and time repress in the drives, appears as their *truth* (if there is no 'absolute', what is truth if not the unspoken of the spoken?) and that this truth can be imagined only as a *woman*. (Kristeva, 1986, 153)

As we saw in chapter three, according to Kristeva, women are ideally qualified to disrupt received truths because of their general estrangement from language and culture. Because of their imperfect separation from the world of the mother, women can never feel at home in the symbolic order; they remain on the boundary between the semiotic and the symbolic. The semiotic breaks down rigidities in thought and language, it undermines meaning, disrupts structures and hints at a new kind of truth. Attached to her mother's world, oscillating between the semiotic and the symbolic, Laura is able to imagine a different sort of truth. When her

---

[9]   A situation which is reflected in a later Johnston novel, *The Illusionist* (1995), where Martyn willfully manipulates the affections of his daughter, Robin, away from Stella with the result that Stella is unable to perform her mothering function effectively and eventually leaves the family home.

husband Maurice, inheritor of his father-in-law's public world, tells her: 'Sometimes I think you're mad', she questions his right to define madness: 'What is madness?' she retorts (Johnston, 1991/1992, 3). Laura's seeming madness may contain a different kind of truth.

Laura's affirmation of her mother's world gives her certain strengths. Membership of the Ascendancy class had bestowed on Laura's mother prestige and glamour, not to mention financial security. She is thus able to hand on to Laura more independence than in O'Brien's novel Mary's Catholic country mother is able to bequeath her daughter. The house in which Laura lives is inherited from her mother and has passed down three generations of the female line: 'I inherited it from my mother and she inherited it from hers' (Johnston, 1991/1992, 4). Thus, like Woolf in 'A Room of One's Own', Laura affirms the importance of a genealogy of women. Laura positions herself as guardian of the house. 'I cannot leave this place' she tells Dominic. 'After all, what would my mother have to say [...] my grandmother, come to that, if I ran away, abandoned them?' (Johnston, 1991/1992, 140). She remains faithful to her female genealogy by living in her mother's house, guarding its treasures and by remaining loyal to her mother's church.

Laura's narrative is interspersed with memories of her mother's strength which in turn nourish her. She recalls her mother's long, determined stride, her wish to have been a pirate like Grace O'Malley and her passion for sailing which was, like Rebecca de Winter's, a protest against restrictions on her sex. She remembers her mother's spirited refusal to convert to Catholicism as her husband wished:

> 'Divil a bit of it,' she said. 'Haven't you got my house and my land and my beautiful body? What makes you think you should have my soul as well?' (Johnston, 1991/1992, 6)

In her essay, 'Public Spaces, Private Lives: Irish Identity and Female Selfhood in the Novels of Jennifer Johnston', Rachel Sealy Lynch comments: 'The male potency of the husband and father figures in this novel is more than countered by the continued tenacious strength of the female line' (Kirkpatrick, 2000, 261). Lynch suggests that the motive behind Senator Quinlan's abuse of Laura is his need to assert his power in the family unit against his Protestant wife (Kirkpatrick, 2000, 264–5). If that is indeed his motive, it fails. Faithful to her female genealogy, Laura reinterprets her family history so as to give the women a larger role: 'Maurice isn't always right, you know. He has odd notions about my family. My father was the same' (Johnston, 1991/1992, 23). She wrests control of the narrative from these two men, rejecting Maurice's imperialist interpretation of her family history. Her great-grandfather was not an empire-builder, she tells Dominic, 'just a traveller' (Johnston, 1991/1992, 22) and she fills him in on the women's side of the story: while her great-grandfather traveled, her great-grandmother kept the mill running. 'Weren't women amazing?' she adds (Johnston, 1991/1992, 22). Her father and her husband may be important in the outside world but in this house Laura rules, as her mother and grandmother did before her. The grown-up Laura rejects her father's attempt to construct her as 'the traditional Irish daughter' who will take care of him (Johnston, 1991/1992, 121). Instead she marries Maurice and throws her father out of the house. Though Laura's domestic space may be marginal to the public world of her father and her husband, in her world, it is these men who are marginal.

Laura is a woman who finds an advantage in being situated on the margins of the nation. By stubbornly clinging to her mother's house and her mother's world, Laura is able to become an unsettling presence in her nation's life, a sign that not everyone in the nation agrees with the world-view of her father and her husband. Broken, fragmented memories of her abuse at the hands of her father pulse through the novel like a semiotic stream, disrupting the surface tale of a hero who fought for his country's independence and prospered in the new Irish nation to such an extent that the President's ADC attends his funeral. Laura's tale is a reminder that, as Kristeva has argued, nationalism is built on exclusions. Laura comes to symbolize all the abused children, battered women, incest survivors whose stories bear witness to the underside of Irish nationalism, stories that men like her father wish to suppress because they do not fit into the image of a glorious new nation: 'We have to keep our suffering to ourselves' (Johnson, 1991/1992, 57), he tells her, warning her to remain silent about the rape. Laura's refusal to be drawn into Maurice's world may be read as strength rather than weakness, a form in fact of political protest against the homogenization of her nation. As Cixous writes in 'The Laugh of the Medusa': 'Woman un-thinks the unifying, regulating history that homogenizes and channels forces, herding contradictions into a single battlefield' (Marks and de Courtivron, 1981, 252). The only man Laura allows in close to the heart of her world is one who is regarded as a failure in public terms, namely Dominic, the ex-priest. To him she confesses her story in the knowledge that this time her words will not kill.

Rüdiger Imhof finds the friendship (he calls it an 'affair' but it is hardly that) between Laura and Dominic 'unconvincing' (Imhof, 2002, 108). However, read against the context of *Tales of Love* and the link Kristeva makes in that work between the Christian notion of agapeic love and the psychoanalytic relationship as a dialogic practice of love between analyst and analysand, the choice of Dominic, an ex-priest who would have been trained in listening to confessions, to assist Laura's healing process seems highly appropriate. Dominic's listening ability allows space for Laura to come to terms with her trauma. As Kristeva envisages in *Tales of Love*, a secular, dialogic therapeutic relationship has replaced the Christian framework of priest and sinner; indeed Laura explicitly rejects the latter context when she evades the Rector's ineffectual offer of help.

After Laura has finally found the words to tell Dominic her story, she surprises him with her energy by burning down the summerhouse where the rape took place, thus purging her home of her father's spirit. In this scene Laura takes charge, reducing Dominic to silence: 'I don't want you to speak. Not a word. I am generalissimo. I am in charge' (Johnston, 1991/1992, 167). Similarly, in the analytic process, Kristeva envisages the moment when the patient is let go to take responsibility for his own life again, as she writes in *Au commencement était l'amour. Psychoanalyse et foi* (1985): 'En fin de cure, l'analyse conduit au détrônement de la fonction de l'analyste lui-même par la dissolution du lien transférentiel' (Kristeva, 1985, 67).[10] In this way, the analytic process contains the

---

[10]   'At the end of the healing process, the analysis leads to the deposing of the function of the analyst through the dissolving of the transferential bond' (my translation).

possibility of leading to psychic and intellectual renewal as the patient regains confidence in himself and his ability to love and to establish relationships with others.

Similarly, Johnston's novel ends on a note of hope. Having told her story and burned down the summerhouse, there is a possibility that the fleeing woman who haunts Laura's imagination may not run away again. The running woman may be Laura herself or it may be her mother, running away from the knowledge of her daughter's rape. Although Laura is in awe of her mother's physical courage, in the end Laura is revealed as the stronger woman. She sees no point in fleeing. Unlike her mother, she has the courage to stay in the house and 'see the whole thing through' (Johnston, 1991/1992, 141). Having told her story, there is a chance she will come alive and 'begin to write my life' (Johnston, 1991/1992, 181). For Kristeva, the psychoanalytic process is always provisional, the subject always 'on-trial'. In the same way, Laura's healing is left open-ended. Nevertheless, in the context of the mother-daughter story, there is hope: so far from fleeing the mother, this daughter takes what inspiration she can find in her mother's life and uses it in her quest to become the subject of her own life.

Belonging

In 'A New Type of Intellectual: the Dissident', Kristeva insists that: 'real female innovation (in whatever social field) will only come about when maternity, female creation and the link between them are better understood' (Kristeva, 1986, 298). The link between maternity and female creation is crucial to an understanding of Clairr O'Connor's luminous and partly comic novel, *Belonging*, published in 1991. Deirdre Pender, a lecturer in feminist literature brought up in Ireland but now living in New York, is dissatisfied with both her mother and her mother country. The novel is an account of her attempt to come to terms with both.

Belonging opens with Deirdre returning to the family home, Field End in West Cork, for her parents' funeral. Deirdre's need to discover an identity of her own is suggested by the rather Woolfian opening scene which finds her writing at her father's desk while wearing one of her mother's black silk dresses. Her insecure national identity, partly the result of her parents' mixed marriage, seems to be confirmed when after the funeral the family lawyer hands her part of her father's diary. The diary implies that Deirdre is not Irish but Hungarian, being the baby of a fifteen-year-old Hungarian refugee, Inga, adopted by the elderly Penders in the 1950s. The discovery provokes in Deirdre a semi-comic, almost adolescent crisis of identity: 'My parents were not my parents so how can I be the person I thought I was?' she wonders (O'Connor, 1991, 12). 'All the Irish national neuroses I claimed naturally, have they to be abandoned now?' (O'Connor, 1991, 18).

For Barry, Deirdre's American lover, fixed national identities are vital to his sense of self. Son of a prostitute and a pimp, Barry has forged an entirely new identity for himself out of an Irish grandfather and a talent for folk music and for him Deirdre's Irish nationality is the perfect adjunct to his new identity. 'Our entire relationship is based on my ethnic identity' she admits (O'Connor, 1991, 12). In the course of the novel Deirdre discovers that rigid national identities may not be as important as Barry thinks: 'He wanted security. I wanted the freedom of ambiguity' (O'Connor, 1991, 143). In the end she opts for a transnational solution to her life: since there are no teaching jobs in Ireland for specialists in feminist literature, she will spend half the year teaching in New York and her summers in Ireland at Field End. As we will see in chapter five, this kind of transnationalism is favored by Kristeva in *Nations without Nationalism* where she writes of her own experience as a Bulgarian living in France.

Deeper than the crisis over her nationality are the fractures Deirdre's supposed new identity reveals in her relationship with her parents, particularly with her invalid mother. As a child Deirdre wanted desperately to pass unnoticed. Her mother's mysterious illness and the elaborate embroidered dresses she made her daughter wear prevented this. Both increased Deirdre's self-consciousness and discomfort: 'I thought of Mam's sewing. Love that had stitched and pinned me to inhibition and wordlessness' (O'Connor, 1991, 65). Unlike Johnston's heroine, Laura, Deirdre does not value silence as a maternal inheritance but spends years with a speech therapist getting rid of her stammer and with a New York therapist, Mark, trying to cure her shyness. Her resentment over her Irish childhood, in particular her relationship with her mother, has stunted Deirdre's development. With her conflicted feelings about her own mother she has not been able to face becoming a mother herself: 'Being a mother was beyond me, territory to be kept at bay. An invasion I couldn't accept' (O'Connor, 1991, 64). The previous year, despite his protests, she aborted the baby she conceived with Barry. In the throes of a nervous breakdown, Deirdre retreats to her old nursery in Field End and embraces her new Hungarian identity and her new Hungarian mother, the self-willed refugee, Inga: 'I have found a mother indeed. Not Mam, the pale invalid. On the prayer list for the sick all my life. Pulling me to her heart by anxious threads' (O'Connor, 1991, 79).

Deirdre believes her creativity is inherited from her father who is rumored to have written a novel. In a scene symbolizing her father's handing on of authorship to his daughter, Deirdre recalls being allowed to fill his fountain pen on the evening before her first communion. However, her father's creativity petered out in later life and, as Deirdre gradually uncovers her mother's story, it becomes clear that her creativity is inherited from her mother rather than from her father.

The shocking news that Barry is expecting a baby with her best friend, Greta, catapults Deirdre out of the nursery and forces her to take a more adult view of things. She moves into her mother's sewing room and starts to take stock. A family friend makes a connection for her between her mother's epilepsy and her own childhood stammer. The stuttering and silences of her childhood are not a sign of some deep psychological flaw as Mark insists but have a physical cause. She begins to appreciate her bond with her mother. The dresses which she so loathed wearing because they made her stand out from other children were sewn with love, she now realizes.

Deirdre turns her mother's sewing room into a study for herself and, surrounded by samples of her mother's lace work hanging on the walls, starts to write her long-delayed book on Emily Dickinson. She is inspired by her mother's creative energies: 'I'm able to work very well in my study. It's as if the years of Mam's stitchery are casting a benign aura and my hands race over the typewriter keys at an impressive pace' (O'Connor, 1991, 159). Deirdre creates a room of her own where she can express her creativity. In order to do so, she draws on her inheritance from her mother rather than from her father and she writes about that icon of feminist literary critics, Emily Dickinson, a woman who, like Deirdre's mother, centered her creative life on withdrawal and reticence.

Despite unpromising beginnings, the mother is not finally in *Belonging* a forbidden place that prevents speech or against which the daughter has to emerge as subject, as in Freud and Lacan. Instead the mother has become, as in Cixous' 'The Laugh of the Medusa', the daughter's source for speaking. There is another mother-daughter story in this novel, between Deirdre's lively friend, Greta, and Mrs Harty, housekeeper at Field End. Deirdre recognizes early on that Greta has inherited her strength from her mother:

> A warrior queen. Greta, her patience and strengths tried by another culture, has to all intents and purposes become an American, taken on the camouflage, the guerrilla uniform and slapstick of the urban survivor, yet she remains her mother's daughter in the face of adversity, cocking a snook at her own Majors, refusing to let anyone colonise her pain. (O'Connor, 1991, 22)

Like Deirdre, Greta is an Irish woman who has learned to move between cultures: despite her seeming Americanization, Greta returns to Ireland every summer and she names her new baby Fionn. Deirdre realizes that the mother-daughter bond has survived Greta being translated into another culture, but only at the end of the novel does she come to terms with her own maternal inheritance.

In her essay 'Motherhood According to Giovanni Bellini', Kristeva breaks the biological connection between motherhood and creation when she links maternal *jouissance* with that of the artist, male or female. In other words, for Kristeva, art mirrors maternal *jouissance*. Operating at the junction between the symbolic and the semiotic, art reveals the artist's debt to the maternal body. Similarly, without being a mother herself, Deirdre evolves to a point where the mother figure becomes central to her creativity. In New York she creates another room of her own. She hangs two pictures in her apartment: Paula Modersohn-Becker's 'Self-Portrait on Sixth Anniversary' of a pregnant woman and a portrait of the twelfth-century Abbess Hildegaard Von Bingen, 'visionary, poet and composer. A late-starter – at forty-three, tongues of fire descended on her in a vision and inspired her to take up the creative arts' (O'Connor, 1991, 204). These two paintings suggest that Deirdre's aborted baby will not be forgotten but that her maternal feelings will henceforth be channeled into creative work:

> I know I will be able to work well in this apartment. Its clear bright lines encourage me to simplicity and clarity. I have begun to write fiction. Short stories. I write them down in hardbacked copybooks and leave them. As yet, I haven't re-read any of them. They write themselves or so it appears to me. I do not want to interrupt their wholeness. (O'Connor, 1991, 204)

As Irish women's writing opens up to more positive aspects of the mother-daughter relationship, the mother-daughter story depicted in contemporary Irish women's fiction lends itself to being read in the light of Kristeva's theories in a way that earlier Irish writing did not. This is not to say that from the 1990s onwards, Irish women begin to write mother-daughter stories in a way which is wholly positive. After *The Invisible Worm*, Jennifer Johnston has written mother-daughter stories where the daughter is seduced away from her mother by her father (*The Illusionist*), where the mother is well-intentioned but perceived by her daughter as interfering (*The Gingerbread Woman*), or judged by her daughter to be self-absorbed and negligent (Grace in *Two Moons*).

Johnston's novel, *The Illusionist*, demonstrates the extent to which nationality can get in the way of effective mothering. Stella's allegiance to her Irish nationality impedes her ability to mother her daughter Robin who identifies with England and her English father. Patterns of mothering are repeated in this novel. Just as Stella has escaped to England to escape her mother's too observant eye, so Stella's daughter, Robin, resists her mother's nurturing, labeling it 'Motherspeak' (Johnston, 1995/1996, 38). It is only as Stella matures that she learns to appreciate both her mother and her mother country. In portraying Robin's shock at discovering she is not the only daughter in her father's life, the novel leaves open the possibility that Stella and Robin may also at some future date be reconciled and that Robin may come to acknowledge the Irish part of her identity. Johnston's most recent novel, *Grace and Truth* (2005), presents an over-controlling mother whose coldness drives her daughter Ruth into her father's arms. Unlike Laura, Ruth never tells the story of her abuse by her father and thus never finds healing. She is consumed by self-hatred and depression which in turn casts a shadow over the life of her own daughter, Sally, who consequently resists the mothering role for herself. *Grace and Truth* is as disempowering a mother-daughter story as any written in Ireland in the middle decades of the twentieth century.

Nevertheless, in the context of the three novels analyzed above, it may be argued that, as the rigid boundaries and exclusions on which earlier Irish nationalism was founded begin to dissolve, the abject maternal body begins to emerge and the mother's story can begin to be heard. All three daughters in the novels discussed above succeed in retrieving something of their mothers' stories despite the near-silencing of the mother by the culture in which they live. Mary's bodily *jouissance*, Laura's ability to live on the margins, Deirdre's creativity all have their sources in their mothers' example.

As we have seen, these mother-daughter stories have implications for the story of the Irish nation. Mary's song cuts through the legal obfuscations of the Irish Constitution, Laura's turns her life on the margins into a protest against the public world of her father and her husband, and Deirdre opts for the sort of transnational solution to her life which calls into question the importance of rigid national identities. As Kristeva has said in an interview:

> I believe we should trust mothers and listen to them. We should recognize the 'civilizing' role that mothers play, not only in psychoanalysis but in general [...] Mothers are the ones who pass along the native tongue, but they also perform an important psychological role that we are still discovering. They perform a sort of miracle by separating themselves from their children while loving them and teaching them to speak. (Gubermann, 1996, 10)

By learning to listen to what their mothers have to teach them, these daughters not only learn 'to speak' in their own voices, they also discover strategies of survival for themselves within the life of the nation.

Chapter 5

Translating Between Cultures: A Kristevan Reading of the Theme of the Foreigner

Introduction

In 1966, Julia Kristeva, a young Bulgarian student, arrived in Paris to pursue her studies. She is now, forty years later, an internationally known figure, regarded as the French intellectual *par excellence* – except, as she has frequently pointed out in interviews, in France where ironically she remains a foreigner and a dissident. In *Julia Kristeva: Speaking the Unspeakable*, Anne-Marie Smith sees foreignness as central to Kristeva's intellectual identity and she elaborates on Kristeva's paradoxical position in French cultural life:

> She has adopted a country which despite its symbolic recognition of her work – in January 1997 she was awarded the prestigious *légion d'honneur* – could never adopt her foreignness; France is a profoundly ethnocentric, phallocentric country, and foreignness, dissidence and femininity are integral factors in Julia Kristeva's construction of her intellectual identity. (Smith, 1998, 2)

In *Nations without Nationalism* Kristeva speaks of her experiences of living in a nation not her own and defines her position as one which cuts across cultural boundaries: 'I have, against origins and starting from them, chosen a transnational or international position situated at the crossing of boundaries' (Kristeva, 1993, 16). In *Strangers to Ourselves*, writing out of personal experience, she speaks of the foreigner's feelings of loss, insecurity, loneliness and nostalgia for the motherland. In discussing this theme of the foreigner, we must also bear in mind Kristeva's arguments that women are often marginalized within the nation and that because of their otherness to the public life of the nation, women find themselves better able to embrace the otherness of strangers. In an interview given in 1985, Kristeva argues the case for regarding 'woman as an irrecuperable foreigner' (Gubermann, 1996, 45).

Kristeva's portrait of the foreigner has particular relevance for Irish women's writing since the experience of being a foreigner in an alien culture was one shared by a fair proportion of Irish women in the twentieth century. As we saw in chapter one, poverty, lack of employment or simple inability to fit into the prevailing ethos of their nation, forced many Irish women to emigrate during the course of the century. The Irish woman obliged to seek domestic work abroad features in short stories by writers as disparate as Norah Hoult and Maeve Brennan.

Norah Hoult's story, 'Bridget Kiernon', published in 1930, provides a rare glimpse into a day in the life of an Irish Catholic maid in England. One of the many Irish women of the period who emigrated in search of work, Bridget Kiernon encounters harshness and anti-Irish prejudice in the household of her Protestant mistress, Mrs Fitzroy. Hoult explores the cultural differences between the employer and her maid. Whereas Mrs Fitzroy prizes efficiency, economy and cleanliness, Bridget values personal contact and human warmth above all else and feels she is being asked to 'work in new ways that no one had ever heard of before' (Hoult, 1930, 284). Even their notions of time are different. Bridget, from the country, works too slowly for Mrs Fitzroy whose day is strictly regulated by clock time. Bridget is alienated by the voice of her English employer:

> She listened to the precise English accent which made her feel she was dealing with someone she could never approach as an ordinary human being; one who must be an inhabitant of a quite different world from herself. (Hoult, 1930, 270)[1]

In Hoult's story Bridget's homesickness and vulnerability are delicately conveyed, together with her fear that she may be pregnant. By the end of the story, however, power shifts from the mistress to the maid as Bridget discovers she is not pregnant and realizes that, given the shortage of domestic labor, she will be able to find another job more easily than Mrs Fitzroy will be able to hire another maid.

A comparison may be drawn between Hoult's story and the power struggles between employers and their Irish maids portrayed in Maeve Brennan's series of stories set in Herbert's Retreat, a wealthy community outside New York. In these stories, published in *The New Yorker* between 1953 and 1956, Irish maids observe their employers' behavior with a satirical eye. In 'The View from the Kitchen', Bridie and Agnes derive much malicious enjoyment from observing the social maneuvering and drinking habits of their employer, Mrs Harkey. In 'The Divine Fireplace', Stasia employs her Irish storytelling abilities in recounting to the other Irish maids on the way to Mass their employers' drunken exploits which have wrecked their luxurious home. Herbert's Retreat is based on an actual community outside New York, Snedens Landing, which Maeve Brennan visited and even inhabited for a while, and it has been suggested that the Irish maids in these stories express Maeve Brennan's own feelings as an Irish woman of being an interloper in this wealthy community (Bourke, 2004, 186–7).

The maids in these stories by Norah Hoult and Maeve Brennan observe their employers' behavior with the envy and rage of the dispossessed, but the maids' inferior economic and social status minimizes their ability to translate between cultures in any meaningful way. Bridget Kiernon, for example, knows that if she is pregnant she will not be able to return home for she will have become the abject, 'bringing scandal into the parish and disgrace on her poor mother' (Hoult, 1930, 284). Bridie may have fantasies of being treated as a friend by her employers

---

[1]   The heroine of *Sarah's Youth*, a novel by Somerville and Ross published in the 1930s, experiences similar alienation in London. Sarah Heritage-Dixon is an Anglo-Irish heiress and therefore of a completely different class from Bridget but she also feels a stranger in London: 'The smart clothes and the high English voices antagonized and scared Sarah. This was enemy country' (Somerville and Ross, 1938, 264).

(Brennan, 2000, 128) and even in 'The Servants' Dance' leads the servants in an act of vengeance against them, but she knows that nothing will ever really change her status, she will always be patronized by them as 'that splendid Irish woman of Leona's' (Brennan, 2000, 112).

In 'The Bride', Margaret Casey daydreams of returning to Ireland with enough money to outshine her elder sister in her mother's eyes, but her mother dies before she is able to save up sufficient money for her fare. Instead she will marry another outsider, Carl, a German plumber whom she knows would never impress the people at home (Brennan, 2000, 156). These maids have no choice but to stay in America. At the same time, they remain 'other' to the culture around them, retaining their Irish Catholic mentality. Mr Runyon mixing drinks strikes Bridie as resembling 'a priest saying Mass' (Brennan, 2000, 8). Mr Harkey who works as a credit manager is described by Agnes as: 'One of the ones that does the dirty work. When our Blessed Lord was crucified, he was standing there holding the box of nails' (Brennan, 2000, 12).

These stories arguably reflect Maeve Brennan's own sense of otherness which increased as time went on until she felt at home neither in Ireland nor America. Her novella, *The Visitor*, depicting Anastasia's exclusion from her grandmother's Dublin home, reflects, it has been suggested, Brennan's sense of alienation from the Ireland that had developed after independence: introverted and xenophobic, with a narrow definition of femininity which had no place for the sophisticated, professional woman she had now become (Bourke, 2004, 154). In America, by contrast, Brennan was always seen as Irish, an outsider (Bourke, 2004, 176, 193). Her many house moves in the States exacerbated her lack of roots until by the end of her life she had become literally homeless, living on the streets of New York. Caught between two cultures, Brennan failed to make the translation and lost herself. In a letter dated 1973, she wrote: 'The most I ever knew was that I "didn't know where I was"' (Bourke, 2004, 266). Homelessness as a theme runs through both her Irish and her American stories: 'What makes a waif?' wonders the wealthy American hostess, Isobel Bailey in 'The Joker' (1952). 'When do people get that fatal separate look? Are waifs born?' (Brennan, 2000, 52).

The theme of the mother-daughter relationship overlaps with the theme of the Irish woman in exile as many stories by Irish women writers portray daughters fleeing not only their mothers, but also their mother countries in search of new and more empowering identities. In many of Edna O'Brien's stories and novels, this search for a new identity remains unfulfilled. The daughters have adopted enough of the new culture in which they find themselves to feel alien towards their mothers who remain locked in the old ways of behavior and thought. At the same time this new identity leaves them dissatisfied; they feel a constant pull back to their mothers and their mother countries. This is apparent, for example, in O'Brien's short story, 'Cords', where a visit from Claire's Irish mother leaves Claire feeling dissatisfied with her life in London: 'her present life, her work, the friends she had, seemed insubstantial compared with all that had happened before' (O'Brien, 1968, 144). In *August is a Wicked Month* (1965), Ellen is introduced to the world 'of ideas and collective thought and flute music' (O'Brien, 1965, 122) by her husband, a successor to the free-thinking Eugene Gaillard of *The Country Girls* trilogy, but that does not prevent her from yearning for Ireland: 'It all sounded grand. Except that it wasn't enough and he didn't buoy her up when she hankered after the proverbs and accordion music and a statue of the Virgin hewn from blackthorn wood' (O'Brien, 1965, 122). Ellen has found no new identity to set against the Irish one she has only partly outgrown.

Nell in *Time and Tide* experiences a similar conflict between her new life in England and life back in Ireland. In London she tries out a series of identities but finds no new identity strong enough to replace the old certainties. The consequence is that she is unable to break her ties entirely with either her mother or her motherland. A chance encounter with an old enemy, a fellow Irish woman, Rita, brings Nell face to face with a truth from which she has tried to hide: 'Always sooner or later we are brought back to the dark stew of ourselves and the ancestry before us, back to the midnight of the race whose sins and whose songs we carry' (O'Brien, 1992/1993, 260). Far from feeling empowered by their life in new surroundings, the conflict between old and new often leaves O'Brien's heroines defeated. They lack the ability to translate between cultures and indeed, in a movement which runs counter to Kristeva's observations, these women often find their new fluid identities unsettling. In O'Brien's short story, 'The Doll', the narrator feels that in her new London life she is only acting a part: 'So I am far from those I am with, and far from those I have left [...] None of us ever says where we come from or what haunts us. Perhaps we are bewildered or ashamed' (O'Brien, 1985/2003, 52). In 'Paradise', the narrator's search for a new identity abroad ends in failure and attempted suicide.

Several of Jennifer Johnston's recent novels portray heroines who flee their mother and their mother country but fail to settle abroad and feel constantly pulled back to Ireland and to their mother's comforting presence. In *The Gingerbread Woman* (2000), Clara travels the world lecturing but always returns to her house in Dalkey and to her mother who lives round the corner and plies her with comforting food: 'I come here to lick my wounds and eat my mother's jam, take deep breaths and get ready to go away again' (Johnston, 2000, 5). In *The Illusionist* (1995), Stella moves to London to escape her mother's controlling eye. In England she marries but feels a constant yearning for Ireland: 'I longed for whin bushes and the lace of dry-stone walls with the light shining through' (Johnston, 1995/1996, 72). She fails to establish a proper connection with the English:

> I had acquaintances all right, people to whom I chatted in the street, people who invited us to dinner and who came to our house for meals. Decent enough people. Just not my people. (Johnston, 1995/1996, 102).

The scorn her husband Martyn pours on her nationality adds to Stella's feeling of alienation. He refuses, for example, to allow their daughter, Robin, to be educated in Ireland even though she is, as Stella reminds him, half-Irish. Indeed Martyn reveals his doubts about the validity of the Irish national identity when he insists that Robin's future lies in England. He tells Stella: 'Don't let's have any more nonsense about this. She's going to be assured, sure of who she is and proud of it' (Johnston, 1995/1996, 170). Though Martyn conceals from Stella any information about his family background and working life, his scorn for the Irish might have some bearing on the manner of his death (he is blown up by an IRA bomb). Eventually Stella escapes this abusive marriage and returns to Ireland, reconciled now to her mother as a 'benign' and 'comfortable' presence (Johnston, 1995/1996, 212) and to Ireland as 'home' (Johnston, 1995/1996, 213).

Stella fails to translate between cultures in any meaningful way. She will always feel an outsider in England and this outsider status facilitates Martyn's seduction of Robin away from her. Just as Ireland will always be home to Stella and England will always be a foreign place, so Ireland is an alien country for her daughter, emphasizing the way in which the mother-daughter relationship in this novel is disrupted by national allegiance. Stella observes that Robin 'feels ill at ease in Dublin. She speaks with an alien voice, looks at the city with the critical eye of a stranger. I love her, but I doubt whether she cares' (Johnston, 1995/1996, 9). Since the bomb which kills Martyn is planted by the IRA, Robin blames her mother's nation for her father's death. The mother-daughter relationship in this novel is fractured by the father's determined seduction of the daughter away from the mother, but even more by the irreconcilable clash between hostile national identities.

Kate O'Riordan's novel, *The Memory Stones* (2003), presents a more positive angle on these tales of exile from the mother and the mother country. *The Memory Stones* depicts the 'simple' and 'obvious story' (O'Riordan, 2003, 259) of Nell, a sixteen-year-old, pregnant, unmarried Irish girl sent over to England to have her baby. Nell's case is rather different from the norm, however. Believing that her mother loves her less than her dead sister, Bridget, and having endured years of bullying at school, Nell actively wishes to escape her mother, her motherland and Ireland's 'snively nationalism' (O'Riordan, 2003, 126). Her stay in England opens up new possibilities for her life. She trains to become a wine expert and eventually moves to Paris where she creates a happy and fulfilling life for herself, albeit at the cost of certain emotional repressions. She lives alone, in a well-ordered flat, sustaining a relationship with a married lover whom she is happy to keep at arm's length. Her relationship with her own daughter, Ali, who identifies with Ireland and her grandmother, remains an uneasy one. Though her mother visits her abroad, Nell does not return to Ireland until thirty-two years later, after her mother's death. This return to Ireland provides a turning point for Nell. It allows her to repair her fractured relationship with Ali and leads her to the discovery that her mother did after all love her. Mother and motherland merge as Nell feels 'the landscape folding around her like arms welcoming her back' (O'Riordan, 2003, 190). No longer a stranger in Ireland, Nell is able, finally, to bring the two parts of her life together, to translate in some sense between the two cultures in which she has lived. In an early introduction of the immigrant theme into writing by Irish women, Nell contrasts her story with that of Bola, an asylum seeker from Nigeria who can never return home and yet for whom Ireland will always be a foreign place.

Remembering Light and Stone (1992)

In many ways no one describes better than Deirdre Madden in her novel, *Remembering Light and Stone* (1992), the peculiar quality of being a foreigner. Like Nell in *The Memory Stones*, Madden's heroine, Aisling, is an Irish woman in flight not only from her country but from a childhood which in Aisling's case contained a violent father. She remains haunted by 'the psychic violence' which she associates with the landscape of her native region, the Burren (Madden, 1992, 32) and by her 'many unhappy experiences in Ireland' (Madden, 1992, 37). She describes herself repeatedly as 'troubled and anxious' (Madden, 1992, 36), prey to terrifying nightmares. The trauma is deep seated enough for her to have preserved an instinct to flinch, as if expecting to be hit (Madden, 1992, 76). She responds violently when she feels herself under threat, as when she punches her ex lover, Bill, or lashes out at her current lover, Ted. She flees any hint of aggression on the part of others and faints when visiting an Italian farm which reminds her 'not always pleasantly, of growing up on my father's farm in Ireland' (Madden, 1992, 122). Although the reader is given few precise details about Aisling's past, it is clear that, like Kristeva's foreigner, Aisling has been propelled into exile by a 'secret wound' (Kristeva, 1991, 5), namely 'the complicated web of lies, secrets and violence' which formed her childhood (Madden, 1992, 61). Fleeing Ireland, she lives first in Paris and then in Italy.

Traumatized and rendered vulnerable by her father's violence, Aisling is, more than most, aware of the stranger inside herself:

> It wasn't other people who bothered me, it all came from inside myself, and the feeling was so strong that it was as if there were another person inside me, a dark self who tormented me. My self was split in two, and one half threatened the other, the weaker half. (Madden, 1992, 65)

Like Albert Camus' Meursault, whose psychological alienation Kristeva analyzes in *Strangers to Ourselves*, Aisling often feels a stranger even to humanity; on her worst days, she prefers the animal world. Like Kristeva's foreigner, Aisling multiplies masks, experimenting with her appearance to such an extent that she is now unrecognizable from her photographs taken in Ireland. One of the happiest moments of her life, she tells us, is when she caught sight of herself in a bar in Paris and saw herself as a stranger, 'as if I were someone other than myself' (Madden, 1992, 36). For most people this experience of otherness would be troubling; for Aisling, in flight from her past, it is a moment to treasure. Early on in the novel she tells us that she associates Northern Europe with violence and death and that she has come south to escape that. When she settles in the small town of S. Giorgio in Umbria, Aisling, like Kristeva's foreigner, feels a sense of 'reprieve, of having gotten away' (Kristeva, 1991, 8).

Conscious that she has come from a tightly homogeneous society and in rebellion against this, Aisling willingly embraces the foreignness of S. Giorgio. She earns her living as a translator, moving with ease between her two languages, English and Italian. She learns to dress well for her job, accepting that that is what Italians expect: 'I went along with it reluctantly, in a spirit of compromise. You have to, at times, if you choose to live in a country which isn't your own' (Madden, 1992, 15).

At the same time, Aisling embodies many of the more unsettling characteristics of the foreigner as described by Kristeva in *Strangers to Ourselves*. Like Kristeva's foreigner, she has a 'passion for solitude' (Kristeva, 1991, 12). Understandably, given what we eventually learn about her childhood, Aisling has a particular dislike of family life. As a young, single woman without obvious family ties, she encounters surprise and some hostility from the family-centered Italians: 'However, the thing that made me a total anomaly in Italy was that I'm a real lone wolf' (Madden, 1992, 15). Her solitary, rootless life seems entirely unnatural to her Umbrian landlady, Franca.

Like Kristeva's immigrant worker, Aisling works hard to establish herself in this foreign country, often taking on several jobs simultaneously in order to make ends meet. At the same time she adopts an arrogant attitude towards her fellow townsmen, many of whom seem to her to be leading the lives prescribed for them by their society without any attempt to think beyond this. According to Kristeva, this arrogant attitude to more rooted people is one to which the foreigner may easily fall prey:

> The foreigner feels strengthened by the distance that detaches him from the others as it does from himself and gives him the lofty sense not so much of holding the truth but of making it and himself relative while others fall into the ruts of monovalency [...] In the eyes of the foreigner those who are not foreign have no life at all. (Kristeva, 1991, 7)

Aisling particularly castigates Fabiola, her employer's wife, for her empty-headed pursuit of a middle-class life fixed by social convention and surrounded by the trappings of wealth: 'She hasn't a thought in her head that hasn't been put there by social and commercial forces' (Madden, 1992, 46). Aisling is grateful for the opportunity to live in a different culture precisely because it enables her to think both beyond the society in which she finds herself and beyond the society in which she was born. 'Maybe one of the hardest things is to see beyond your own society' she suggests (Madden, 1992, 7). In 'A New Type of Intellectual: The Dissident' Kristeva argues:

> How can one avoid sinking into the mire of common sense, if not by becoming a stranger to one's own country, language, sex and identity? [...] Exile is already in itself a form of *dissidence*, since it involves uprooting oneself from a family, a country or a language. (Kristeva, 1986, 298)

For Aisling, as for Kristeva, exile grants one the power to dissent from the values of the culture in which one has been born.

In Madden's novel, Aisling's encounter with a foreign culture is performed with relative ease. Associating the north with 'violence and death', she has been seduced by the myth of the south as a warm and happy place (Madden, 1992, 2). Her stay in Italy shows her that unhappiness can be found anywhere (Franca, her landlady, commits suicide). But what is more significant than anything she learns about Italy is the way in which living in a foreign culture begins the healing process which gradually leads Aisling back to her home in Ireland: 'more than learning anything about Italy, I had found out more about my own country, simply by not being in it' (Madden, 1992, 2). For Aisling, it is not the encounter with the foreign other that is significant – she embraces otherness – but the way in which living outside Ireland allows her to get her country into perspective. In that sense it does not much matter to her in which foreign country she lives: 'in many ways I felt I could have gone anywhere, so long as it was far away and provided me with privacy, so that I could forget all about Ireland and then remember it, undisturbed'

(Madden, 1992, 2). In Italy she finds the necessary separation from Ireland to allow her to remember the past without becoming engulfed by it. And she is able, finally, to exorcise the pain of her childhood, as in the church of S. Giorgio, in the fresco that so unsettles her, the blank-faced friar exorcises the devil. When Aisling revisits her family home she hears the call of a corn-crake, like herself a rare migratory bird returned to Ireland. Nearby on a wall sits a large cat. Later, having made her decision to stay in Ireland, Aisling walks back down the same road and hears the corn-crake again, but now the menacing cat has disappeared. Her father is dead and the threat of 'the psychic violence' which she associates with Ireland has disappeared.

If Aisling's encounter with the foreign other serves primarily to heal the divide within herself, by contrast, two earlier novels by Irish women portray the experience of a foreign culture as initiating a difficult negotiation between the self and the other.

Mary Lavelle (1936)

Kate O'Brien's novel, *Mary Lavelle*, opens with the eponymous heroine arriving in Spain in 1922 to take up a post as English language governess to the Areavaga family. Unlike Deirdre Madden's heroine, Mary Lavelle does not eagerly embrace otherness: her feelings of exasperation with a foreign language she barely understands, her loneliness and her nostalgia for her home country mirror the foreigner's emotions described by Kristeva in *Strangers to Ourselves*. A foreigner, Kristeva remarks, has little social standing and, as governess, Mary is expected to be invisible, a passive presence in the Areavaga girls' lives. At the same time, though she barely understands why, Mary is pleased to escape for a while a life that is only too clearly marked out for her at home. 'A secret wound, often unknown to himself, drives the foreigner to wandering' says Kristeva in *Strangers to Ourselves* (Kristeva, 1991, 5). While Deirdre Madden's heroine, Aisling, is well aware of the 'wound' which propelled her abroad, for Mary this wound is, at the beginning of the novel, barely understood.

Though she can as yet hardly articulate it even to herself, there is plenty for Mary to feel dissatisfied about at home. Her family is middle-class and Catholic but is far from forming the happy family unit envisaged by Eamon de Valera. Mary's mother died when she was ten and her father's peevishness and critical attitude towards his children remain unchecked by the ineffectual Aunt Cissy who comes to care for them. The stunted fig tree in the garden of the family house in Mellick (always a stand-in in O'Brien's novels for her native Limerick) becomes in Spain a recurring symbol in Mary's memories of Ireland.

Mary is dimly aware of the limitations of life in Mellick but sees no possibility of another sort of life. She has inherited a hundred pounds from her godmother but her father refuses to spend it ('waste it' he calls it) on training her for employment, believing that, since she is a beauty, she will not lack proposals of marriage. Mary's role is to play daughter of the house and her destiny is marriage. She becomes engaged to John, the nearest conventional young man. Only when Mother Liguori, the history teacher in her convent school, mentions a vacant post of governess with a family in Spain does Mary, half blindly, seize her chance for a brief respite from the rigidities of life in Mellick. This mirrors the actual situation in Ireland at the time when convent schools like the one Kate O'Brien herself attended had excellent networks in Europe and often sent young Irish women to study abroad (Ward, 1997, 10). Though there is no mention of the order to which Mother Liguori belongs, in Kate O'Brien's novels Irish convents are frequently part of a European network, allowing O'Brien to juxtapose the internationalism of these female-run convents with the narrow nationalism prevalent in Ireland, as for example in her later novel, *The Land of Spices*, discussed below.

Mary's months in Spain as governess for the Areavaga family are intended to be no more than an interval of freedom:

A tiny hiatus between her life's two accepted phases. To cease being a daughter without immediately becoming a wife. To be a free lance, to belong to no one place or family or person. (O'Brien, 1936/2000, 34)

This point is emphasized in the Prologue, with its ironic commentary on those middle-class Catholic Irish Misses who go abroad with trunks which, like their owners, possess 'the air of never having wandered far from parish bounds' (O'Brien, 1936/2000, xv). In the usual course of events, an Irish Miss will remain unchanged by her encounter with a foreign culture. By contrast, Mary Lavelle's time in Spain leads her to re-evaluate the life awaiting her back in Ireland.

Mary's imagination is engaged by being in a foreign country and puzzled curiosity drives her to discover more about the place in which she finds herself. Kate O'Brien's novel carefully charts Mary's emotional surrender to the other as represented by Spain. Mary takes pains to learn the Spanish language and to adapt to the customs of the country which from the first has startled her into awareness by being 'not a bit what I expected Spain to be' (O'Brien, 1936/2000, 2).

Mary's willingness to go beyond her preconceptions of Spain marks her out from the other Irish Misses who, in their refusal to surrender to the experience of living in Spain or even to learn the language, cling to their Irish nationalism or, as the narrator puts it, retain 'their violent and terrible Irish purity' (O'Brien, 1936/2000, 94). For these Irish Misses, the Spanish with their bullfights and their preference for hot chocolate over tea, truly are the foreigner as 'image of hatred and of the other' (Kristeva, 1991, 1). The company of these xenophobic fellow-countrywomen speeds Mary's growth in maturity as she defines herself against them.

An exception to the xenophobic Irish Misses is Agatha Conlan, who speaks Spanish fluently. At Agatha's prompting, Mary attends a bullfight and its beauty and violence, piercing her senses in a way John never did, become a symbol of the pain and knowledge Spain is imposing on her. The maturing process Mary is undergoing in Spain bewilders her Irish fiancé. John disapproves of her attendance at a bullfight. His narrow judgments in his letters on Mary's life in Spain start to irritate her and make her feel 'remote' from life back in Ireland (O'Brien, 1936/2000, 125). The emotional cost of entering into a culture not one's own is made clear in the descriptions of Mary's moments of exhaustion and self-doubt: 'She had not known that life and travel and experiment could maim one thus' (O'Brien, 1936/2000, 240).

She reads Spanish newspapers and books about Spain and she visits the Prado in Madrid but it is the bullfight which remains a pivotal episode in Mary's development, introducing her simultaneously to life's violence and life's sensuality, things from which, as daughter of the house in Ireland, she was supposed to be sheltered. In her response to the bullfight, Mary becomes vaguely conscious of her own potential for sexual passion: 'uneasily aware that some nerve in her waited to be [...] disturbed' (O'Brien, 1936/2000, 151). Immediately after this she meets the Areavaga heir, Juanito, a married man. Through him, Mary's experience of Spain will be completed.

Mary's emotional surrender to Spain is paralleled by her surrender to her Spanish lover. Like Spain, the mutual passion between Juanito and Mary brings her both pleasure and pain as she struggles against their adulterous love. In the end, her desire not to impede his life as much as her Catholic conscience forbids her to continue the liaison with Juanito. Nevertheless it has startled her into an awareness of life's possibilities: 'she knew now about regrets and griefs and faithlessness' (O'Brien, 1936/2000, 253). According to Kristeva in *Strangers to Ourselves*, such sexual awakening is not untypical of the foreigner's experience (Kristeva, 1991, 30–31). By the end of the novel, Mary has learned that sexual passion is not reasonable or manageable; that, unlike her feeling for John, it has nothing to do with social convention or conformity to tradition. It cannot be legislated for and is only with difficulty restrained. She knows from her own experience that sometimes a woman can take the lead in sexual passion. This knowledge puts her at odds with her nation's view of womanhood where the sexual purity of the Irish woman guarantees the purity of the nation. Mary knows she is returning to Ireland with a tale that will revolt John into rejecting her.

Spain has imposed upon Mary a new identity, that of lover of a married man. It is an identity which puritanical Irish society will not allow her. She has become excluded from her nation's construct of womanhood which denies unprompted sexual passion in females: 'John had told her that he, having seen her across a room, was in love then and for ever, but that that sort of thing never happened to a girl' (O'Brien, 1936/2000, 185). Her love affair with Juanito has placed Mary at odds with her nation. She knows that, whatever she may become in the future, she will no longer fit into the stereotyped role of wife awaiting her back in Ireland. She has moved from acceptance of the foreign other to finding what is foreign to her nation inside herself.

Mary's future after her emotional awakening is uncertain. She will return to Ireland to break off her engagement and collect her godmother's legacy and then she intends to 'go away' (O'Brien, 1936/2000, 344). It is suggested that, awakened to the reality of female sexual desire, it will be impossible for her to stay in her native country. Her encounter with the foreign other has brought Mary into conflict with her nation to whose traditions and orthodoxies she has been 'deliberately faithless' (O'Brien, 1936/2000, 253). Ireland's rigid national identity precludes Mary's ability to translate her new knowledge back to her nation and thwarts her ability to mediate between cultures. By the end of the novel, Mary has become akin to the Kristevan abject, that which has to be excluded from the self or the nation in order for identity to form.

At the same time her weeks in Spain have awoken Mary to a larger experience of life than would have been available in Ireland. 'Happiness seems to prevail, *in spite of everything*, because something has definitely been exceeded: it is the happiness of tearing away, of racing, the space of a promised infinite' says Kristeva of the often tormenting experience of being a foreigner (Kristeva, 1991, 4). Like Lois in *The Last September* or Claire Mackey in Leland's *Approaching Priests*, Mary has become a Kristevan 'subject-in-process': her life, the reader feels, will be one of perpetual wandering and exploration, in keeping with Kristeva's view of women as exemplary as strangers and exiles.

This theme of women as wanderers and exiles is taken up in a later O'Brien novel, *As Music and Splendour* (1958). Set in the latter part of the nineteenth century, *As Music and Splendour* traces the fortunes of Clare and Rosa who have been sent away from Ireland as teenagers in order to earn money for their families by training to be opera singers, first in Paris, then in Italy. The novel recounts their growth to maturity and the various love affairs the young women experience (heterosexual in Rosa's case, lesbian in Clare's). These love affairs make the women – and this is ground-breaking in terms of the treatment of lesbianism in Irish women's fiction – equal sinners in the eyes of their Church and their nation. Clare is always clear that her love for Luisa is no more sinful than Rose's affairs with René and Antonio, or any other kind of love outside marriage. She tells Thomas:

> I am, I suppose, a sinner – certainly I am a sinner in the argument of my Church. But so would I be if I were your lover. So is Rose a sinner – and she knows it – in reference to our education and faith [...] We are so well instructed that we can decide for ourselves. There's no vagueness in Catholic instruction. (O'Brien, 1958, 207)

Thinking about their years abroad, Clare recognizes that she and Rose have been 'refashioned altogether' by their experience (O'Brien, 1958, 189). They are no longer the people they would have been if they had stayed in Ireland; they have been 'parted from their obvious selves' (O'Brien, 1958, 190). Reflecting on 'how uniform and rule-of-thumb everyone is expected to be at home' (O'Brien, 1958, 189), they agree that if they had stayed in Ireland Rose would be married by now and Clare might have become a nun. Clare's last visit to Ireland to see her dying grandmother prompts her realization that her previous nostalgia for Ireland has been a fantasy. Life in Ireland, while not without its virtues, is too narrow to accommodate the woman Clare has become: 'She could not ever live now the simple, clean, courageous and uncomforted life' (O'Brien, 1958, 343). Clare's acknowledgment that there is no longer a place for her in the life of her nation is matched by Rose's realization that: 'there could never be return to Lackanashee in the old and simple sense' (O'Brien, 1958, 128). As in *Mary Lavelle*, Ireland's rigid national identity precludes these young women's ability to translate their new knowledge back to their nation. However much Clare yearns for home, and indeed the Catholic values in which she has been raised determine her preference for sacred music over opera, she knows that she will end her days outside Ireland, like Kristeva's foreigner who 'survives with a tearful face turned toward the lost homeland' (Kristeva, 1997, 271).

The House in Paris (1935)

Elizabeth Bowen's novel, *The House in Paris*, published a year earlier than *Mary Lavelle*, in 1935, opens with a description of a young English girl, Henrietta, encountering Paris for the first time. The novel gradually weaves back in time to portray the reaction of another English girl, Karen Michaelis, to her year spent as a paying guest in the house of Madame Fisher in Paris. For the eleven-year-old Henrietta her encounter with Paris and with Leopold confirms her in her Englishness: 'She might marvel, but nothing, thought Leopold, would ever really happen to her' (Bowen, 1935/1976, 28). By contrast, Karen allows her encounter with the foreign other, in the form of Max Ebhart, to alter her life forever.

At eighteen, Karen's first reaction to Max, a regular visitor to Madame Fisher's house, is one of fascination and fear. For the whole of Karen's year abroad Max, a Jew of mixed English and French descent, disconcerts and troubles her. Returning to England, Karen allows herself to fall back on her mother's view of things. She associates only with members of her own, upper middle class and becomes engaged to the reassuringly conventional Englishman, Ray Forrestier. Her visit to Ireland, a country which gives her a feeling of 'troubling strangeness' (Bowen, 1935/1976, 76), takes Karen sufficiently out of herself to realize that Max was someone who made her deeply unhappy. Here Ireland functions, in inverse fashion, as the foreign space in which re-evaluation takes place.[2] This trip begins to awaken Karen to awareness of the other inside herself: 'Something in Ireland bends one back on oneself' she writes to Ray (Bowen, 1935/1976, 89). When her friend from Paris, Madame Fisher's daughter Naomi, arrives in London to announce that she has become engaged to Max, Karen knows the moment she has been dreading has come; she must encounter Max again.

At first, meeting Max as Naomi's fiancé, Karen is able to fit him into her English life. In his domestic role of Naomi's fiancé Max appears solid and dependable. Karen wonders why she had been so afraid of him: 'her Michaelis view of life quickly fitted him in' (Bowen, 1935/1976, 108). At their second meeting, Max and Karen begin to acknowledge their feelings for each other. This is done in an edgy, roundabout way, for each is suspicious of the other's foreignness. Max continually stresses the fact that he and Naomi are outsiders in England whereas Karen is firmly rooted in upper-middle-class English life.

For Karen it is Max's hybrid nationality which renders him strange. If he is a foreigner in England, so he is also to some extent in France since, though his mother was French, his father was an English Jew. Max in fact embodies many of the qualities of the foreigner as portrayed by Kristeva in *Strangers to Ourselves*. He is restless, hypersensitive and aloof. Lacking a secure national identity, he finds his identity in his work. 'The foreigner is the one who works,' says Kristeva in *Strangers to Ourselves*, arguing that the foreigner substitutes his work for a nation: 'as if *it* were the chosen soil, the only source of possible success' (Kristeva, 1991, 18). Max possesses the fierce determination of an outsider to establish himself in

---

[2]   Compare Orla Murphy's novel, *The Sway of Winter* (2002), where Birgit, a young
       Scandinavian woman, comes to spend winter on the island of Inis Breac. For Birgit, as
       for Karen, Ireland functions as a foreign place where she can rethink her life.

France, a country which Kristeva describes as particularly difficult for foreigners: 'Nowhere is one *more* a foreigner than in France [...] the French set a compact social texture and an unbeatable national pride against foreigners' (Kristeva, 1991, 38). Madame Fisher, Max's guide and mentor, warns Max that as an outsider in France he must expect to be distrusted and to wait longer for success than his less gifted colleagues. Max himself acknowledges that: 'in France to have no family can be more humbling than poverty' (Kristeva, 1991, 163).

Karen is both afraid of and fascinated by Max's passion and his restless intellect which make him so different from Ray, the reliable Englishman. Max reveals to her depths in life which are smothered by the Michaelis world of breeding, good manners and calm reasonableness. Mrs Michaelis' facile dismissal of Max as a Jew who is touchy about his background underestimates his complexity for Karen. Falling in love with him makes her realize how much in herself is secretly in rebellion against the Michaelis world she has inherited. 'The foreigner's friends', writes Kristeva in *Strangers to Ourselves*, 'could only be those who feel foreign to themselves' (Kristeva, 1991, 23). Max, the half French Jew, the other, makes Karen aware of the other in herself. It could in fact be argued that Max functions as the abject for Karen. He remains a figure of fascination and dread, threatening the borders of her identity to such an extent that at times she is happy to exclude him from her line of vision.[3]

Cracks begin to appear in the life of the Michaelis family. Aunt Violet's sudden death causes Mrs Michaelis to lose confidence in the old calm way of going about things. Influenced by this, Karen begins an affair with Max which runs counter to all the values instilled in her by her mother. It is an affair that is still tinged with apprehension on both sides. The narrator comments: 'Their worlds were so much unlike that no experience had the same value for both of them' (Bowen, 1935/1976, 143). Max feels unnerved by Karen's class superiority which casts doubts on his motives for loving her. He emphasizes their difference: 'We should never tolerate one another if we were not in love. Even today here, we are both estranged from half of ourselves. You would find my life mean. A good deal of what you are I should not care to touch' (Bowen, 1935/1976, 142). Both of them are cautious creatures, wishing to succeed in their own worlds. He warns her: 'You were not made to leap in the dark either' (Bowen, 1935/1976, 142). Neither of them happily embraces the foreignness of the other. Indeed Max continues to insist that he must marry Naomi with whom he feels 'at home'. He tells Karen: 'You should stay with your own people' (Bowen, 1935/1976, 146). However Karen is willing to risk going further in the encounter with the other and she persuades Max to meet again.

After they have slept together, Karen believes that nothing else can come of their relationship. Max will marry Naomi. She will return to her old life and no one will ever know. In rebellion against the safety of this, she envisages the possibility of a child by Max. A child would be proof of her revolt against her parents' world, tangible evidence of her encounter with the foreigner, the other: 'He would be the

---

[3] For a general discussion of the foreigner as abject, see N. McAfee, 1993 and see also *Strangers to Ourselves* (Kristeva, 1991, 187), quoted below.

Max I heard talking when I stood outside the salon, the Max I rang up: that other we were both looking for' (Bowen, 1935/1976, 153). She would no longer be able to return safely to her home, she would remain cut off. Though this, their second meeting, takes place in England, 'Karen, walking by Max, felt more isolated with him, more cut off from her own country than if they had been in Peru. You feel most foreign when you no longer belong where you did' (Bowen 1935/1976, 157). Like Mary Lavelle, Karen's encounter with the foreign other has made her aware of how much in herself is foreign to her nation and her class.

Though it is eventually agreed between them that Max must break off his engagement with Naomi and they must marry, their return to their respective countries jolts each of them back into an awareness of how difficult it will be to escape their separate worlds and be together. Madame Fisher, seeking to retain her power over him, destroys Max's belief in his love for Karen by casting doubt on his motives: she congratulates him on being self-seeking and ambitious even in love. In despair and self-loathing, Max kills himself. For her part, Karen becomes involved in a struggle to get her mother to acknowledge the seriousness of her feelings for Max which run so entirely counter to the Michealis social code. After Max's death, she abandons the struggle and retreats into the safety of the Michaelis life. When she discovers she is pregnant she becomes afraid of what the unborn child represents, namely the strangeness of the other which threatens to disrupt her English way of life. As Kristeva says in a passage from *Strangers to Ourselves* quoted earlier: 'The foreigner is within us. And when we flee from or struggle against the foreigner, we are fighting our unconscious' (Kristeva, 1991, 191). In allowing Naomi to place Leopold for adoption, Karen is fighting both the disruptive memory of her affair with Max and her consciousness of the other inside herself. She tells Ray: 'He is more than a little boy. He is Leopold. You don't know what he is' (Bowen, 1935/1976, 215).

Karen attempts to suppress all memory of her encounter with the other by adopting the persona of a conventionally submissive wife to Ray: 'Feverishly, she simulated the married peace women seemed to inherit, wanting most of all to live like her mother' (Bowen 1935/1976, 218). She has become terrified of what her experience with Max has revealed to her of life. As Kristeva has said, in a sentence which recalls her description of the abject: 'Confronting the foreigner whom I reject and with whom at the same time I identify, I lose my boundaries' (Kristeva, 1991, 187). This is in effect what has happened to Karen and it is why she is so determined to re-establish those known boundaries of her upbringing in her marriage to Ray. It is Ray now who urges her to remember Leopold and it is Ray finally who crosses cultural boundaries to bring Leopold home.

Ray knows that the future with Leopold will not be easy: 'Ray saw for the moment what he was up against: the force of a foreign cold personality' (Bowen 1935/1976, 221). Their difference strikes even passers-by: 'Their inappropriateness to each other made people stare' (Bowen, 1935/1976, 238). He, the calm Englishman, recognizes Leopold's foreignness, yet he acknowledges that the child represents something in Karen which he values but which she has tried to stifle in the conventional life they lead. Contrary to Kristeva's argument that women because of their boundary position are best positioned to welcome foreigners, in this novel it is a man, Ray, who is more adept at welcoming the stranger into their lives. Leopold, too, welcomes the unfamiliar English world of his mother just because it is his mother's country and he suspects that this foreign other will for him contain the familiar: 'his own moments, hands approaching making him unsuspicious' (Bowen, 1935/1976, 196). The novel ends with the recognition that Ray and Leopold in crossing cultural boundaries to reach one another have done something heroic.

For the heroines of Kate O'Brien, and for Deirdre Madden's heroine, Aisling, the encounter with another culture is creative, providing them with an opportunity to break through habits of thought and behavior formed at home. Aisling's stay abroad, like that of Nell in *The Memory Stones*, allows her to begin the healing process necessary after her traumatic childhood in Ireland. Out of Mary Lavelle's dialog with another culture comes a questioning of the received assumptions of her home culture. Clare's life abroad allows her to explore those aspects of her identity – opera singer and lesbian – in a way which would not be possible in Ireland. Elizabeth Bowen, on the other hand, presents the encounter with the foreign other as perplexing and confusing for her heroine. Karen's encounter with the other in the form of Max unnerves her through the revelation of the foreign other in herself. With none of these heroines, however, does the encounter with the other impinge on the wider society in which she finds herself. Their recognition of the foreign within themselves does not have the impact on wider national life that Kristeva hoped for in *Nations without Nationalism*. These are private, interior accounts of encounters with the other. For the setting of the theme of the foreigner within the wider context of the life of a nation, we may turn to another novel by Kate O'Brien, *The Land of Spices*, published in 1941.

The Land of Spices (1941)

The Land of Spices is centered around a convent school in Ireland run by a French order, La Compagnie de la Sainte Famille, similar to the French-run convent, Laurel Hill, which Kate O'Brien herself attended in Limerick.[4] Laurel Hill was run by the Faithful Companions of Jesus and known locally as 'the French convent'. The novel is set between the years 1904 and 1914, a time when nationalist ideas were taking hold in Ireland. This has an impact on Helen Archer, the Reverend Mother of the convent. Helen is English and, as an English woman, she finds herself in a particularly difficult situation in a country where she is regarded as the foreign enemy. In fact at the beginning of the novel she has decided to resign because she feels she will never be accepted by the Irish.

The novel opens with a scene where the European or transnational ethos of the convent is juxtaposed to the narrow forms of Irish nationalism espoused by the convent chaplain, Father Conroy, and the local Catholic Bishop. Father Conroy, 'a country boy fresh from Maynooth'(O'Brien, 1941/2000, 13), thinks it is a pity that a foreign Order is running a school in Ireland and that Irish girls have to go abroad to receive their training in the Order's novitiate in Bruges. He tells Helen: 'Our

---

[4]　For further details of Kate O'Brien's life, see Éibhear Walshe, *Kate O'Brien: a Writing Life*, Irish Academic Press, Dublin and Portland, 2006. Walshe's biography came out after this study was completed.

young girls must be educated *nationally* now, Reverend Mother – to be the wives of *Irishmen* and to meet the changing times!' (O'Brien, 1941/2000, 92). Both the Bishop and Father Conroy anticipate an Irish education system which will endorse what the Bishop calls 'the establishment of a national character' (O'Brien, 1941/2000, 14). This Irish nationalism will be, the Bishop tells the Reverend Mother, closely 'bound up with its religion' (O'Brien, 1941/2000, 15). The narrowly nationalistic and Catholic ethos of the future Irish nation is prefigured here.

The Bishop and Father Conroy perceive the French-run convent school as a threat to the emerging Irish national identity whereas the Reverend Mother, English but brought up in Brussels, argues for the educational advantages of familiarity with several different cultures. In opposition to the Irish clergy's narrow brand of nationalism she sets out her concept of transnationalism, emphasizing that her Order cuts across national boundaries. It has nuns teaching in Canada, Portugal, Poland, England, the States and South America. 'Our nuns are *not* a nation' she tells the Bishop, 'and our business is not with national matters' (O'Brien, 1941/2000, 15). The Order is willing to adapt to the culture in which its nuns find themselves: Helen permits her pupils to study the Irish language but as 'a choice of cultures offered to them' (O'Brien, 1941/2000, 168). Her pupils use French as their everyday language and also learn German. The convent encourages its pupils to transcend local nationalisms by educating them into a European outlook. Kate O'Brien's novel thus provides an interesting juxtaposition of masculinist Irish nationalism with a transnational female network of convents. It annoys the Bishop intensely that the convent of La Compagnie de la Sainte Famille is autonomous and lies outside his jurisdiction. The brief presence in the novel of the English suffragist, Miss Robertson, underlines the link O'Brien is making between women and transnationalism by reminding us that the struggle to gain the vote was one which crossed national boundaries. The Bishop has his arguments with Miss Robertson too, and in conversation with him she states her specific approval of the convent school's ethos of 'detachment of spirit' from narrow forms of nationalism (O'Brien, 1941/2000, 210).

Despite her spirited defense to the Bishop, Helen Archer feels discouraged in her task, believing that the convent would do better headed by a nun who is not a foreigner and not regarded by others as 'a cold English fish' (O'Brien, 1941/2000, 13). In *Strangers to Ourselves*, Kristeva describes feelings of hatred produced by the foreigner, 'image of hatred and of the other', in terms which have bearing on Helen's situation:

> Detestation tells you that you are an intruder, that you are irritating, and that this will be shown to you frankly and without caution. No one in this country can either defend or avenge you. You do not count for anyone, you should be grateful for being tolerated among us. Civilised people need not be gentle with foreigners. (Kristeva, 1991, 14)

Helen is about to hand in her resignation and allow the convent to be given over to the leadership of Mother Mary Andrew, a nationalist nun from Northern Ireland, when a moment of empathy with the youngest pupil at the school, Anna Murphy, changes her mind.

The Land of Spices is partly a female *Bildungsroman*. It portrays, over the course of ten years, Anna's growth to maturity and, in the final epiphany, points to her future as an artist.[5] The novel shows how, under Helen's leadership, the convent's detachment from narrow forms of nationalism saves the young Anna from the traps set for her by her life in Ireland. The most evident of these traps is Anna's financial dependence on members of her family who, though they are prepared to finance her elder brother's university studies, do not believe in higher education for women. Whereas the nationalist nun, Mother Mary Andrew, hinders Anna's development in all sorts of ways, Helen opens up the future for her by supporting and facilitating her desire to go to university despite the Murphy family's opposition. In this respect, as Ann Owens Weekes has pointed out, the Order of La Sainte Famille is more truly nurturing of Anna's potential than is her biological family (Weekes, 1991, 127).

Despite the obstacles to a young girl's liberty posed by life in Ireland and by the pressures to conform to certain expectations of womanhood, by the end of the novel, Helen has helped Anna to become a Kristevan subject-in-process, her future evolving and open-ended. For Anna, too, her awareness of how much in herself is other to the life she sees around her, with its limited expectations of women, encourages her to cross national boundaries and reach out to the example of foreign others – Helen Archer, Miss Robertson – in order to move into a wider and more adventurous future than the one laid down for her by her family.

Writing on *The Land of Spices*, Mary Breen sees the French-run convent as marginalized and therefore powerless (Walshe, 1993, 167–90). While it may be true that the convent is somewhat marginalized in the life of the Irish nation, it gains strength and power from its network of influences abroad. 'Our Order is world-wide and powerful' Helen tells Anna's grandmother, in the course of her battle with her for Anna's future (O'Brien, 1941/2000, 262). Relying on the authority invested in this transnational network of power, Helen helps Anna take her place in the world. Not only that: as an educator, Helen has the power to shape the future generation of Irish women, as even the hostile Father Conroy acknowledges (indeed Helen's power over Irish girls is partly the reason for his hostility): 'Nuns shouldn't trouble themselves with these secular things, I suppose. And yet you know, Reverend Mother, a convent like this wields great influence – through its girls afterwards – in the world' (O'Brien, 1941/2000, 91–2). The European-centered convent in *The Land of Spices*, with its international network and its emphasis on the individual's right to a choice of cultures, has the potential to make its girls, as Julia Kristeva has argued in *Nations without Nationalism* women should be, unsettling presences in the life of the Irish nation. In the figure of Helen Archer, *The Land of Spices* portrays a foreigner whose ability to translate between cultures may indeed have an influence on the life of the nation.

---

[5] For this theme see Ann Owens Weekes' discussion of *The Land of Spices* in *Irish Women Writers* (Weekes, 1991, 120–32).

Chapter 6

The Feminine and the Sacred

Introduction

In recent years there has been increasing interest in the element of spirituality in Julia Kristeva's writings. Works such as *Transfigurations: Theology and the French Feminists* edited by Kim, St Ville and Simonaitis (1993), *French Feminists on Religion* edited by Joy, O'Grady and Poxon (2002) and my own *Women's Spirituality in the Twentieth Century* (2004) have highlighted Kristeva's often provocative writing on religion and the way in which her theories may be used to illuminate the frequently neglected topic, at least amongst literary critics, of spirituality in women's fiction.

In her native Bulgaria, Kristeva was raised in the twin dogmas of Marxism and Roman Catholicism. As outlined both in *Au commencement était l'amour* (1985) and in *The Feminine and the Sacred* (2001), she discarded Roman Catholicism during her teenage years. Facing up to the fact of her own mortality, she could not, she writes in *The Feminine and the Sacred*, believe either in an after-life or in a supreme being. Whilst she had faith that the thought of the species would continue (the only kind of after-life in which she believes), she felt obliged to concede that her individual mind would perish with her body (Kristeva, 2001, 47–8).

Despite her abandonment of formal belief, Kristeva's work continues to be informed by the Judeo-Christian tradition even when she seeks to challenge it. Indeed the development of her punning redefinition of heresy as 'herethics', a word used to express the type of reaching out to the other in love which she sees as characteristic of women, demonstrates the close link in Kristeva's work between heretical thinking and a new type of feminist ethics. The evolution of her work has shown a continued interest in the loss of security caused by the break-up of religion in Western culture and the way in which psychoanalysis has taken over from religion in healing psychic wounds. In *Tales of Love*, Kristeva draws parallels between the Christian discourse of love and the psychoanalyst's relationship with her client and she introduces religious terms such as agapeic love into psychoanalytical discourse. In an interview she has stated: 'For me, in a very Christian fashion, ethics merges with love, which is why ethics also merges with the psychoanalytic relationship' (Kristeva, 1986, 20).

Two of Kristeva's essays, 'Stabat Mater' and 'Motherhood According to Bellini', contrast idealizations of motherhood in Roman Catholicism with the mother in psychoanalytical discourse in order to elaborate a new psychoanalytic understanding of motherhood based on an herethics of love. In 'Stabat Mater', following Marina Warner, Kristeva argues that the orthodox view of the Virgin Mary has often been used to suppress dissent. Her arguments, as we saw in chapter four, are very relevant to the way in which the Catholic religion developed in

Ireland, where the patriarchal construct of the Virgin was used to control and define women. 'Our queen of heaven may dominate the mystic depths, but she is rarely seen along the byways of power within the Church community' comments Kristeva dryly in *The Feminine and the Sacred* (Clément and Kristeva, 2001, 71).

In this chapter I explore different aspects of Kristeva's writing on spirituality in the context of Irish women's writing. I first look at the way in which religion was used in Ireland to control and suppress women, as illustrated in the writing of Mary Lavin. I then discuss the portrayal in two of Kate O'Brien's novels, *The Ante-Room* and *That Lady*, of the way in which their private faith enables her heroines to resist pressure from the symbolic order. In the third section I explore Kristeva's anxieties about the loss of soul in modern society in the context of Elizabeth Bowen's novel, *Eva Trout* (1968). Finally, following Kristeva's argument, in *Revolt, She Said*, that new forms of spirituality are a necessary defense against institutionalism and political dogmatism, I examine Éilís Ní Dhuibhne's novel, *Dancers Dancing*, which presents a young woman who, through her discovery of a sense of the sacred in nature, creates a private space for herself within the life of the nation. For Kristeva, as she makes clear in *The Feminine and the Sacred* (Clément and Kristeva, 2001, 26), there is a definite distinction to be drawn between religion and a sense of the sacred (hence the title of this chapter). Religion and belief, interpreted in the widest sense, are, she explains, always consolatory, proposing omnipotent father figures and the comforting illusion that we are not subject to nature, biology or mortality. In this sense she associates orthodox religion with the symbolic order. A sense of the sacred, for Kristeva, involves celebrating the border between nature and culture, a border of which women, she believes, are particularly conscious (Clément and Kristeva, 2001, 27).

Religion as suppression: Mary Lavin

In chapter four we looked at the way in which in 'Stabat Mater' Kristeva juxtaposes women's bodily experience of motherhood, based on her own experience of giving birth, with the abstractions of the Virgin Mary in order to expose the idealizations inherent in the latter, idealizations which have been unhelpful to women. In her essay, Kristeva's reflections on her own bodily experience of motherhood break up the analysis of the historical development of the cult of the Virgin Mary by emphasizing what that cult has suppressed or ignored, namely the pain, tears, sweat of childbirth, the sleeplessness, the milk, the eroticism of motherhood.

We also looked at *Powers of Horror* where Kristeva examines the religious prohibitions on the maternal body which figures in Judaism and Christianity as the abject, that which must at all costs be repressed in the name of the Father. Jewish purity rituals arose, she argues, from a desire to distinguish Judaism from the maternal cults by which it was surrounded. It was a matter 'of separating oneself from the phantasmatic power of the mother, that archaic Mother Goddess who actually haunted the imagination of a nation at war with the surrounding polytheism' (Kristeva, 1982, 100). She concludes that both Judaism and Christianity seek to stifle our awareness of the body, sex, mortality in the name of a logocentric connection with ultimate reality, 'subordinating maternal power (whether historical or phantasmic, natural or reproductive) to the symbolic order as pure logical order regulating social performance, as divine Law attended to in the Temple' (Kristeva, 1982, 91).

Kristeva's analysis of the suppression of the body is very relevant to Ireland where, as Cheryl Herr argues in 'The Erotics of Irishness', the various ideologies which have held Ireland in their grip during the twentieth century have been responsible for a general suppression of the body in Irish society (Herr, 1990, 1–34). In her article, 'The Family and The Female Body in the Novels of Edna O'Brien and Julia O'Faolain', Lorna Rooks-Hughes agrees with Herr's analysis and argues that the idealization of motherhood in Ireland has led to a desexualization of the female body which has been damaging to women's sense of self (Rooks-Hughes, 1996, 83–97).

The theme of religious prohibitions used by church and society to control and police the female body is one which figures prominently in the short stories of Mary Lavin. Lavin's writing life extended from 1939 to the late 1970s, that is, she was writing at a time when the female body was severely censored and restricted by Irish social mores and by a narrowly puritanical form of Roman Catholicism. In *Inventing Ireland: The Literature of the Modern Nation* (1995), Declan Kiberd sees Mary Lavin as writing from within her community: 'Her touch was ever light and easy. She had no desire to dig society up by its roots' (Kiberd, 1995/1996, 409). Seamus Deane makes a similar claim: 'Mary Lavin very largely shares the mores of her society' (Rafroidi and Brown, 1979, 238). The fact that her mother-daughter stories, as we saw in chapter four, portray women unable to disentangle themselves from social conditioning may seem to bear out Deane's point. Against this it could be claimed that, by placing the mother-daughter relationship at the center of her work, Lavin indicates a desire to mark a shift from the traditional Irish emphasis on fathers and sons or mothers and sons.

Certainly I would argue that on the theme of sexuality and the female body, Lavin is a more radical writer than has been allowed. One of her earliest short stories, 'Sunday brings Sunday' (1944), criticizes the sexual repressions of rural Ireland which leave a young girl dangerously ignorant about sexuality. The curate preaches against 'company-keeping' (Lavin, 1974, 112), but this term is not precise enough for Mona who sees many people around her keeping company without running into danger: 'Company-keeping was no harm. The priest meant something else. Why couldn't he speak more particular?' (Lavin, 1974, 113). Inevitably, without quite knowing how it has happened, Mona becomes pregnant. The implication of Lavin's story is that church and society are to blame for keeping a young girl in ignorance about her own body.

In story after story Lavin depicts Ireland as a society which censors information about women's bodies. As late as 1974, in 'The Shrine', she depicts a Canon obsessed with controlling his female parishioners' sexuality. If their bodies escape his control and they become pregnant outside marriage, he quickly arranges to have them married off. Women collude in policing the female body. The women the Canon marries off precipitately turn round and help him marry off others. They learn to be ashamed of their bodies. In 'Chamois Gloves' (1956), Mabel's liberated talk about induced childbirth, labor pains and breast feeding causes several embarrassed silences in the convent parlor. Mabel's sister, Veronica, who has just taken her novice's vows, is disturbed by this discussion of the female body: 'A nervous feeling came into her stomach, and she didn't want to hear any more details' (Lavin, 1999, 124–5). Already she has learned to censor the body in the interests of her religion: 'If God ordained that certain things were to be outside her experience, she didn't want to know anything about them' (Lavin, 1999, 125).

One of Lavin's most forceful indictments of the censoring of Irish women's bodies comes in 'The Nun's Mother' (1944), where Mrs Latimer's convent training in prudery affects her relationship with her daughter, Angela, to such an extent that when Angela announces that she wishes to enter a convent, her mother is unable, despite her husband's urgings, to talk to her daughter about the sexual pleasure she will be missing out on. 'A curious embarrassment – it would not be going too far to call it revulsion' (Lavin, 1974, 51) – causes Mrs Latimer to keep quiet, with the result that Angela will enter a convent where all bodily pleasure is censored and where the body is humiliated and restricted by strange kinds of undergarments that appall her mother. The story ends with Mrs Latimer herself, now the mother of a nun, training herself to suppress 'her thoughts with regard to – how should she say it – with regard to the pleasures of the body' (Lavin, 1974, 54). This is despite the fact that she has previously enjoyed a healthy sexual relationship with her husband. The social and religious restrictions on speaking of the body thus result in impoverishment for both mother and daughter. In stories such as these, Lavin questions her nation's normalizing discourse concerning women's bodies.

Occasionally Lavin goes further and depicts female bodies bursting through the religious and social prohibitions placed on them. Her short story, 'A Memory' (1972), portrays the female body erupting in violent protest against the restrictions on it. 'A Memory' recounts the relationship between James, a research professor who fell in love once in his youth and self-protectively will never allow himself to do so again, and Myra, who for ten years has served as his form of relaxation from work. Myra, an independent professional woman, is well aware of James' fear of being possessed and has gradually suppressed in herself any trace of behavior that might seem 'wifey', a word they smugly coin 'to describe a certain type of woman they both abhorred' (Lavin, 1972, 188). Femaleness becomes the abject in this relationship and Myra forms the sort of defense against the mother which Kristeva warns can lead to psychosis (Oliver, 1993a, 62). In order to maintain her relationship with James, who loathes any sign of womanliness, Myra relinquishes her domestic skills and restricts her domesticity to ordering takeaways which they pay for separately.

In order to preserve her relationship with James, Myra suppresses all trace of female desire. Her flat takes on 'a marvellously masculine air' (Lavin, 1972, 165). This relationship suits James but the cost to Myra of suppressing the body is hinted at: 'It was – she said – as if part of her had become palsied' (Lavin, 1972, 165). As Kristeva has argued, a woman cannot suppress the body without suppressing part of herself. Far from oscillating between the symbolic and the semiotic, Myra identifies so completely with the symbolic order that she becomes a pseudo male, a danger of which Kristeva warns in 'About Chinese Women'. Myra is aware of the peculiarly cerebral nature of their relationship: 'this curious transference – this drawing off of energies – from the body to the brain' (Lavin 1972, 164). She is a woman who, in order to please a man has, to use Kristevan terminology, annihilated her difference. This leads eventually to her breakdown.

One evening, after a spectacularly casual piece of behavior by James, Myra's feelings erupt. Her body, long suppressed, erupts in a storm of tears. James, who sealed off his emotions many years ago, remains impervious, dismissing Myra's outburst as 'a performance' and 'hysterical'. When he prepares to leave, Myra tries physically to stop him by throwing out her arms in 'an outrageous gesture of crucifixion' (Lavin, 1972, 198). The image, though strong, does not seem inappropriate. Myra has indeed crucified her emotional life and her physical desires for James' sake. She has recently undergone a hysterectomy, which is presented as another mutilation of her bodily desires for the sake of pleasing James, whose abhorrence of children has long been plain. Myra indeed wonders whether she has not 'denatured herself for James' (Lavin, 1972, 195). Kristeva's words in 'Women's Time' (1979), about women's desire to free themselves from society's suppression of the female body, seem applicable to Mona's eventual rebellion against all she has sacrificed to please James. Kristeva speaks of:

> Women's desire to lift the weight of what is sacrificial in the social contract from their shoulders, to nourish our societies with a more flexible and free discourse, one able to name what has thus far never been an object of circulation in the community: the enigmas of the body, the dreams, secret joys, shames, hatreds of the second sex. (Kristeva, 1986, 207)

Myra does indeed explode against the restraints on her female desire exacted by James. James is left feeling nauseated by her outburst, a typical male reaction in Lavin's stories to evidence of female desire (see Matthew in 'Love is for Lovers').

Although on one level Lavin's story dangerously skirts essentialism in the notion that there is an essential female nature that Myra has sacrificed, a danger from which Kristeva's own analysis is not at times exempt, it does bear out Kristeva's warning of the risks to women of complete identification with the symbolic order. Myra's attitude of crucifixion has resonance with Kristeva's analysis of those moments in the lives of the female mystics when they expressed their sense of the sacred and the unnameable in bodily swoons and ecstasies which marked a deliberate protest against societal and religious prohibitions. In *The Feminine and the Sacred*, discussing the ecstasies of Saint Teresa of Avila, Hildegard of Bingen and Angela of Foligno she says:

> Indeed, that unspeakable jouissance is at once *provoked* in me by the other – by "my neighbor", by language – and *irreducible* to their transparency. The indomitable excitability of the hysterical body attests to that paradox, and the sacred was the space where woman could give free rein to that abjection and to that pleasure, to nothingness and to glory (Clément and Kristeva, 2001, 38)

Through her bodily protest, Myra reclaims her difference from James and perhaps in the process discovers her own sacred space, as Kristeva suggests hysterical women do.

Mary Lavin's much-neglected novel, *The House in Clewe Street* (1945), depicts another heroine, Onny Soraghan, resisting, by means of her body, the narrow puritanical society in which she lives. The novel is set in Castlerampart, a fictionalized version of Athenry, the twelfth-century walled town in County Galway, birthplace of Lavin's mother, to which Lavin returned at the age of nine from America and which therefore she always saw to some extent with the eyes of an outsider. In *The House in Clewe Street* the stultifying middle class values of the leaders of Castlerampart society are established from the outset. It is a world dominated by class, property and Catholicism with the Coniffe family at the center as the largest property owners of all.

Onny lives on the outskirts of Castlerampart beyond which lies the ruined castle and wild parkland where she will hold her trysts with the heir to the Coniffe property, Gabriel. Many of Lavin's stories feature such a wilderness outside the town walls. These wildernesses come to symbolize all that the town rejects: the parkland in *The House in Clewe Street* is described as 'vacant and waste land that is seldom entered by the people of the town' (Lavin, 1945/1987, 6). In the short story, 'A Bevy of Aunts', the wilderness outside the town (another fictionalized version of Athenry) becomes a metaphorical 'forbidden domain' (Lavin, 1985, 160). Wandering there, the young narrator meets a wise old woman who tells her she has learned her wisdom from this wilderness. In 'A Bevy of Aunts' the wilderness is associated with the bodily pleasures this society tries to restrict: it is where Tim and Milly give way to their outlaw desire. Predictably the narrator's bourgeois family in 'A Bevy of Aunts' are horrified to discover the narrator has been wandering in the wilderness: 'That's no fit place for you or any proper person' her uncle Vance tells her (Lavin, 1985, 164). At times like these, Lavin's wilderness comes close to the Kristevan notion of a psychic wilderness embodying all that society wishes to suppress. Kristeva notes that because of their marginal position within the symbolic order, male culture associates women in particular with this wilderness (see Moi, 1990, 167) and indeed many of Lavin's stories portray mad women lurking in the wild places on the edge of Irish communities, unable to be absorbed by them: Mad Mary in 'Sunday Brings Sunday', for example. Significantly, then, it is in the fields outside Castlerampart that six-year-old Gabriel Coniffe first encounters Onny and becomes fascinated by her naked body.

When they are both grown up and Onny has come to work in Gabriel's household as a servant, her body continues to exert its fascination over Gabriel. Her brightly colored clothes show off her body and express a spirit of rebellion 'in the dull walled town' (Lavin, 1945/1987, 257). To wear yellow silk stockings to Church is to challenge her society's equation of the female body with modesty and humility. It is in the wilderness outside the town that Gabriel and Onny first embrace, breaking through the class distinctions of their society which would keep them apart. For Gabriel this wilderness is like an entry into another world away from the 'dull world of routine and convention':

> Crossing the river he seemed to have stepped into an enchanted land where everything wore a new shape, a new colour, and where the sounds of the earth were different. (Lavin, 1945/1987, 259)

The wilderness contains all the sensuality that his society has tried to suppress. In its association with color and sound it represents in Gabriel's life the momentary triumph of the semiotic over the symbolic: 'the river seemed to have widened until he felt that never again would he recross it and go back to the old flat life of obedience and self-abasement' (Lavin, 1945/1987, 260).

Eventually the strain of keeping their relationship a secret in Castlerampart becomes too difficult for the couple and they move to Dublin, where Onny's body exerts its charms over the artists among whom she and Gabriel live. Jealous of her success, Gabriel tries to assert his authority over Onny: he wants to bring her outlaw and untamed body inside the Catholic Church by marrying her. However Onny, though by now pregnant, refuses to be owned either by Gabriel or by the Church. She asserts her rights over her own body, including her right to have an abortion: 'I'm not your wife! You have no rights over me; I am free. I can do what I like' she tells Gabriel (Lavin, 1945/1987, 438). The illegal abortion is botched and Onny dies but, despite the urging of his artist friends, Gabriel will not disown her even if it means making himself, under the Irish law of that time, an accessory to murder.

Onny's body features in the novel as the abject, disowned by both the hidebound inhabitants of Castlerampart and the supposedly free-thinking bohemians of Dublin whose rebellion against the mores of their society turns out to be shallow. The continuing fascination Onny's body exerts over Gabriel allows him to see through the feminine masquerade. It allows him to discern the hypocrisy of Agnes Finnerty, a woman whose clothes and behavior, unlike Onny's, exactly conform to her society's construct of femininity and who employs a pretended piety to try to entrap Gabriel. Through her body, Onny subverts the Coniffe values of restraint, prudence and respectability. There is a moment at the end of the novel when Castlerampart almost triumphs as Gabriel dreams of returning home after his adventures in the city to ask forgiveness of his aunts, but the memory of Onny and what he owes her prevents him.[1] Though the portrayal of Gabriel and his aunts is not without sympathy, in the end it is Onny who grips the reader's imagination, as she gripped Gabriel's and as indeed she seems to have gripped Lavin's (Lavin, 1945/1987, 470).

Onny's use of her body as a means to subvert the values of the society around her finds an echo in Lavin's novella, 'The Becker Wives', where the small, bird-like Flora uses her body to parody the heavy movements of the other Becker wives, all solid, middle-class women with bodies amply built for child-bearing. Flora's imitative gestures emphasize the bourgeois entrapment of the other Becker wives; they constitute a protest against what Hélène Cixous in 'Sorties' calls 'the merry-go-round of bourgeois-conjugal pettiness' (Cixous and Clément, 1996, 99). Like Cixous' hysterics, Lavin's women reveal the return of what is repressed in their society through their bodies. Flora's eventual drift into insanity aligns her with other women whose protest against the symbolic order ended with slippage into madness (Kristeva, 1986, 157).

---

[1]   The Virago edition of *The House in Clewe Street* contains an afterword by Augustine Martin which seems to me to contain a fundamental misreading of the ending of Lavin's novel. Martin claims that Gabriel returns to his aunts, but in fact Gabriel only dreams of returning to Castlerampart before realizing that this would be an evasion of his duty to Onny. The ending shows him firmly directing his steps to the morgue to acknowledge his relationship with Onny and accept whatever legal consequences may follow.

By writing the female body, its pains, its *jouissances*, its humiliations (miscarriage in 'The Lost Child', incontinence in 'Senility'), Lavin succeeds in depicting, and on occasion challenging, the severely restricting Catholic discourses of her nation surrounding women's bodies. Renee's miscarriage in 'The Lost Child', for instance, causes her to question Roman Catholic belief in limbo. Rather than fitting in with the prevailing ethos of their time, Lavin's stories may be read, at least in the context of her treatment of the theme of the female body, as marking the return of the repressed other.

Resisting the symbolic order

The Ante-Room

The spiritual theme in Kristeva's work continues the theme of the relationship between the symbolic and the semiotic for, in Kristeva's view, institutional religion upholds the symbolic and suppresses the semiotic and this is why she privileges psychoanalytic over religious discourse since she believes the former allows for a more provisional and flexible sense of identity while the latter, with its insistence on authority, in her view closes down discussion. As Cleo Kearns argues in 'Kristeva and Feminist Theology': 'Kristeva's critique of theology rests on the assumption that, taken straight, and without the benefit of postmodern reading, it leans so heavily to the symbolic level that it violently represses the semiotic' (Kim, St Ville, Simonaitis, 1993, 66–7). Feminist theologians like Cleo Kearns have questioned Kristeva's analysis of the Judaeo-Christian tradition as predicated on a series of master discourses which deny heterogeneity and thus hinder the development of a provisional and flexible sense of self. In particular, Kearns argues in the above article that Thomas Aquinas' concept of the sacrament as mediation between the word and the body may be translated into contemporary terms as an attempt to negotiate between the symbolic and the semiotic. Kate O'Brien's novel, *The Ante-Room*, published in 1934, portrays a woman attempting to use the sacramental rituals of the Catholic religion in just such a way.

The very structure of *The Ante-Room*, built around three successive feast-days in the Catholic Church calendar, The Eve of All Saints, The Feast of All Saints and The Feast of All Souls, takes us away from the romance plot. The feast-days are days both inside time, being marked on the Church calendar, and outside, in that they focus believers' attention on the lives of those who have passed into a dimension beyond time. The novel centers on a pair of star-crossed lovers, Agnes and Vincent. Vincent, handsome, moody and selfish, is unhappily married to Agnes' sister, Marie-Rose, and in love with Agnes. Agnes is a deeply devout Catholic tormented by guilt over her love for her sister's husband. Punctuated by religious services for the feast-days, the novel moves inside and out of time.

Both Agnes and Vincent seek in different ways to escape time. Vincent longs to find a place outside time with Agnes: 'an escape through time or space [...] in which he and she could speak and be their real selves' (O'Brien, 1934/1988, 127). He rails against the fact that: 'There was no place in time where she could love him, where he could have her in honour or dishonour' (O'Brien, 1934/1988, 158).

Agnes too wishes to escape 'the rigidity of time' (O'Brien, 1934/1988, 10), marked in the novel by the tolling of the bells for Mass and the clock in the hall at Roseholm. We first see her waking reluctantly from sleep into linear time: 'Bells and clock and thin autumnal light were calling her back to things she did not wish to face' (O'Brien, 1934/1988, 4). For Kristeva, linear time is always connected with the father and is part of the symbolic order: 'The symbolic order – the order of verbal communication, the paternal order of genealogy – is a temporal order' (Kristeva, 1986, 152). Only a woman, Kristeva argues, can escape time: 'outside time, with neither a before nor an after, neither true nor false' (Kristeva, 1986, 153). Whenever a woman identifies with the archaic maternal, Kristeva argues, she breaks the symbolic chain.

In *The Ante-Room*, however, Agnes escapes time rather differently, by adhering to the rituals of her Catholic religion. These remind her of another dimension, eternal life, and in turn this reminder gives her the strength to resist Vincent. When she guesses that Vincent is likely to follow his wife down to Roseholm, Agnes seeks to armor herself against him by going to Benediction and Confession: 'Faith a cold thing, a fact – that was what she must use to destroy fantasy' (O'Brien, 1934/1988, 84). After confessing her sinful daydreams to the priest and receiving understanding and absolution, Agnes is left feeling detached and courageous. Earthly love, the priest reminds her, has a time limit whereas the search for God leads us outside time.

When Vincent surprises Agnes in the corridor by laying a hand on her shoulder, her momentary temptation to yield to him is restrained by the sound of Sister Emmanuel moving around in her mother's room. To Agnes, Sister Emmanuel's cough is 'a sound almost holy in its repression':

> It brought back the idea of holiness, the idea of pain. It brought back prayer and duty and the memory of her own confession. Dazedly her spirit moved from its moment of righteousness under his loved hand to its outer, older knowledge of another rectitude. (O'Brien, 1934/1988, 140)

Later, going to meet Vincent in the garden, she uses Saint Bernard's prayer as 'her shield' (O'Brien, 1934/1988, 242). Agnes employs the rituals of the Catholic religion in order to evade the romance plot in which Vincent seeks to place her. Though Agnes is passionately in love with Vincent, the romantic fancies he weaves around her feel like a trap: 'He thought it was an escape, apparently, but it had been her prison' (O'Brien, 1934/1988, 192). Vincent's love is a snare for Agnes because she knows that giving in to his love would destroy irrevocably the bond with her sister which runs back to her earliest childhood: 'through that time the thread of Marie-Rose indeed ran vividly' (O'Brien, 1934/1988, 5).

For Agnes, this bond with Marie-Rose is the only thing which seems to make sense of her life and bring together all its scattered parts: 'the unrelated phases of her life, through which the only unifying thread was Marie-Rose' (O'Brien, 1934/1988, 9). For Marie-Rose, too, her relationship with her sister represents 'that harmony of innocence and irresponsibility in which Agnes and she had flowered, their spirits nurturing each other' (O'Brien, 1934/1988, 145-6). For both sisters their bond is an appeal 'against time' (O'Brien, 1934/1988, 146) but neither is able to articulate the bond very clearly. It seems to lie outside time, and therefore

outside the symbolic order, and beyond words, as Kristeva says in 'Stabat Mater'
the bonds between women often do:

> Women doubtless reproduce among themselves the strange gamut of forgotten body
> relationships with their mothers. Complicity in the unspoken, connivance of the
> inexpressible, of a wink, a tone of voice, a gesture, a tinge, a scent [...] No
> communication between individuals but connections between atoms, molecules, wisps
> of words, droplets of sentences. The community of women is a community of dolphins.
> (Kristeva, 1997, 323)

Nevertheless, though Agnes is not able to articulate clearly all that Marie-Rose
means to her, it is this bond with her sister, bolstered by the imperatives of her
Catholic faith, which gives her strength to resist Vincent:

> She said: 'We'll never be together.'
> She spoke softly, yet to both the words were a hard ripple of pistol-shots. But Agnes, as
> she heard them issue from her astonished lips, understood their truth. For a ghost passed
> before her eyes then, and had no doubt selected them.
> Marie-Rose was the ghost, and she had chosen well. They were the only possible words.
> (O'Brien, 1934/1988, 261–2)

Dr Curran, who is also in love with Agnes, shares Kristeva's view of institutional
religion as serving primarily to shore up the social system: 'it seemed to him that
the Catholic Church provided as good a system as might be found for keeping the
human animal in order' (O'Brien, 1934/1988, 67). But that is not how Agnes sees
it and the doctor freely admits that her soul escapes him: 'in the dark regions of her
essential self, he had no light by which to grope' (O'Brien, 1934/1988, 59). So far
from suppressing the semiotic, as Kristeva claims, so far from being merely a
necessary part of the social system as Dr Curran believes, Catholicism allows
Agnes to maintain the semiotic bond with her sister:

> And now, with heart cleaned of offence against her, now cooled by the antiseptic of
> confession, to be able to turn to her, with the old, deep, unstained affection – it was
> glorious! (O'Brien, 1934/1988, 106).

> Violence and passion could have their tortured minute if he insisted, but they could not
> retrace, unplait, unravel the long slow weaving of childhood. (O'Brien, 1934/1988, 267–
> 8).

By the end of the novel, Vincent too has escaped time and the symbolic order. He
commits suicide in order to free Marie-Rose for a happier life (in 1880 there could
be no divorce) and to escape the misery of his unrequited passion for Agnes. He is
also, however, motivated by a desire to be reunited with the mother he adored and
who by her early death has left him forever haunted by her image. In other words,
Vincent accedes to the call of the mother beyond time which Kristeva in 'About
Chinese Women' sees as the prerogative of women:

> For a woman, the call of the mother is not only a call from beyond time, or beyond the
> socio-political battle [...] this call troubles the word: it generates hallucinations, voices,

'madness'. After the superego, the ego founders and sinks. It is a fragile envelope, incapable of staving off the irruption of this conflict, of this love which had bound the little girl to her mother, and which then, like black lava, had lain in wait for her all along the path of her desperate attempts to identify with the symbolic paternal order. Once the moorings of the word, the ego, the superego, begin to slip, life itself can't hang on: death moves quietly in. Suicide without a cause, or sacrifice without fuss [...] a woman can carry off such things without tragedy, even without drama. (Kristeva, 1986, 157)

The examples Kristeva cites at the end of 'About Chinese Women' are Virginia Woolf, Maria Tsvetaeva and Sylvia Plath. However, in *The Ante-Room* it is a man, Vincent, who commits suicide and who is haunted in his dying moments by the memory of his mother with whom he longs to be reunited: 'Darling mother. He smiled. He could see every detail of her smile. Darling mother. He pulled the trigger, his thoughts far off in boyhood' (O'Brien, 1934/1988, 306).

The Ante-Room, though it can be read in the light of Kristeva's writings, in several important ways – the use of sacramental religion to support the semiotic, the portrayal of a man's pull towards the maternal – resists Kristevan theory. Her adherence to Catholicism allows Agnes to escape from the patriarchal romance plot and maintain her semiotic bond with her sister. The novel provides an illustration of Myrtle Hill's argument that the centrality of the Catholic faith to Irish women's sense of self during this period has been seriously underestimated by commentators eager to dwell on the oppressive nature of Catholicism (Hill, 2003, 107–8).

That Lady

A similar theme, though set in sixteenth-century Spain, features in O'Brien's later novel, *That Lady* (1946), where the heroine, Ana, Princess of Eboli, relies on her Catholic faith in her defense of the rights of the individual against the increasing tyranny and political dogmatism of the King of Spain. As Éibhear Walshe has argued in his illuminating analysis of *That Lady*, O'Brien's novel is among other things a protest against Franco's Spain, 'a political fable' (Walshe, 1993, 165), but he also points out that it can be read as a protest against the authoritarianism and narrowness of Eamon de Valera's Ireland where O'Brien's books had lately been censored.

For Kristeva, despite the modern trend to submit everything to political analysis, politics is not a discourse adequate to cover all aspects of life; it neglects, for instance, the importance of the individual. In an interview with Rosalind Coward, Kristeva makes this point: 'My reproach to some political discourses with which I am disillusioned is that they don't consider the individual as a value' (Kristeva, 1997, 347). In a separate interview, with Elaine Hoffman Baruch, she specifically defines women's protest as 'a protest which consists in demanding that attention be paid to the subjective particularity which an individual represents' (Kristeva, 1997, 370). Belief in the importance of the individual is central for the heroine of Kate O'Brien's novel, *That Lady*. However O'Brien's novel resists Kristevan theory in that, rather than developing 'new forms of spirituality', Ana uses institutional religion, namely her adherence to Roman Catholicism, to challenge the political order.

Ana de Mendoza is a widow and a Castilian aristocrat who possesses all the pride of her lineage. At the age of fourteen she fought a duel with a page who had insulted the honor of Castile. She lost an eye during the duel, an incident she has come to believe has determined the course of her life. The silk patch over her eye becomes a talisman for her, a reminder of this early spirited defense of her beliefs. In times of crisis she gains reassurance from touching it. However, despite the fact that Ana is a believer in individual freedom, the constraints of her life as a woman and subject of Philip II and her marriage to the much older Ruy Gomez, have largely forced this independent spirit underground. In marriage, Ruy's purpose has been, or so Ana feels, 'to train her out of being herself' (O'Brien, 1946/1985, 4), as Philip II and his father have trained the Castilian nobility out of any pretension to participate in ruling Spain. In contrast to her husband who approved of this policy, Ana frets against the growing indolence and indifference of the Spanish nobility and Philip's tendency to gather all the reins of power for himself. In public Ana gives Philip her political support as a loyal subject; as an aristocrat and the most powerful female in Spain, she reserves the right in their private conversations to address him on a human level and even to remind him of the time he was in love with her.

Ana comes to stand for a private space within the nation's life and for the importance of the individual, whereas for Philip there is no private space; every aspect of his subjects' lives belongs to him. This especially applies to Ana since he was once in love, or half in love, with her, and the former object of a King's affections must never be unworthy or unfaithful. As the novel progresses, Ana makes an ever more sharp divide between her duty to Philip and her private life when she takes as her lover Don Antonio Perez, a married man.

In her resistance to Philip's encroachment on her private life, Ana is helped by her spirituality which has, paradoxically, been awakened by her affair with Antonio. All her life, Ana has been a good Catholic and kept to the rules of her Church. In the first moments of panic after Ruy's death, Ana turned to Teresa of Avila for help, pleading to be allowed to join the Carmelite Order. She was refused and this caused a knock to her self-confidence as sharp as the loss of her eye. At the start of her affair with Antonio, a married man, though knowing she is committing a mortal sin, Ana is prepared to take her chances. Juan de Escovedo's intrusion into her private bedchamber and his subsequent public denunciation of the adulterous pair shocks her into spiritual awareness. For the first time she turns Antonio away. News of Escovedo's murder for state reasons at the King's command but colluded in by Antonio for private reasons of revenge, leads her into a period of prolonged spiritual reflection. She withdraws from both Philip and Antonio to her country estate at Pastrana. Her spiritual life is something apart from both of them, a private space of her own. In her final interview with Philip, Ana invokes God as a bulwark against tyranny, telling the King: 'My private life is all that I own, and I insist on managing it myself, under God' (O'Brien, 1946/1985, 236). Philip is amazed to be spoken to like this and Ana has her reply when his guards come to take her to jail. Her spirit has defied him and it is her spirit he hopes to break.

So begin Ana's long years of incarceration, first in prison and then under house arrest at Pastrana. At Pastrana, in the company of her housekeeper Bernardina and her daughter Anichu, Ana creates a place of spiritual resistance to Philip, 'an alternative religious community' as Éibhear Walshe calls it (Walshe, 1993, 164). Walshe sees Pastrana as the place where Ana finally realizes her vocation as a holy woman, thwarted all those years ago by the Carmelites. He points out that the fact that Anichu becomes a nun after her mother's death underlines the spirituality of the community at Pastrana. Anichu's action in rejecting an arranged marriage and returning instead to Pastrana to enter the Franciscan convent emphasizes the close bond between mother and daughter. It is a bond which, as he acknowledges at the end of the novel, Philip has been unable to break. In this novel the mother-daughter relationship is presented as an outlaw bond which resists the symbolic order. Though she ends, on the King's command, living and dying in one walled-up room in the dark, Ana feels grateful to Philip for her long incarceration which has allowed her to grow spiritually. Anichu's entrance into the convent at Pastrana suggests that her mother's spiritual influence will continue and work itself out in the life of her daughter.

Though Ana's resistance to Philip is a private matter, it has national resonance. Her friend, the Cardinal, recognizes the rightness of her resistance: 'This stand of yours against blackmail is one of Spain's few good deeds at present [...] you are fighting quite simply for your idea of human conduct' (O'Brien, 1946/1985, 322–3). Ana is resisting tyranny on behalf of all the people of Spain and especially on behalf of her beloved Castile. 'You're the only subject of Philip's who hasn't compromised with his dishonesty' her companion, Bernardina, declares (O'Brien, 1946/1985, 339). The implications for Franco's Spain or even for de Valera's Ireland are clear. Rulers may try to impose a homogeneous identity on their nation but they cannot legislate for what goes on in the individual soul. In turn, by clearing a private space in the nation, be it a convent or a room, the individual may function as a site of dissidence on behalf of the whole nation. Kate O'Brien's novel vividly depicts the clash Kristeva delineates in *Revolt, She Said*, between political discourse and the rights of the individual. However, as in *The Ante-Room*, *That Lady* resists Kristevan theory by presenting a heroine who uses her adherence to orthodox Catholicism in order to challenge the symbolic order.

Loss of the Soul: *Eva Trout* (1968)

In *New Maladies of the Soul* (1995), Kristeva laments the moral and spiritual decline of Western culture which has resulted, she believes, in a subject who is no longer capable of sustaining a rich inner life. In 'The Soul and the Image' she poses the question:

> Do you have a soul? This question, which may be philosophical, theological, or simply misguided in nature, has a particular relevance for our time. In the wake of psychiatric medicines, aerobics, and media zapping, does the soul still exist? (Kristeva, 1995, 3)

Our modern media-obsessed and consumer-driven society has led, she believes, to impoverished imaginations. As an analyst she increasingly comes across patients who have no meaningful inner life:

> An affirmation emerges: today's men and women – who are stress-ridden and eager to achieve, to spend money, have fun, and die – dispense with the representation of their experience that we call psychic life. (Kristeva, 1995, 7)

> We have neither the time nor the space needed to create a soul for ourselves, and the mere hint of such activity seems frivolous and ill-advised. (Kristeva, 1995, 7)

Society's temporary answers to the modern loss of soul are 'dependence on medicines and refuge in the image' (Kristeva, 1995, 9). Since for Kristeva there can be no return to orthodox religion, it is left to analysts to come up with a more permanent solution. Psychoanalysis has replaced religion in tending to the soul: 'the psychoanalyst is then asked to restore psychic life and to enable the speaking entity to live life to its fullest' (Kristeva, 1995, 9). She argues:

> [...] in our world, both the producer and the consumer of images suffer from lack of imagination. Their helplessness results in impairment. What do they want from their analyst? A new psychic apparatus. (Kristeva, 1995, 10)

She gives the example of her patient, Didier, an artist who lived off the images of his paintings but was unable to construct a story of his life or maintain relationships with others. For Kristeva, Didier is a 'symbolic emblem of contemporary man – an actor or consumer of the society of the spectacle who has run out of imagination' (Kristeva, 1995, 10). The way he employed language, speaking in a monotone as if to ward off communication, illustrated his inability to sustain relationships with other human beings: 'Didier wished to convince himself (and his analyst) that he had no soul, as if he were nothing but a robot' (Kristeva, 1995, 12). To come out of his autistic world, Didier needed to be given language and the capacity for human intimacy. In other words, he needed to be given a soul.

For Kristeva psychoanalysis can be a secular replacement for religion, giving back the patient faith in his inner life and providing meaning in an otherwise meaningless existence (without of course providing hope for the next life). In *The Feminine and the Sacred* she asks the question: 'What if what we call the "sacred" were the celebration of a mystery, the mystery of the emergence of meaning?' (Clément and Kristeva, 2001, 13). For Kristeva, to find meaning in life is to find the sacred: 'I claim that what comes back to us as "sacred" in the experience of a woman is the impossible and nevertheless sustained connection between life and meaning' (Clément and Kristeva, 2001, 14).

Kristeva's observations on the emptiness of what she terms 'the society of the spectacle', on the loss of soul in the modern consumer society and on the loss of meaning may be applied to Elizabeth Bowen's last novel, *Eva Trout*. Indeed, the novel's subtitle, *Changing Scenes*, points us towards the visual, as if we were about to watch a movie rather than read a novel. The novel's heroine, Eva Trout, is adept at creating scenes, and the novel opens with a scene carefully set up by Eva, namely a view of the castle where she was to have spent her honeymoon. The castle looks artificial, like a stage set, but is in fact real. The honeymoon, on the other hand, is fake since there has been no engagement; it is merely one of a series of fantasies by which Eva tries to write herself into the life of a woman. As Maud Ellmann argues, in her excellent analysis of *Eva Trout*: 'Eva uses spectacle to construct her relation to society' (Ellmann, 2003, 215). Several critics have argued that Eva in her sexlessness and her inability to settle anywhere incorporates aspects of the Anglo-Irish. Though we never get to know Eva's exact identity (she is described merely as partly foreign), in this context it is interesting to note that Bowen likened the impact on outsiders of the Anglo-Irish way of life as possessing 'something of the trance-like quality of a spectacle' (Bowen, 1986/1999, 276).

Like Bowen's earlier heroines, Lois and Portia, Eva is a motherless heroine who has to make her own way in the world. Eva's mother is even less of a help to her daughter than those earlier mothers. Cissie fled the family home when Eva was two months old and subsequently died in a plane crash. Eva has, her guardian, Constantine, asserts, been 'motherless from the cradle' (Bowen, 1968/1982, 39). All Eva recalls of Cissie is a 'shriek' (Bowen, 1968/1982, 40), a maternal protest reminiscent of Laura's rebellious scratchings on the windowpane in *The Last September*. Eva's father, Willy Trout, tortured by his masochistic love affair with Constantine, leaves his daughter's care to the 'scanty attention' of foreign women hired by the various hotels from where he pursues his international business interests (Bowen, 1968/1982, 46). Willy then sacrifices Eva to his desire to impress Constantine by sending her to the highly dubious, experimental boarding school for wealthy delinquents run by Constantine's friend, Kenneth.

Unmothered, Eva is left yearning for the wordless union with the pre-oedipal mother, a union she attempts to play out with her roommate, Elsinore, abandoned in a coma by the school authorities. Watching over her, Eva feels as if the two of them are together in a moment outside time: 'This deathly yet living stillness, together, of two beings, this unapartness, came to be the requital of all longing' (Bowen, 1968/1982, 56). This back to the womb interlude is, however, broken off when Elsinore's mother arrives to take her daughter away. In this episode, Elsinore's mother acts as the third party, 'the agent of language and society' (Ellmann, 2003, 218), breaking up the symbiotic relationship. In chapter 12, Eva has another chance to recreate this relationship when she encounters the grown-up Elsinore in America, but by then it is too late: Eva has decided to write herself another script (or 'scene'), by adopting a baby.

At another, more appropriate school, Iseult Smith, an inspirational and brilliant teacher, recognizes that Eva has difficulty adapting to language. She speaks, Iseult realizes, 'like a displaced person' (Bowen, 1968/1982, 17). This is accurate in two senses: Eva has been cared for by a series of displaced women, but also she has not yet found her place in the symbolic order, the world of language and civilization. She is afraid of books and is unable to produce any written work. She speaks in a way that forms a barrier to communication: 'she was unable to speak – talk, be understood, converse' (Bowen, 1968/1982, 63). She constantly misunderstands: when Mr Denge speaks of 'plate and linen' she has no idea what he means (Bowen, 1968/1982, 77). When Iseult's husband, Eric, says of Mr Denge: 'He's the big noise round here?' Eva takes him up literally: 'He was noisy, but he is quite small, though' (Bowen, 1968/1982, 85). In an effort to establish some sort of communication (he, after all, as Iseult recognizes, 'has a soul'), Eric is forced to abandon words and resort to putting a hand on Eva's shoulder.

Lacking language, Eva lacks any meaningful inner life. In *New Maladies of the Soul*, Kristeva describes the speech of her patient Didier as: 'delivered in a monotone [...] I was completely convinced that he spoke for the sole purpose of ignoring me' (Kristeva, 1995, 10–11). Iseult defines Eva's speech similarly: 'It's pompous, it's unnatural-sounding, it's wooden, it's deadly, it's hopeless, it's shutting-off' (Bowen, 1968/1982, 65). The modern world, Kristeva argues, produces people who speak as if alienated from their own words. Kristeva likens Didier to a robot, and Eva similarly lacks the human dimension, being variously described as a 'giantess' (Bowen, 1968/1982, 13), 'an astray moose' (Bowen, 1968/1982, 14), an 'organism' (Bowen, 1968/1982, 33), 'a ghost' (Bowen, 1968/1982, 50). When Eric shakes her, it is more like shaking a doll than a human being: 'her head rolled on her shoulders, her arms swung from them' (Bowen, 1968/1982, 88). Eva has been 'left unfinished' (Bowen, 1968/1982, 51) with the result that she hardly recognizes herself as human. Arriving at Kenneth's experimental school, she takes care to study the other children: 'So these were humans, and this was what it was like being amongst them?' (Bowen, 1968/1982, 51). The other children recognize her oddity: '"Trout, are you a hermaphrodite?" one did ask' (Bowen, 1968/1982, 51).

Iseult tries to bring Eva into the symbolic order by encouraging her to think rationally: 'Try joining things together: this, then that, then the other. That's thinking; at least, that's beginning to think' (Bowen, 1968/1982, 62). But Iseult has taken on a task beyond her powers. In her unmothered, homeless state, Eva misinterprets the attention Iseult pays to her as love and she quickly exhausts Iseult's never very strong capacity to nurture. Iseult is, as she warns Eva, easily rendered 'claustrophobic' (Bowen, 1968/1982, 60). Faced with Eva's relentless pressure, Iseult abandons her task, leaving Eva's identity unformed. Eva tells Father Clavering-Height that she had hoped Iseult would teach her how 'to be, to become – I had never been', but Iseult abandoned her task: '[she] sent me back again – to be nothing [...] I remain gone. Where am I? I do not know' (Bowen, 1968/1982, 185). Iseult follows in the line of Bowen's intellectual, sophisticated, resisting mothers: 'I am not loving by nature' she warns Eva (Bowen, 1968/1982, 92). *Eva Trout* opens at the point where *The Death of the Heart* left off: like Portia, Eva has recognized that the longed for mother-daughter relationship is not working and has precipitated a crisis by demanding to leave Iseult's house.

The novel documents Eva's subsequent struggles with language and intimacy. The opening of chapter 5 gives us an insight into Eva's thought processes. She can remember time only in fragments: 'She remembered, that is to say, disjectedly' (Bowen, 1968/1982, 46). Sometimes it is possible to bring her memories together to form patterns but she does not bother to look for the meaning in them: 'Each pattern had a predominant colour; and each probably *had* meaning, though that she did not seek' (Bowen, 1968/1982, 46). Typical of someone nourished on 'the society of the spectacle', Eva thinks in images, but lacks the words to give her inner life meaning. Her words constantly betray her inability to form meaningful human relationships. Instead of inquiring of Constantine whether he is feeling well, Eva asks, 'Are you deteriorating?' (Bowen, 1968/1982, 100), as if he were an object. Similarly she says later, of her adopted son Jeremy, 'Jeremy is being put right' (Bowen, 1968/1982, 217) and, replying to an inquiry about his health, 'Jeremy is in good condition' (Bowen, 1968/1982, 257).

Eva's studies into how to be a human being continue. 'What a slippery fish is identity [...] What *is* a person?' she wonders (Bowen, 1968/1982, 193).[2] Lacking any inner life, she buys heavily into the consumer society. When we first see her she is driving an enormous Jaguar. Mrs Dancey, observing her, doubts whether Eva has an inner life: '*Is* she thinking? Mrs Dancey thought not. Monolithic, Eva's attitude was. It was not, somehow, the attitude of a thinking person' (Bowen, 1968/1982, 12). Like Kristeva's patient, Didier, Eva sustains her lack of inner life through feeding off images. When Iseult comes to visit, she finds Eva's house full of 'outstanding examples of everything auro-visual on the market this year' (Bowen, 1968/1982, 118) and Eva informs her she is intending to purchase a computer in order to teach herself how to think.

These scenes recall Jean Baudrillard's definition of consumption as founded on 'a lack' and his argument that our desires are not our own, but have been artificially manufactured so that we consume to meet the economy's needs rather than our own (Baudrillard, 2001, 30). Far from exercising consumer choice, Baudrillard argues, the consumer is manipulated to conform to society's values: 'The fundamental, unconscious and automatic choice of the consumer is to accept the life-style of a particular society (no longer therefore a real choice: the theory of the autonomy and sovereignty of the consumer is thus refuted)' (Baudrillard, 2001, 40). Eva half blindly purchases all those objects advertised as up-to-the-minute aids to language and communication in 1959, including a large-screen television set, radio-gramophone, projector and screen, and recording instrument. Since consumerism can never satisfy, only stimulate, desire, it is not from these purchased consumer goods that Eva's enhanced self-confidence arises, as Iseult recognizes. The puzzle of Eva's new self-confidence becomes clear by the end of the chapter: after the fantasy of the fake engagement, Eva will make another attempt to enter the human race. She will mimic motherhood by adopting a child.

Since Jeremy is a deaf-mute who, like herself, feeds off the images with which contemporary society provides him, he is no help in pulling Eva into the world of language. For eight years she and her 'simulacrum of a son' (Bennett and Royle, 1995, 141), live together in a pre-oedipal, wordless communication:

> His and her cinematographic existence, with no sound-track, in successive American cities made still more similar by their continuous manner of being in them, had had a sufficiency which was perfect. Sublimated monotony had cocooned the two of them, making them as near as twins in a womb. (Bowen, 1968/1982, 188)

Apart from intermittent tussles with medical experts over Jeremy's condition, this wordless world excludes outsiders and indeed much contact with external reality: 'They came to distinguish little between what went on inside and what went on outside the diurnal movies' (Bowen, 1968/1982, 189). In the movie world Eva and Jeremy inhabit, boundaries between illusion and reality are dissolved, as are the boundaries between self and other. Eva has finally achieved the symbiotic bond she longed for with Elsinore and therefore, until her return to England, she is quite happy to prolong her inhabitation of this world of simulacra.

---

2   For a discussion of the phrase 'a slippery fish' in relation to Eva's identity and surname, see Bennett and Royle, 1995, 152.

Returning to England, Eva's rejection of the world of language and civilization begins to soften. Her meeting with Henry Dancey, now a clever Oxford undergraduate, and several conversations during which various people – Reverend Dancey, Constantine, Father Clavering-Height – urge her to do more for Jeremy, inspire in her the feeling that she is lacking something:

> What was this lack she had felt? – it was foreign to her. How came it that she could feel? The fact was, since her return to England her mistrust of or objection to verbal intercourse – which she had understood to be fundamental – began to be undermined [...] She was ready to talk. (Bowen, 1968/1982, 188)

Eva discounts the fact that by moving out of the wordless, pre-oedipal bond with Jeremy, she is betraying their years together: 'She had not computed the cost for him of entry into another dimension' (Bowen, 1968/1982, 189). Added to this betrayal, is the fact that she continually reneges on her promise to find them both a home:

> And, so far, he had been denied a home. That England was to provide one had been implicit. What an error, to grant him a glimpse of Larkins, an afternoon's habitation of Cathay. Eva had broken a pact, which was very grievous. (Bowen, 1968/1982, 190)

Jeremy's growing hostility to Eva is expressed visually in the sculptured head he models of her, its sightless eyes exuding 'non-humanity' (Bowen, 1968/1982, 190). Jeremy's sculpture resembles Jung's Great Mother, the loving and terrible mother originally worshiped as a goddess and now surviving as part of the collective unconscious, inspiring fear and awe in males. Elias-Button has described how this Great Mother has come to represent 'within male mythology and psychology, the grasping (female) unconscious whose power to fascinate and ultimately castrate, must be permanently destroyed by the (male) hero' (Davidson and Broner, 1980, 202). This description goes some way to explaining the novel's *dénouement*.

As Eva loses her objection to language, so her interest in what a human being consists of grows. 'What *is* a person?' she asks herself and studies the portraits in the National Portrait Gallery in an effort to find out (Bowen, 1968/1982, 194). The effort fails, the pictures remain two-dimensional, confirming her belief that there is no inner life:

> But, upstairs or down, they *were* all 'pictures'. Images. 'Nothing but a pack of cards'? – not quite, but nearly enough that to defeat Eva [...] No, no getting through to them. They were on show only [...] Nothing was to be learned from them [...] every soul Eva knew became no longer anything but a Portrait. There was no 'real life'; no life was more real than this. This she had long suspected. She now was certain. (Bowen, 1968/1982, 195–6)

Nevertheless, Eva continues the attempt to write herself into human life, this time through marriage to Henry. When he jibes at her proposal, she arranges for them to go through a simulacrum of marriage by appearing to board a train together in order to be married abroad. At the last moment, Henry surprises her by deciding to remain on the train. Henry's words succeed, where Iseult's failed, in bringing Eva to life. She bursts into tears, the very first tears she has ever shed, suggesting that she is at last moving beyond spectacle into the human condition.

However Eva has no further chance to develop. Jeremy's growing hostility to her was expressed, as we have seen, through his model of the sightless head. After Iseult's intervention, he begins to desire to separate himself from Eva by entering the world of language. Iseult, whether provoked by a desire to avenge herself on Eva for her false claim that Eric was Jeremy's father, or by a wish to succeed with Jeremy where she failed with Eva, conveys to Jeremy the dangers of relying on Eva now that she has begun to look outside their relationship. Iseult's role here parallels that of Elsinore's mother in that she is the third party, the agent of language and culture which breaks up the symbiotic relationship between mother and child. Inspired by Iseult's view of him as having the capacity to exceed others (Bowen, 1968/1982, 215), Jeremy begins to want to come out of his silence.[3] He willingly submits to treatment by French doctors whose methods, 'in the main psychic' (Bowen, 1968/1982, 215), recall Kristeva's view that the intervention of psychoanalysis may provide a cure for the emptiness of the modern psyche.

The Bonnards give Jeremy not only language (significantly French rather than Eva's mother tongue, English), but an inner life. With Jeremy's discovery of language and his first efforts at speech, comes resentment of the shady transaction by which Eva acquired him. With language, Jeremy begins to develop a self apart from Eva, symbolized by his new dispatch case containing all the paraphernalia for his speech exercises. He carries this case around with him as if he has already become fully grown and taken his place in the world of business: 'About his entrance there was already a touch of the executive, however junior' (Bowen, 1968/1982, 254). Jeremy's new self judges Eva for the way in which she has attempted to mold his life. What was between them was not a flesh and blood tie, he realizes, only a simulacrum of the mother-child relationship, a 'game' (Bowen, 1968/1982, 254).[4]

In an appropriately cinematic ending Jeremy guns down Eva. Is his act intentional, a punishment for Eva's attempt to fake a mother-son relationship, or an accident? Bowen leaves this open.[5] At the same time, she takes care to make the ending plausible: a number of people warn Eva of the danger of diverting a person's destiny through her initial act of adoption and then of forcing Jeremy to watch her departure with Henry. Whether her death is an accident or murder, it ensures that Eva never makes it into the symbolic. Her last words reflect her continuing difficulty with language, meaning and connection: '"Constantine," asked Eva, "what is concatenation?"' (Bowen, 1968/82, 268). Despite her last frantic efforts Eva is never able to establish a meaning for her life and therefore, in Kristevan terms, she has failed to find the sacred: 'I claim that what comes back to

---

[3]   Iseult's actions here may be compared with those of Madame Fisher in Bowen's earlier novel, *The House in Paris*. Madame Fisher tries similarly to mold the future of the bright, adopted boy, Leopold, by implanting in him the notion of his genius.

[4]   Adoption has a bad press in Bowen's works. In *The House in Paris*, Leopold's adoptive parents, the Grant Moodys, come across as obtuse and slightly ludicrous. The topic seems to have touched a raw nerve, perhaps because of Bowen's own childlessness. The impact of Bowen's childlessness on her life and work has yet to be fully explored.

[5]   For a discussion of the fortuitous nature of events in *Eva Trout*, see Ellmann, 2003, 212.

us as "sacred" in the experience of a woman is the impossible and nevertheless sustained connection between life and meaning' (Kristeva, 2001, 14).

Sacred Spaces: *The Dancers Dancing* (1999)

If modern man is losing his soul, what is to be done? In *Revolt, She Said*, Kristeva argues that new forms of spirituality are a necessary defense of individual freedom against institutionalism and political dogmatism: 'Aside from political life, we need other spaces, new forms of spirituality where people can attempt to find this kind of freedom that politics cannot provide' (Kristeva, 2002c, 109). This statement is perhaps best understood when set in the context of Kristeva's upbringing in Bulgaria where, as she has often remarked, religious discourse provided one of the few areas of resistance to the totalizing force of Communism. However, Kristeva is not arguing for a return to the Catholicism of her childhood. In *The Feminine and the Sacred* she confesses that she does not understand women who seek to become priests in the Catholic Church. She argues that women can gain nothing by becoming priests in a church dedicated to the cult of the father and son. Instead she urges women to find their own sacred spaces: 'Shouldn't these anxious women found another sacred space, other spaces for questioning the sacred?' (Clément and Kristeva, 2001, 64).

For Kristeva, the sacred is located, exactly as women are located, on the borders between nature and culture. In Kristevan theory, then, since borders are their place, women are in a privileged position in regard to the sacred. This argument is most succinctly put in her correspondence with Catherine Clément which forms the basis of their book, *The Feminine and the Sacred*:

> What if the sacred were the unconscious perception the human being has of its untenable eroticism: always on the borderline between nature and culture, the animalistic and the verbal, the sensible and the nameable? What if the sacred were not the religious *need* for protection and omnipotence that institutions exploit but the jouissance of that *cleavage* – of that power/powerlessness – of that exquisite lapse? [...] Women might therefore be otherwise placed, even, I daresay, better placed, to stand on that "roof". (Clément and Kristeva, 2001, 26–7)

In passages such as these, Kristeva dangerously skirts but, I would argue, avoids the age-old essentialist link between women and nature. This link has not altogether been avoided by some ecofeminist theorists who link women and nature in order to argue that both have suffered exploitation by the destructive technologies of patriarchal society (Merchant, 1982; Radford Ruether, 1992). In seeking to break down the binaries on which Western civilization has been based (nature versus culture, body versus mind), the danger is that ecofeminist theorists may end up merely redrawing these dualisms, celebrating nature instead of culture, body instead of mind, female instead of male, in a way which reverses rather than replaces these Cartesian dualisms. To counter this sort of dualism, the major ecofeminist thinker, Val Plumwood, has drawn on Jessica Benjamin's relational account of the self in which the self develops both through relationality (interaction with the other) and mutuality (recognition of the other's difference) (Benjamin,

1990). Plumwood proposes Benjamin's theory as a model for our interaction with nature, that is, recognition of our kinship with but also our difference from nature (Plumwood, 1993, 160). Thus the identification of women with nature is avoided. We shall come back to Plumwood in our analysis of Ní Dhuibhne's novel. However it must be emphasized that Kristeva is concerned not with women's identification with nature, but with the *border* between nature and culture, which is where she locates women.

Orla, the thirteen-year-old heroine of Éilís Ní Dhuibhne's novel, *The Dancers Dancing*, learns to inhabit just this border between nature and culture when she is sent, like hundreds of other Irish girls and boys, to the Gaeltacht for a month at summer camp to study Irish language and culture. Her time in the west of Ireland leads Orla to question the repressive Catholic and patriarchal ethos of her urban environment. *The Dancers Dancing* is another example of an Irish female *Bildungsroman*, with nature in this case stimulating the heroine's awakening as Orla becomes aware of the gap between culture and nature and learns to inhabit and to celebrate that cleavage. As we have seen, in the above quotation from *The Feminine and the Sacred*, Kristeva argues that such awareness of the borderline between nature and culture is a mark of the sacred which, she believes, is particularly possessed by women.

The culture Orla leaves behind in the city is patriarchal. The Roman Catholic Church still rules the lives of its adherents and enforces strict gender divisions which confirm the inferior status of women. The Church allows Roddy to serve at the altar, but not Orla. Despite Vatican II, women are still uneasy about appearing at Mass bare-headed. This privileging of the male extends into the domestic sphere. Orla's mother, Elizabeth, preserves sharp gender distinctions in her home: Orla is expected to help in the house while her brother Roddy is allowed to spend his time playing football. Elizabeth believes that girls are hardy and do not need much food or attention whereas boys need lots of both:

> Girls are often oul-fashioned, their eyes are cunning and knowing, peering from their polite and silent faces, while boys are innocent, loveable and cherished. Orla has been taught this since she was about two years old. (Ní Dhuibhne, 1999/2001, 34)

The culture in which Orla has been raised is one in which the body is repressed. The narrator remarks laconically that: 'Church and State in Ireland have recently been aiming to eliminate sex from the Irish way of life' (Ní Dhuibhne, 1999/2001, 12). Women are particularly affected by this suppression of the body. They refuse to breast feed their babies since they are reluctant to acknowledge they have breasts at all. They encase their bodies in rigid roll-ons and impenetrable layers of clothing. They hand on vague, and not strictly accurate, accounts of the facts of life to their daughters. The picture of Irish society portrayed in Ní Dhuibhne's novel bears out Kristeva's conclusions, in *Powers of Horror*, that Christianity seeks to suppress the female body, the abject, in the name of the Father. It is very hard for Orla to rebel against this. Irish girls at this period, the narrator states, were brought up to obey anyone in authority, parents, church, teachers, government: 'That is how it is for girls, in 1972. Doing what you are told is ethics, philosophy, morality, religion, all rolled into one' (Ní Dhuibhne, 1999/2001, 145). It is clear that such a culture cannot give Orla a sense of pride in her body and her sexuality. To find this she must carve out a sacred space of her own.

During her stay in the west, the influence of her urban culture on Orla gradually diminishes. Her concern over details of social hierarchy, the shameful poverty of her home in comparison with Aisling's, for example, lessens: 'She is beginning to feel liberated from the comparisons that rule her life in Dublin' (Ní Dhuibhne, 1999/2001, 136). The life of the body becomes important. She swims in the sea. She has her first period. She experiences sexual attraction to Micheál which aligns her body even more closely with nature: 'Her head, her body, her blood are filled with a sweetness like the raspberries on the bank of the burn' (Ní Dhuibhne, 1999/2001, 226). By the end of their time in the west, Orla and her friends have so divested themselves of social constraints that in appearance they seem to Aisling's parents to have reverted to a state of nature: 'They look like orphans! Like children who belong to nobody: they've got that wildness' (Ní Dhuibhne, 1999/2001, 173).

If in passages such as these, Ní Dhuibhne's novel seems to skirt the essentialist link between women and nature referred to above, the presence of the narrator, an older Orla who comments on the experiences of her younger self in a detached and ironic manner, prevents us, the readers, from making this link. The narrator points out how little Orla, the city girl, really understands nature. She mistakes a magpie's cry for a bomb-making factory. She ignores real dangers (slipping into the burn which may not be as shallow as she thinks) for unreal (vindictive otters). In this way the narrator underlines the otherness of nature which, for theorists such as Val Plumwood, provides an argument against the essentialist link between women and nature. Even the younger Orla is aware that nature possesses a dangerous edge: 'the glaucous cavern seems not enchanted and protective but dangerous – or dangerous at the same time as it is more magically seductive than any place she has ever been' (Ní Dhuibhne, 1999/2001, 71). Nature is harsh and tough and women are tough too; their power can be death-dealing. Orla learns this about herself when, out of a spurious sense of social shame, she abandons her sick old Aunt Annie on the floor of her barn. As Kristeva warns in *The Feminine and the Sacred*, if the sacred is a place where women can give free rein to their *jouissance*, it can also bring them face to face with their own abjection (Kristeva, 2001, 38).

In contrast with life in Dublin where girls are told what they must do so often that they lose all sense of themselves, immersion in the otherness of nature reveals to Orla a primal, instinctual, fearless self:

> In the burn, she was a part of whatever whole encompassed the water and the weeds and the raspberries and the drooping willows. Her heart beat in time with the babble of the burn down there [...] Orla belonged with the river. She was nothing there, nothing more than a berry dipping to the water or a minnow floating under the surface of a pool. Nothing. And completely herself. Orla Herself. Not Orla the Daughter of Elizabeth, Orla the Pride of Rathmines, Orla the Betrayer of Tubber. Just Orla. (Ní Dhuibhne, 1999/2001, 73)

In the burn Orla yells all the taboo words she can think of and for the first time in her life finds her own voice. In Kristevan terms, this is Orla celebrating her *jouissance* of the cleavage between nature and culture, between the animal and the verbal. She loses her sense of shame over her family's lowly social status. She feels that it will be all right to tell people about her family for: 'who now has the power to harm her? Now that she has found her own place?' (Ní Dhuibhne, 1999/2001, 73). She learns not to be ashamed of relatives like simple Aunt Annie who, having lived all her life in the west, is ignorant of the social codes in which Orla has been raised. Orla learns that she is not all culture but can inhabit the wild space between nature and culture and rejoice in that as liberation.

From Orla's perspective, *The Dancers Dancing* would seem to endorse the notion, prevalent since the Irish Literary Revival, that the landscape of the west of Ireland is purer and somehow more 'Irish' than the rest of the country (see Nash, 1993, 86–111). As Katie Soper points out in *What is Nature? Culture, Politics and the non-Human*, cultural constructions of nature have always played a key role in nationalisms where nature is seen as a wholesome salvation from societal decadence: 'an aesthetic of "nature" as source of purity and authentic self-identification has been a component of all forms of racism, tribalism and nationalism' she argues (Soper, 1995, 32). But, Soper continues, to replace culture with nature is to fall into an essentialist view of nature that has been conditioned into us since the Romantic poets. Though, when speaking of women as the bridge between nature and culture, Kristeva does avoid an essentialist view of the link between women and nature, when speaking of nature as the opposite of culture she does not seem altogether to avoid essentialism. In *The Dancers Dancing* however, Ní Dhuibhne does succeed in avoiding this essentialist view of nature by means of the older Orla's narrative voice.

Ní Dhuibhne's narrator acknowledges that though Orla may experience the west as somehow purer than the urban culture she has left behind, this view is in itself a construct, programmed into her, the narrator comments dryly, 'by history and the tourist board' (Ní Dhuibhne, 1999/2001, 163). Sending their children to Irish summer school, their parents hope that their offspring will learn something more than the language:

> [...] it is believed that by getting to know native Irish speakers, inhabitants of a rural, western, relict zone, the children will learn something other than Irish, something cultural, the nature of which nobody quite understands. All that is known about this quality is that it is healthier than the culture the students are accustomed to in the city – as the air is fresher, the fields greener, and the water clearer, so is the culture itself more spontaneous, fresh and unadulterated. (Ní Dhuibhne, 1999/2001, 38)

By using the phrase 'something cultural' the narrator underlines the fact that whatever the children may learn out in the west (spontaneity, liberation, wildness) will be just as much culturally conditioned as 'the culture' with which they are familiar in the city. In this way, *The Dancers Dancing* avoids an unexamined dualist notion of nature as free from social constructs. There is in fact plenty of evidence in the novel that this landscape is not as pure and untouched as Orla's scenes in the burn might lead us to believe. This is countryside which has long been subject to human habitation – the skeletons Orla finds in the creek, the Mass rocks that dot the countryside.

The return to the 1990s at the end of *The Dancers Dancing* demonstrates how once again the landscape in the west of Ireland is changing as the result of economic and cultural forces from outside. A heritage center now stands in the middle of Orla's wild valley. The farm house of Maisie and Denis has been lifted stone by stone and rebuilt in a park near Belfast. The wild raspberries Orla ate by the side of the burn are not 'a taste of a wonderful future', as she thought at the time, but 'a residue of a wild world that is past, or passing' (Ní Dhuibhne, 1999/2001, 72). In this way the ending of the novel bears out the narrator's view that nature does not exist in the pure state imagined by the youthful Orla. It is always being tampered with and changed by human beings.

Nevertheless, at the end of *The Dancers Dancing* there remains the feeling that, as Katie Soper has argued, there is more to nature than cultural constructs. While our view of nature is always conditioned by the ideologies of our period, there still remains, Soper argues, beyond ideology, an external nature, apart from our constructions of it:

> Yet none of these points about the constructed nature of 'nature', its pseudo or ideological status, can be registered without at least implicitly invoking the extra-discursive reality of the nature that is distorted or misrepresented through these cultural appropriations of the term. (Soper, 1995, 250)

Similarly the narrator of *The Dancers Dancing* concedes that Orla and the other children experience something powerful in the west which cannot be explained away merely as a cultural construct: 'the smells of the Gaeltacht enhance the atmosphere of goodness: the turf smoke, the salt breeze, the tang of cow dung relax Orla, and the other students. Their noses recognise that they are undergoing a purifying experience' (Ní Dhuibhne, 1999/2001, 38). There is no doubt that Orla is acted upon in some way by her experience in the west and that her experience of a rural way of life leads her to query what she has hitherto regarded as givens in her upbringing. The west becomes for Orla a sacred space, one not untouched by cultural constructs but different from the Dublin culture in which she has grown up, and this sacred space allows Orla to begin to cast off the constraints of her Dublin life. As the narrator warns us at the beginning of the novel, this is a story about border places: 'in between, in between, in between, that is the truth and that is the story' (Ní Dhuibhne, 1999/2001, 3). The borders, however, are not so much, as in Kristeva, between culture and some primitive untouched nature, as between culture and nature as *experienced* as untouched by a young girl. The novelist here is more sophisticated than the theorist.

The question *The Dancers Dancing* leaves us with, underlined by Ní Dhuibhne's use of Gerald Manley Hopkins' poem, 'Inversnaid', is where will a girl like Orla go in the future to free herself from the restrictions of her environment? If the west has been appropriated by the demands of tourists from elsewhere and by a heritage industry which threatens to congeal its identity, where will Orla go in the future to find her sacred space? As well as questioning cultural assumptions about nature and the west of Ireland, *The Dancers Dancing* interrogates the ethos of a nation which places such an emphasis on the land yet is a bad custodian of it.

The theme of the feminine and the sacred has thrown up some examples of resistance to Kristevan theory. Though Éilís Ní Dhuibhne's novel and much of Mary Lavin's writing bear out Kristeva's argument that institutional religion seeks to stifle women's awareness of their bodies and Kate O'Brien's novel, *That Lady*, portrays a woman who speaks up for the rights of the individual against a homogenizing political discourse, both this novel and the earlier one by O'Brien, *The Ante-Room*, rather than endorsing Kristeva's view of religion as upholding the symbolic order and suppressing the semiotic, portray women who find strength in their adherence to institutional religion to enable them to resist the symbolic order. *The Dancers Dancing,* however, while resisting Kristeva's unexamined essentialist assumptions about nature, illustrates Kristeva's argument that new spaces need to be found for celebrating the sacred.

Chapter 7

Northern Ireland

Historical Introduction

For much of the twentieth century, feminists in Northern Ireland have operated under exceedingly difficult, not to say dangerous, circumstances. Like feminists in the early decades of the century in what was later to become the Republic, Northern Irish feminists have constantly had to decide whether to prioritize their feminism or their politics. Feminists on both sides of the divide in Northern Ireland have found that their feminism has brought them into conflict with their communities. Nationalist women have been wary of supporting any demands of the state, for example for state-sponsored nurseries, which might seem to imply recognition of the legitimacy of British rule. Unionist women, on the other hand, have wished to avoid seeming to challenge state institutions. Deeply held religious beliefs too have often demanded women's loyalty and prevented them from speaking out on women's issues. For all these reasons, Northern Irish feminism cannot be compared straightforwardly with the development of feminism in the Republic.

The extremely polarized political situation in Northern Ireland has created particular difficulties for women attempting to unite around feminist issues. A lucid and witty account of this effect is contained in Edna Longley's pamphlet, 'From Cathleen to Anorexia: The Breakdown of Irelands'. Longley argues that masculinist ideologies such as Protestantism, Catholicism, nationalism and unionism, have exercised and continue to exercise a stronger hold in the North than in the Republic: 'Ulster's territorial imperative has produced a politics which pivots on male refusal to give an inch' (Longley, 1994, 183). In Northern Ireland, Cathleen Ní Houlihan has been turned into a death-cult by Catholic nationalists, she argues, while Ulster Protestantism, though lacking Cathleen Ní Houlihan, is just as patriarchal as republican nationalism. She cites its numerous lodges, brotherhoods, sodalities all of which exclude women. Longley argues that the effect on women is that they have been 'starved' and 'squeezed' by these different masculinist ideologies with the result that 'the northern women's movement has been divided and retarded' (Longley, 1994, 162).

Not all feminist writers on Northern Ireland would agree with Longley's analysis: Geraldine Meaney, for example, argues that it is possible to be both a republican and a feminist and she refutes any notion of women as victims (Meaney, 1991, 12). On the contrary, she argues, women have often been active supporters of both nationalism and unionism. In *Literature, Rhetoric and Violence in Northern Ireland, 1968–98*, Patrick Grant points out that what is implicit in Longley's argument, however, is not the notion that women are inherently more pacifist than men, but that because of their long history of oppression, women especially should understand the way oppression operates and should take care to resist rather than to collude in it (Grant, 2001, 119). Whatever the merits of Longley's analysis, it remains the case, as I hope the following brief outline of women in Northern Ireland will make clear, that the highly polarized politics of the North has often resulted in the subordination of gender loyalty to loyalty to one's community. Sometimes women have been willing to accept this prioritizing of their loyalties, sometimes they have struggled against it. The violent situation in the North has made that struggle difficult and at times dangerous.

In their analysis of 'Women, Politics and the State in Northern Ireland, 1918–66' (*The Field Day Anthology*, V, 353–4), Ruth Taillon and Diane Urquhart describe the weaknesses of feminism amongst both unionist and nationalist women in the North. The Ulster Women's Unionist Council (UWUC) was established in 1911 to campaign against the Home Rule Bill. It mobilized popular support for the unionist cause and by 1913 it represented the largest female political organization in Ireland with between 115,000 and 200,000 members. Following the passage of the Government of Ireland Act in 1920 partitioning Ireland and establishing a separate six-county state of Northern Ireland, the UWUC continued its work for unionism. Taillon and Urquhart point out that it was not an especially feminist organization, however. It was always ancillary to the Ulster Unionist Council and it never actively encouraged women to come forward as parliamentary candidates. In *The Hidden Tradition: Feminism, Women and Nationalism in Ireland*, Carol Coulter traces the weakness of feminism among Northern Protestant women even today to the fact that, unlike James Connolly, for instance, Edward Carson refused to take up the issue of women's suffrage and hence: 'Unionist women had nowhere to go without breaking with Unionism' (Coulter, 1993, 29).

After the partitioning of Ireland no nationalist woman was elected to the parliament of Northern Ireland, and the only female nationalist association was the Ladies' Auxiliary of the Ancient Order of Hibernians which, as its name suggests, was, like the UWUC, ancillary to a male organization. It too did not encourage its members to stand as parliamentary candidates. If the situation of women in the Republic was weak during the middle decades of the twentieth century, that of women in Northern Ireland was, if anything, worse. Only nine women were elected to the Northern Irish parliament between 1921 and 1972. Six of these were representatives of the Ulster Unionist Party. Only three women represented Northern Ireland at Westminster, two Ulster Unionists and Bernadette Devlin (now McAliskey), a 'nationalist unity' candidate who represented mid Ulster at Stormont in 1969 and at Westminster from 1970 to 1974.

Most commentators would agree that the conflict in Northern Ireland is fundamentally about national identity, or even about the state versus nation, rather than about religion.[1] Nevertheless because the division between nationalist/ republican and unionist/ loyalist coincides in the main with a Catholic/ Protestant divide, religious ideology has figured largely in the debate over national identity and is woven tightly into the fabric of daily life in Northern Ireland.

---

[1]   For the argument that the conflict is essentially about a Protestant state versus a Catholic nation, see Mary K. Meyer, 'Gender, identity, and sectarian conflict in Northern Ireland' in Ranchod-Nilsson and Tétreault, 2000.

Catholicism in the North, as in the Republic, fostered the equation of women with the Virgin Mary, encouraging Catholic women to be pure, chaste and, above all, submissive. In her autobiographical memoir, *All of Us There*, recounting her Catholic childhood in rural County Tyrone, Polly Devlin describes the punitive, guilt-ridden religion indoctrinated into herself and her sisters, not by their parents, but by the convent schools they attended. There, as in the Republic, the model of the Virgin Mary was set before them:

> Mary, the Holy Mother and Blessed Virgin, standing in utter resignation at the foot of the Cross waiting to receive the battered body of her son, was presented as the perfect role model; her passivity, her lack of protest, was the only way to greet adversity and evil. (Devlin, 1983, 148).

Murals in West Belfast depicting Irish mothers holding their dead IRA sons in a Pietà pose were a vivid pictorial underlining of the sacrifice Catholic women were supposed to make. Nationalism added to the figure of Mary republican heroines like Maude Gonne and Constance Markievicz in order to encourage women to enter the armed struggle, though usually only in a subordinate role. Women were allowed to participate in the fighting but not to sit on the IRA Army Council.[2]

Kathleen Ferguson's novel, *The Maid's Tale* (1994), recounted through the voice of Brigid Keen, housekeeper for thirty years to Father Mann in Derry, illustrates the tight hold the Catholic Church kept over women in Northern Ireland. Brought up in an orphanage run by the Sisters of Charity, Brigid is trained into obedience and humility by the nuns. She becomes housekeeper to a priest who takes her services for granted and seldom remembers to pay her wages. 'Being born a woman wasn't a thing to be proud and pleased about in our day [...] A woman's very eyes wasn't her own, least not as far as the Catholic Church was concerned' Brigid comments (Ferguson, 1994/1995, 5). It takes Brigid fifty years to free herself from the Church's influence.

Protestant women did not escape the impact of religious ideology in their lives. Indeed, feminist writers like Marina Warner have argued that the Protestant religion, lacking imagery of female saints, leaves women even more disempowered than the Catholic religion:

> Although Mary cannot be a model for the New Woman, a goddess is better than no goddess at all, for the sombre-suited masculine world of the Protestant religion is altogether too much like a gentlemen's club to which the ladies are only admitted on special days. (Warner, 1976/1985, 338)

This sounds very like a description of the masculine world of Northern Protestantism. In her chapter, 'Gender, identity and sectarian conflict in Northern Ireland', Mary K. Meyer comments particularly on the absence of female symbols in loyalist murals, in the unionist founding myths and in Orangism (Ranchod-Nilsson and Tétreault, 2000). Even if the Virgin Mary was lacking as a means of control, Calvinist theology was there to step in and emphasize women's role as

---

[2]   For the lack of consultation of women activists by the male hierarchy within the IRA, see Aretxaga, 1997.

homemakers subordinate to the authority of their husbands as head of the household. Ian Paisley, for instance, has frequently emphasized the authority of fathers and husbands in the home and his wife endorses his views. Ian Paisley's daughter, Rhonda, who was for a while active in the DUP, wrote an article, 'Feminism, Unionism and "The Brotherhood"' (1992), which was highly critical of male-dominated unionism. In it she declared: 'There exists very little room for feminism within Unionism' (*The Field Day Anthology*, V, 1515). The novels of Janet McNeill illustrate the fact that modesty, humility and repression of the body were just as likely to be inculcated into Protestant women living in the North as Catholic. 'Modesty and duty,' says Addie in *The Maiden Dinosaur*, 'what do you think we expected to get out of that little lot?' (McNeill, 1964, 177).

The masculinism of the two religious traditions in Northern Ireland was demonstrated in 1945 when both Catholic bishops and unionist MPs agreed to the closure of day nurseries, arguing that they destroyed family life. After a flurry of activity during the war when their help was needed in the factories, after the war women lost their jobs in the clothing and textile industries and once again became isolated in the home. The general decline in manufacturing in Northern Ireland after the war and the high level of unemployment ensured that any available jobs went to the men. As we have seen, Protestant ideology stressed the status of men as breadwinners and women as dependents. In the case of Catholics, however, the high level of Catholic male unemployment meant that Catholic married women were more likely than Protestant women to work outside the home. Mary Beckett's novel, *Give Them Stones*, highlights this fact: since Martha's father is long-term unemployed, it is her mother who is responsible for providing the family income. Most of this female work though was in low paid, unskilled jobs. Martha's mother works in the linen mills. As in the Republic, married women were barred from working in the civil service, teaching and banking until the late 1960s. Rates of pay for women were lower too: when Ann McGlone in Frances Molloy's novel, *No Mate for the Magpie* (1985), gets a job in supermarket as a bacon slicer her boss is delighted 'because he only had te give me half the pay a man would get' (Molloy, 1985, 110). This was in Belfast in the 1960s. Ann eventually loses her job because her boss's wife is prejudiced against Catholics. Her fate aptly bears out Rosemary Sales' conclusion that: 'The labour market in Northern Ireland is structured by both gender and religion' (Sales, 1997, 167). After working at a variety of jobs both in Northern Ireland and in the Republic during the 1960s and 70s, Ann finally turns her back on Ireland and determines to go 'to a place where life resembled life more than it did here' (Molloy, 1985, 170).

In Christina Reid's play, *The Belle of the Belfast City*, first performed in 1989, Rose points out to her loyalist sister, Vi, that their cousin Jack's 'right-wing Protestant Church is in total agreement with the right-wing Catholic Church on issues like divorce and abortion, on a woman's right to be anything other than a mother or a daughter or a sister or a wife' (Reid, 1997, 221). Rose's observation is borne out by the findings of Monica McWilliams in her article on 'The Church, the State and the Women's Movement in Northern Ireland' (McWilliams, 1993). McWilliams underlines the conservative nature of church and state ideologies in the North and the way in which they exerted pressure on women in both communities to confine their activities to the home. She points out that both

Catholic bishops and the Democratic Unionist Party under Ian Paisley opposed the introduction of divorce on the grounds of irreconcilability, arguing its damage to family life. It was eventually introduced in 1978, ten years after the rest of the UK. McWilliams also emphasizes that there was opposition in both communities in Northern Ireland to the introduction of barring orders against violent males. Other evidence of the conservative nature of forces in the North is reflected in opposition to the UK's 1967 Homosexual Law Reform Act, which was brought into Northern Ireland only in 1981 after a ruling by the European Court. Both Paisley's Free Presbyterian Church and the Catholic Church opposed the legalization of homosexuality. The law on abortion remains ambiguous: the 1967 UK Abortion Act has never been extended to Northern Ireland. Though doctors in the North do perform abortions, few are prepared to acknowledge this openly, and political parties on both sides of the divide have been reluctant to engage in public debate on the question. The Northern Ireland Abortion Campaign first brought abortion into the public arena in 1980. However, as in the Republic, the majority of women still travel to Britain for abortions.

Unlike feminism in the Republic, feminism in Northern Ireland has not been predominantly a middle-class movement. Rather, it has developed out of a network of autonomous women's groups, often focused on single issues and community campaigns. Monica McWilliams traces the growth of the women's movement in Northern Ireland to grass-roots activism by women during the 1960s. Nationalist women played an active role in the mid-1960s on the housing action committees which eventually led to the demands articulated by the Northern Ireland Civil Rights Association, founded in 1967. When Catholic men began to be interned after August 1971 as a result of the civil rights protests, it was the women who stepped in and took over the campaign, much as women had taken over when the men were imprisoned after the 1916 Rising. It was women who, in July 1970, broke the Falls Road curfew to bring food to families in the Lower Falls Road which had been cordoned off illegally for a brutal house-to-house search by the British Army. This event is described in Mary Beckett's novel, *Give Them Stones*, through the mouth of Martha, a Catholic working-class woman who endorses the women's gender and class based politics:

> The Falls Road curfew happened at the beginning of July 1970 after the Conservatives won the election in England. The people in those wee old streets just like ours were shut in and not allowed out for any messages while the soldiers searched all the houses for guns. They didn't find much – a few old guns from years past and they broke up the houses. We saw it on the television. I was crying, first with vexation and then with pride when a whole army of women with bread and milk came marching down from other streets further up and pushed the soldiers away, shouting at them to go home to England and learn manners. They handed the food in to the besieged houses. (Beckett, 1987, 121)

Nationalist women campaigned against cutbacks that would directly affect their families: they were at the forefront of the rent and rates strike and campaigns for better housing. In 1971 a group of women in the Lower Ormeau area of Belfast organized a 'Milk Campaign' to protest against the British government's decision under Margaret Thatcher as Minister for Education to abolish free milk. That particular protest was unsuccessful, but the political experience women gained in these sorts of campaigns ensured that when the movement for women's rights started up in Northern Ireland in the mid-1970s there were already some seasoned female activists. Moreover, as a result of these local campaigns, the Northern Irish women's movement was more representative of working-class women than elsewhere in Europe.

The Northern Ireland Women's Rights Movement (NIWRM) was founded in 1975 to campaign for equal pay and an end to sex discrimination. It fought to extend Britain's Sex Discrimination Act to Northern Ireland. In this it was successful. The Act was introduced in Northern Ireland in 1976 and an Equal Opportunities Commission was established. In 1980 the NIWRM opened the first women's center in Belfast. However, its deliberately non-sectarian stance proved difficult to maintain and there were splits in the movement, for example, the Socialist Women's group, believing that women's liberation was tied up with liberation from British imperialism, broke away. Divisions in the movement accelerated during the hunger strikes of the 1980s. Opinions were divided as to whether the NIWRM should adopt a unified position on the strip-searching of female prisoners in Armagh jail. Through all this, the NIWRM held to its non-sectarian stance, but the divisions it experienced at this time demonstrated the difficulty of getting women to unite across the communities.

Poverty has been a pressing concern in Northern Ireland and in this area Protestant working-class women have worked together with Catholic women. The 1971 'Milk Campaign' was originally non-sectarian, but Protestant women fell away under threats from their own community which saw any attack on the state as disloyal (*The Field Day Anthology*, V, 382). In 1985 both Catholic and Protestant women campaigned to oppose the Social Security Bill going through Parliament and they traveled to London to lobby MPs against the cuts. In a society where there are many long-term unemployed and where the violent political situation has rendered many women widows, single parents or involved in raising a family while their male partners are in prison, issues such as housing, social benefits, bereavement counseling have taken on priority among the work of women's groups. Women in both communities have created support groups for families of prisoners.

Work with victims of violence has also been a priority, violence in the political arena having a habit of spilling over into the domestic sphere, a point emphasized by Catherine Shannon in her article, 'The Woman Writer as Historical Witness: Northern Ireland, 1968–1994. An Interdisciplinary Perspective':

> Oral material as well as official studies have shown that women in heavily-armed areas of the north were more vulnerable to sexual harassment, exploitation and domestic violence, owing to the easy availability of guns. (Shannon, 1997, 249)

Belfast Women's Aid was set up in 1974 to provide a refuge for women subject to violence from male partners. The Belfast Rape Crisis Centre opened in 1982. Eileen Evason's study, *Against the Grain: The Contemporary Women's Movement in Northern Ireland* (1991), provides a list of women's groups established in Northern Ireland. In 1978 all these groups united to campaign successfully for the release of Noreen Winchester jailed for killing her father following years of sexual abuse. Thus women have worked together across the sectarian divide on issues which most concerned their everyday lives and which they felt were being ignored by the male-dominated mainstream political parties. To do this they have often had to separate themselves from the formal political process in order to voice their concerns on issues which affected them as women. The Women's Information Group has been particularly active in working with women across the sectarian divide, holding monthly meetings across Belfast, alternating between Protestant and Catholic areas.

In the article referred to above, Catherine Shannon points out that the 1990s brought significant cross-community contacts. She cites the coming together in 1990 of Protestant and Catholic women to protest successfully against the decision of the unionist-dominated Belfast City Council to cut funding for the Falls Road Women's Centre (Shannon, 1997, 256). 1992 was the year of President Mary Robinson's historic visit to Belfast, the first time an Irish President had crossed the border. In the course of her visit Mary Robinson met women from all sections of the community. In 1996 the Northern Ireland Women's Coalition was established to ensure women's political representation in the peace process. The Coalition secured two seats at the Northern Ireland Forum designed to shape the political future of Northern Ireland. One delegate was a Catholic, the other a Protestant, emphasizing the cross-community principles of the coalition. The NIWC has adhered to these principles despite difficult debates over parades by the Orange Order, as well as over the treatment of Roisin McAlisky, imprisoned while pregnant and seriously ill. In their account of the NIWC, Kate Fearon and Monica McWilliams conclude: 'The NIWC had managed to do something that had eluded the women's movement in Northern Ireland for many years: unite and organize around an identity as women' (Roulston and Davies, 2000, 132).[3]

In the 1990s, women began to be slightly more visible in Northern Ireland's political life. All political parties in the North began to take notice of women's issues and the SDLP and Sinn Féin both introduced quotas for women on its policy-making bodies and women's sections. Women were encouraged to run for public office, though the UUP and the DUP have a poorer record at putting women forward for election than the nationalist parties. In 1994 Baroness Denton became the first woman Minister of State in Northern Ireland and in 1997 Tony Blair appointed Mo Mowlam Secretary of State for Northern Ireland.

In the 1990s there was progress too in the peace process. In autumn 1997 multi-party talks began under the chairmanship of George Mitchell and ended in April 1998 with the Good Friday Agreement providing for an elected Assembly in Northern Ireland. In May 1998, referendums on the Agreement in the Republic and Northern Ireland indicated support for the new constitutional arrangements. The Good Friday Agreement marked a turning point in the history of these islands. It removed Articles 2 and 3 from the Irish constitution, in effect withdrawing the Republic's constitutional claim over the Six Counties. In turn, the British government revised the 1920 Government of Ireland Act, thereby renouncing claims to exclusive sovereignty over Northern Ireland. As several contributors to the volume *Ireland in the New Century: Politics, Culture and Identity* argue, the 1998 Agreement marked a move towards a more flexible form of Irish national

---

[3] For a fuller account of the Northern Ireland Women's Coalition, see Fearon, 1999.

identity, Richard Kearney even going so far as to state that the Agreement ushered
in a 'post-nationalist constellation in the British-Irish context' (Savage, 2003, 37).

When elections were held to the new Northern Ireland Assembly in June 1998,
out of 108 members of the new Assembly, fourteen were women, a significant gain
for Northern Irish women. Sinn Féin's Bairbe de Brún was Minister for Health in
the new Assembly and SDLP's Brid Rodgers was Minister for Agriculture.
However, in October 2002 the Assembly was suspended due to arguments over
procedures for IRA decommissioning. These procedures remained a sticking-point
for several years. The IRA and independent witnesses insist that the
decommissioning process has now been completed but the DUP dispute that and
are reluctant to share power with Sinn Féin. Despite efforts on all sides to revive
the peace process, the Assembly is still, at the time of writing, suspended.

Feminism in Northern Ireland has been complicated by many factors. Even for
women themselves, gender may have a lower priority than the conflict over the
political future of Northern Ireland. Carol Coulter has argued that feminism has yet
to come to grips with the importance of their political allegiances to the women of
Northern Ireland:

> If feminists are to have a lasting influence there, it is necessary to empathise with the
> experiences which lead women from oppressed nations and communities to support
> nationalist movements which arise out of their history. (Coulter, 1998, 177).

As we have seen, women's motivation to become active in public life in Northern
Ireland arises as much from their political as their gender affiliations. Many of the
women involved in community politics would not in fact call themselves feminists
since it is often the case that they are drawn into campaigning on behalf of their
families and their communities rather than their gender. This being so, in an echo
of Kristeva's wariness about feminism's totalitarian impulses, Coulter warns
against imposing a single voice on the women of Northern Ireland.

Even when women have broken into mainstream politics this has not always
brought about the changes which feminists want. Conservative religious ideologies
have made it difficult for Northern Irish women to raise issues relating to sexuality
and women's rights and, in any gathering of women in the North, the divisive
question of how far politics should be prioritized has to be addressed. More bridges
need to be built linking mainstream politicians with grass-roots groups. Added to
this, the violence and poverty endemic in Northern Ireland for many years have
meant that women's day-to-day energies have gone into simply surviving and
ensuring the safety of their families. It is not surprising if they have had little time
left over for campaigning.

Daily Life for Women in Northern Ireland

The day-to-day pressures experienced by women living since 1968 in the shadow
of the euphemistically named Troubles are vividly portrayed in Jennifer Johnston's
novel, *Shadows on Our Skin* (1977). *Shadows on Our Skin* is set in the 1970s in
Derry and deals with a Catholic working-class family, the Logans. Mrs Logan is
presented as a woman worn down with worry for the safety of her younger son,

Joe, and anxiety over her elder son, Brendan, who has been inspired by his father's tales of heroism in the old IRA to become involved in the fringes of paramilitary activity. The atmosphere of Derry is well conveyed: the constant sound of gunfire, the boarded-up shops and burnt-out houses, the soldiers patrolling the streets, the noise of British Army helicopters circling overhead. Mrs Logan's anxiety expresses itself in over-protectiveness of Joe and in excessive and symbolic cleaning of the family home. Since her husband is one of the long-term unemployed, it is Mrs Logan who is the family bread-winner, working as a waitress in Strand's café. As is the case with so many Northern Irish women, it is up to her to ensure the family's survival, perform all the domestic chores, clean up the house after it has been raided by the British Army and comfort the neighbors. Small wonder then that she can spare little energy for demonstrations of affection to her son. The daily effort of living with the effects of violence has hardened and soured her: 'Death can't come quick enough for me' she tells Joe (Johnston, 1977/1991, 42).

Anne Devlin's play, *Ourselves Alone,* first performed in 1985, likewise reveals the psychological stresses on women in Northern Ireland. Like *Shadows on Our Skin,* Devlin's play centers on a working-class Catholic family but one more heavily involved than the Logans in IRA activity. The McCoys live in Andersonstown in West Belfast and the play is set against a similar background to Johnston's novel, namely constant gunfire, army helicopters and house raids. Donna, waiting for Liam McCoy to get out of Long Kesh, is dependent on valium to keep her going: Northern Irish women's excessive dependence on cigarettes and tranquillizers is a well recorded fact (Shannon, 1997, 251). The British Army raids which wreck houses in Johnston's novel and Devlin's play illustrate the intrusion of politics into the private sphere. There is no safe domestic space: Brendan brings a gun into the Logan household and there is ammunition in Donna's house. Malachy McCoy's sister, Cora, has been severely mutilated by ammunition stored in her bedroom. Added to this, the political violence outside the home frequently spills over in Devlin's play into domestic violence against the female McCoys.

Titanic Town (1992) by Mary Costello, subtitled *Memoirs of a Belfast Girlhood,* provides another vivid picture of the strains of daily life in Andersonstown during the 1960s and 1970s. The McPhelimy family lives in the heart of the violence. Army raids and shooting in the streets are a nightly occurrence. Annie McPhelimy's mother calms her nerves by taking valium and she lives in constant fear for her sons' safety: 'If Thomas or Brendan were late in coming home from school Mother would ring the Incident centre to see if they'd been shot or arrested' (Costello, 1992, 2). [4] Annie herself is allowed out only to go to school or to Mass. As Joe Logan in *Shadows on Our Skin* lies in bed watching the flames from burnt-out houses flicker on his ceiling, so the violence intrudes even into Annie's bedroom: 'But from my bedroom window, under a ceiling black with night and creeping mould I could see the goings-on. The boys and the Brits, and the RUC' (Costello, 1992, 3). There is no safe domestic sphere. 'The trouble with the troubles,' reflects Annie, 'was that it was impossible to leave them at the

---

[4]   Compare Colette's mother in Una Woods' novel, *the Dark Hole Days* (1984), set in Belfast during the Troubles: 'Mam says she doesn't rest till the door's closed and we're all safe' (Woods, 1984, 1).

front door' (Costello, 1992, 84). She too ends up taking valium and, despite her mother's best efforts, her schooling is disrupted by the violence.

What Johnston, Devlin and Costello do for the Catholic working-class community, Christina Reid's plays do for the Protestant working classes. *Tea in a China Cup*, first performed in 1983, portrays a Protestant working-class Belfast family gradually destroyed from within by external events: grandfather and son fight in the First and Second World Wars respectively, the grandfather is gassed, the son loses his life, while the grandson, unable to find a job in Belfast joins the British Army and can no longer return home for fear of IRA reprisals. Meanwhile the mother is threatened with being burned out of her home by paramilitaries on both sides. Both novels and plays demonstrate that there is no safe, private sphere; the private has become politicized. In this sense, though these texts are centered around domestic life, through their interrogation of the ideologies which weigh on private lives, they connect with the public discourse of Northern Ireland.

Both novels and plays emphasize women's different priorities from their male relatives. When her husband and elder son insist that the British must be resisted, Mrs Logan asks: 'What good does killing do?' (Johnston, 1977/1991, 67). To Mrs Logan the two dead British soldiers are not the enemy but simply two dead boys. Her priority is not political freedom so much as economic. She points out that the political freedom enjoyed by Catholics in the Republic does not necessarily mean freedom for working-class women, preoccupied as they are with providing for their families: 'Have they any more freedom down there than we have up here' she asks her husband. 'Is there a job for every man? And a home for everyone? Have all the children got shoes on their feet?' (Johnston, 1977/1991, 154). In this way, Mrs Logan challenges the male-authored text of Northern nationalism.

The plays of Christina Reid and Anne Devlin present a younger generation of women who question the masculinism of loyalist and nationalist ideologies respectively: Beth in *Tea in a China Cup,* Rose in *The Belle of the Belfast City,* Andrea in *My Name, Shall I tell You My Name?* and Frieda in *Ourselves Alone.* In Devlin's play, Frieda is well aware of the masculinism of the republican paramilitaries. She tells Joe Conran: 'And when there's a tricolour over the City Hall, Donna will still be making coffee for Joe Conran, and Josie will still be keeping house for her daddy' (Devlin, 1986/1990, 30). Frieda knows that the fight for political freedom does not include freedom for women. The opening scene of the play shows her refusing any longer to sing republican songs 'I'm fed up with songs where the women are doormats!' (Devlin, 1986/1990, 13). Issues of gender are not, however, over-simplified by these playwrights: both Devlin and Reid present women who collude in this masculinism. Often these are older women such as Beth's mother in *Tea in a China Cup* or Vi in *The Belle of the Belfast City* or politically active women, like Frieda's elder sister Josie in *Ourselves Alone.* Josie has worked for the IRA for many years, carrying messages and moving ammunition or people. When she becomes pregnant by Joe, however, Josie's priorities change. She loses the killing instinct and wants to leave the movement in order to lead a normal life. The end of the play reveals that Josie will never be free.

Her father and brother fight over the future of her unborn baby, emphasizing the patriarchal nature of the tribal warfare in which she is involved.[5]

Because women's priorities are sometimes different from those of the men with whom they live, they are often shown engaged in crossing borders.[6] In *Shadows on Our Skin*, as both Rachel Sealy Lynch (Kirkpatrick, 2000, 253–4) and Ann Owens Weekes (Weekes, 1991, 198) have pointed out, Kathleen Doherty, a school teacher from the Republic intent on keeping 'an open mind' (Johnston, 1977/1991, 51), tries to cut across the sectarian divide in her country. Though engaged to a soldier in the British Army stationed in Germany, Kathleen has moved to Northern Ireland in order to try to understand what is going on: 'I didn't understand before I came [...] no one can understand [...] I thought it would be a good thing to do' she tells Joe Logan (Johnston, 1977/1991, 120). She makes friends with Joe but her efforts to reach across sectarian divisions come to a sticky end when Joe's brother Brendan finds out about her engagement to a British soldier. She undergoes a punishment beating at the hands of Brendan's mates and is forced to leave Ireland.

Similarly in *Ourselves Alone* Frieda McCoy hopes that by moving in with John McDermot, a member of the Workers' Party and a Protestant, she will be able to escape the violent republicanism espoused by her family and find her own identity. There is no escape. She is driven out by Protestants who object to a Catholic living on their street. Like Kathleen, Frieda will leave Ireland behind, her efforts to cross the sectarian divide having come to naught.

In *Titanic Town*, the killing of a local woman caught in cross-fire between the IRA and the British Army inspires Annie's mother, Bernie McPhelimy, and her friend, Deirdre, to try to negotiate a halt to the shooting, at least during the daytime, in order to make the streets safe. In keeping with the bleakly comic tone of the novel, the women's efforts are portrayed as farcical since, as Elmer Kennedy-Andrews has pointed out, the women lack 'any political analysis and any clear programme for social change' (Kennedy-Andrews, 2003, 267). Their wish for an end to the violence has great emotional appeal but lacks a specific strategy to deal with its causes. Bernie and Deirdre end up being manipulated by all sides, by the media, by the Catholic Church, by the IRA who use them to present their demands to the British, demands they know have no chance of succeeding, and by the British who turn the women's desire for peace into anti-IRA propaganda. Kennedy-Andrews comments:

> The Peace Women constitute an emblem of female energy, determination and commitment, but they are shown to be pathetically inadequate to deal with the establishment and counter-hegemonic power structures, both exclusively male, which would thwart, marginalise and take over those who seek to work through new channels. (Kennedy-Andrews, 2003, 266)

---

[5] On this theme of the patriarchal control of the women in *Ourselves Alone*, see Ann Rea's analysis in 'Reproducing the Nation: Nationalism, Reproduction, and Paternalism in Anne Devlin's *Ourselves Alone*' (Kirkpatrick, 2000, 204–26).

[6] See the volume devoted to this topic, *Border Crossings: Irish Women Writers and National Identities* ed. K. Kirkpatrick, 2000.

This failed effort to ensure a more normal life for the people of Andersonstown reflects the failed attempt of the cross-community Women's Peace Movement founded in 1976 by Mairéad Corrigan and Betty Williams to shame politicians and paramilitaries into a solution. The movement, later called the Peace People, won more sympathy abroad than at home where it was criticized for its lack of a specific political strategy and for its failure to investigate British Army violence. Though its founders won the Nobel Peace Prize in 1977, the movement eventually collapsed through internal dissension. In the novel, Bernie's initiative differs from that of the Peace People in being a localized Catholic West Belfast initiative rather than a cross-community effort; indeed Bernie is anxious to repudiate any connection with the middle-class Protestant Peace Women led by Mrs Lockhart. But both fiction and fact reveal that while some women in Northern Ireland are engaged in the Kristevan project of reaching out to the other, good intentions on the part of women are not sufficient to counter the violence. Indeed, as Jennifer Jeffers argues in the course of her discussion of this novel, gender constraints on both sides of the divide in Northern Ireland will always ensure that the contribution of women to the political process is not taken seriously: 'One basic idea that the British, the IRA, and the Protestants all agree upon is that women have no place in the political process: "Women are there to make the sandwiches"' (Jeffers, 2002, 69). The ending of *Titanic Town* foresees no cessation of violence since neither side is about to give way:

> Sons, sisters, fathers, daughters, husbands and brothers will not be grudged, though they go out to break their strength and die. We will not give an inch and shall not be moved, till the last drops of blood, orange and green, run down the street, through our four green fields, one of them in bondage, to mingle with the rivers of ceaseless rain, seep into the brown sucking bog, and piss, peacefully at last, out into Belfast Lough, in the wake of the Titanic. (Costello, 1992, 340)

A novel by Deirdre Madden, *Hidden Symptoms* (1986), depressingly underlines the impossibility of escape from sectarian divisions. *Hidden Symptoms* portrays Belfast as a city paralyzed by hatred and fear. Twenty-two-year old Theresa has been traumatized by the random sectarian killing of her twin brother Francis two years previously and she is unable to move beyond this. She retains her Catholic faith but refuses to be comforted by it. Her mental stasis is paralleled by that of the city in which she lives: 'It remained an introverted city, narcissistic, nostalgic and profoundly un-European' (Madden, 1986/1988, 80). The novel presents little hope of escape from the city's warring ideologies. Theresa tells Robert that even though he has abandoned his faith, he will always be labeled Catholic: 'If you think that you can escape tribal loyalty in Belfast today you're betraying your people and fooling yourself' (Madden, 1986/1988, 46).

The weight of inherited narratives of Irish history and the difficulty of escaping from them is a central theme of Briege Duffaud's novel, *A Wreath Upon the Dead* (1993). The narrator, Maureen Murphy, brought up in Claghan, a town based on Duffaud's native Crossmaglen, has been indoctrinated by her grandmother from an early age into a Catholic version of Irish history where all the blame is laid upon 'Cromwell's mad dogs of Protestant soldiers' (Duffaud, 1993, 19). Maureen eventually learns to question her grandmother's version of history and reaches out to the other to the extent of making Protestant friends in her teenage years before escaping to England and then to France where she establishes herself as a writer of romantic fiction. Though she intends to write about the story of the nineteenth-century lovers, Catholic Cormac O'Flaherty and Protestant Marianne McLeod, 'from both sides' (Duffaud, 1993, 8), in the end Maureen is still too tied to the people of Claghan to bring herself to write 'anything that sort of questioned their values. It would break their hearts' (Duffaud, 1993, 327). As in Madden's novel, so in *A Wreath Upon the Dead* no escape is envisioned possible from the dead hand of Irish history, at least for the inhabitants of Claghan where history re-emerges as violence with the reformation of the IRA. The house in which Cormac O'Flaherty and Marianne McLeod took refuge has been saved from demolition by a group of liberal Protestants and preserved in the hope that it might become a place where Catholics and Protestants could reach across the sectarian divide. The fact that the house eventually collapses in on itself, blown apart from within by one of Cormac's descendants and from outside by the British Army, turns it into a symbol of the Northern Irish situation where future possibilities are portrayed as doomed in this novel by endless recountings of old grievances: 'in a hundred years time, in a thousand, it'll be the self-same play over and over and over again with another band of poor eejits playing it' (Duffaud, 1993, 44).

Campaigns like the Women's Peace movement tend to bring to the fore essentialist notions of women as peacemakers. However, women's opposition to the violence in Northern Ireland is very far from being the whole story. In her book, *Shattering Silence: Women, Nationalism and Political Subjectivity in Northern Ireland*, Begoña Aretxaga investigates the experience of female nationalist activists. In the 1970s, when the men were interned, women volunteered their services to the IRA not only as couriers but as bomb-makers. They became active in directing operations and setting up training camps. At the time of the 1980s hunger strikes, around thirty women were on 'dirty protest' in Armagh jail. One of these was Mairéad Farrell, serving a fourteen year sentence for planting a bomb. Released in 1986, she was later shot by the Special Air Service (SAS) in Gibraltar. At various times Maíre Drumm who had a daughter on dirty protest was acting president of Sinn Féin. She was murdered while in hospital in 1976.

Loyalist women paramilitaries also exist but are apparently less militant (Sales, 1997, 71). However Woman's Action was founded in 1971 to involve women in active service on behalf of the Ulster Defence Association (UDA). In 1974 a number of loyalist women from this group savagely murdered Ann Ogilby, a married woman who had been taking food to an unmarried prisoner. Loyalist women have been vocal, also, in their support for the men of the Orange Order in their stand at Drumcree. They made application for a women's march down Garvaghy Road and in 1998 they were prominent in setting up roadblocks. While the involvement of some loyalist women in paramilitary violence is clear, much more information about them is needed (see Grant, 2001, 104).

These real-life female activists have their counterparts in Irish women's fiction. In *A Wreath Upon the Dead*, the IRA is represented by a young middle-class woman, Nuala McCormack, while Anne Devlin's play, *Ourselves Alone,* depicts Josie McCoy participating in the violence and expressing revolutionary rhetoric about political freedom indistinguishable from that of men. Devlin's short story,

'Passages', published in her collection *The Way-Paver* (1986) recounts the story of a woman brought to a nervous breakdown by the political situation in Northern Ireland as the civil rights movement becomes swamped by increasingly militant unionist and republican groups. But this is balanced by another story in the collection, 'Naming the Names', in which a Catholic teenage girl, Finn McQuillen, is drawn into actively supporting the republican paramilitaries. Inspired by her Granny's stories of Eamon de Valera and Constance Markievicz, Finn's romantic republican sympathies harden after her Granny's home is burned by Protestant mobs from Shankill. When the British introduce internment, Finn offers her services to the IRA and helps set up the assassination of her lover who is the son of a British judge. These examples show that writing by women on the violence in Northern Ireland does not necessarily endorse essentialist views about women as natural peacemakers.

In her influential essay, 'Fiction in conflict: Northern Ireland's prodigal novelists' (Bell, 1995, 128–48), Eve Patten criticizes Northern Irish fiction for its over-simplified division between the public, political realm, a place of violence, and the private, domestic sphere depicted as a place of authentic feeling and personal relationships under constant threat from outside forces. Detaching itself from the sphere of conflict the liberal humanist novel, she argues, retreats into the safety of the apolitical domestic, providing 'consolatory images' at the expense of a more complex examination of the political conflict (Bell, 1995, 132). This chapter will suggest that a Kristevan reading of fiction by women from Northern Ireland may provide a way out of this dilemma. Kristevan theory, as Marilyn Edelstein has pointed out, deconstructs the seeming binary opposition between the private, ethical sphere and the public, political domain. It does this by linking ethical practice with political in Kristeva's argument that politics is not opposed to ethics but involves a continuation of the dialogic relation between self and other: as we have seen in previous chapters, Kristeva's insistence on the necessity of reaching out to the other is central to her writings on nationalism. Similarly, her emphasis on recognizing the subjectivity of the other is central to her writing on politics. Edelstein comments:

> Kristeva's deconstruction of the seeming binary opposition between ethics and politics is a postmodernist but also a feminist move, in keeping with other feminist critiques of traditional oppositions between public and private, or between the personal and the political. (Edelstein, 1993, 206)

Clearly Kristevan theory, with its rejection of binary thinking, its recognition of difference and its emphasis on inclusiveness and on breaking down rigid forms of nationalism, might have something to say to the situation in Northern Ireland. Reading women's writing through a Kristevan lens may provide for alternative female identities and suggest a way out of the stereotypes of Northern Irish women as either passive victims of violence or bomb-throwing viragoes. In the following analysis we shall be investigating whether women writers on Northern Ireland uphold what Edna Longley calls 'the binary shapes cut out by nationalism and unionism' (Longley, 1994, 185), or whether they use their fiction to explore more fluid and varied kinds of identity than the ones traditionally on offer in Northern Ireland. We shall look for links and comparisons with women's writing from the

Republic, continuing our discussion of the Kristevan themes of the other, the semiotic, the foreigner, the mother and the sacred in the very different political context of Northern Ireland.

Reaching out to the Other: To Stay Alive (1984)

In Northern Ireland, as the preceding analysis has demonstrated, identity has very often been formed on the basis of the exclusion of the other. In the polarized atmosphere of the Troubles particularly, reaching out to the other could be an extremely risky business. Nevertheless this is what Rosaleen, the nineteen-year-old heroine of Linda Anderson's harrowing portrayal of life in Belfast during the Troubles, attempts to do. *To Stay Alive* is set in 1979, a period when IRA prisoners were engaged in the 'dirty protest' which preceded the hunger strikes. The theme of the body, particularly the female body as a site of resistance to patriarchal ideologies, to pick up a topic from chapter 6 of this study, is central to Anderson's novel.

At first sight the theme of the female body is not a promising one: born into a Catholic working-class family, Rosaleen has found her life scarred not only by poverty and violence, but also by sexism. Her family life is highly gendered. Despite her university ambitions, Rosaleen is expected to care for her younger siblings while her mother nurses the latest baby and her long-term unemployed father is out drinking. There is no private space in the family home for her to study and in any case her brother, Leo, who resents her academic ambitions, takes every opportunity to load her with the domestic chores from which his gender exempts him. The fact of her femaleness disadvantages Rosaleen from the outset. A comparison may be drawn with that other nineteen-year-old heroine, Lois, in Elizabeth Bowen's novel, *The Last September.* Though not over-burdened by domestic chores, Lois is disadvantaged by her gender in comparison with her cousin Laurence whose future at least contains the possibility of serious study.

School is no more empowering for Rosaleen than her home life. The nuns do little to encourage Rosaleen's ambition to get to university, distrusting university as 'a cesspit of carnal temptations and revolutionary politics' (Anderson, 1984/1985, 35). Like the nuns in the convent school Cait and Baba attend in *The Country Girls*, Rosaleen's teachers add to the gender constraints on her life by equating femaleness with chastity and humility. Rosaleen believes her convent education has simply programmed her 'for motherhood, nationalism and eternity!' (Anderson, 1984/1985, 96). The result is that Rosaleen feels uncomfortable about her female body, believing that it gets in the way of her serious ambitions: 'She experienced her body as some clownish uncomfortable double of herself' (Anderson, 1984/1985, 86).

Anderson's novel makes clear that Rosaleen's contempt for her body, like that of Mary Lavin's female characters, is socially conditioned: all the various ideologies weighing on her life hold the body in low esteem. Not only the nuns, but also Catholic priests have instilled in her a belief in the inferiority of the body in comparison with the soul. She regards their prohibition on birth control as an effort to turn young Catholic women like herself into what she scornfully describes as 'biddable little breeders' (Anderson, 1984/1985, 45). The only person who encourages Rosaleen's ambitions is Dan, a medical student, but by the time she has been accepted for Queens she is pregnant by him. Rosaleen's body has betrayed her, a fact which would seem to confirm her distrust of her body. Instead of the freedom she had imagined at university, marriage and motherhood have become her fate.

The ideologies which weigh on Rosaleen's life are very real: gender, class and the Catholic Church's prohibition against contraception have stymied her life from the outset. She accepts that Queens University, occupied by Protestants, men and English professors is not the place for a Catholic working-class girl. At a later stage in the novel, Rosaleen is afraid she is pregnant again:

> The period was so late. She hesitated, praying, willing the menstrual flow, then pressed her hand between her legs, withdrawing it smeared with blood. She ran out of the room and downstairs, her whole body light and swift with the astonishment of relief.
>
> It was a reprieve. A sign. She could have a new life, scoured clean of everything that had happened. (Anderson, 1984/1985, 94)

Rosaleen's rejoicing that she is not pregnant runs counter to the Catholic ideology of motherhood instilled in her by the nuns and priests. It also, as Jayne Steel has pointed out, presents menstruation as liberating and cleansing, as opposed to the patriarchal and misogynistic view which associates menstrual blood with the abject (Steel, 2004, 63).

Not only does Rosaleen seek to resist the discourses surrounding the female body, she also questions the nationalist assumptions of the Catholic working-class environment in which she has grown up. Like the young heroines of Elizabeth Bowen, Jennifer Johnston and Edna O'Brien, the ironically named Rosaleen feels an outsider to her environment. When a baby is killed by the IRA in crossfire, she questions the right of the IRA to justify their violence on the grounds that they are acting on behalf of the Irish nation: 'They act in the name of dead Irishmen, future Irishmen. In the name of what does not exist' (Anderson, 1984/1985, 33). Rosaleen feels an outsider to a nationalism that is gendered as male. Irish men carry out violence on behalf of other Irish men while women and children get caught in the crossfire. Rosaleen has chosen none of the oppressions which weigh on her life – neither her religion, her class, her gender nor her nationality. When Marty's grandfather, an old IRA man, reminds her that good men are laying down their lives for her, she replies: 'I don't require it, I assure you' (Anderson, 1984/1985, 104). Echoing Eavan Boland's view about women in the Irish poetic tradition, Rosaleen argues that women may be powerful symbols in Irish music and poetry but in real life they are invisible: 'It annoys me, the way lovely songs and poems are written about Irishwomen but we're treated like zeros' she tells her sister, Katrin (Anderson, 1984/1985, 40). Rosaleen perceives the Irish nation as constructed by the nationalists to be male property.

Even in her own community, then, Rosaleen is positioned as an outsider. She lives in an environment where every statement she makes is examined for its loyalty or otherwise to the nationalist cause. When, in an off-guard moment, she questions the heroism of the men on dirty protest in the H block, she becomes afraid that her friend, Marty, a republican hard-liner who insists on the homogeneity of the nationalist community, will denounce her as a traitor. The themes of the oppressions of nationalism and the oppression of the female body dovetail in Rosaleen's resistance to her body being appropriated by marriage. As Lois in *The Last September* finds parallels between Gerald's attitude to Ireland and his attitude towards herself, so Rosaleen equates Dan's possessiveness about his country with his possessiveness towards her as his wife: 'This is your country. And I'm your cunt' she thinks (Anderson, 1984/1985, 44).

Questioning many of the values of her community, both political and religious, Rosaleen is determined to break free from the conditions of her life: 'Rosaleen set her heart against sacrifice. Church, family, country, were like so many voracious mouths' (Anderson, 1984/1985, 36). Awareness of her otherness causes her to reach out to the other and who could be more other in her environment than a British soldier? Despite the fact that her republican friend, Marty, insists that to love an Englishman would involve 'Spitting on every belief. Betraying everyone' (Anderson, 1984/1985, 106), Rosaleen seeks escape from the conditions of her life through sex with Gerry, a British soldier newly arrived in the country. Their first encounter takes place in a graveyard where Rosaleen has gone to mourn the death of her friend Aidan, killed by the IRA who believe him to have been an informer. Gerry, horrified by the violence of Belfast for which nothing in his training has prepared him, is also grieving for a fellow soldier who has been killed. In this way sex and death become intertwined. For both Rosaleen and Gerry sex is a form of escapism from the claims laid on them by the communities to which they belong. Sex is a protest against the different ideologies which govern their lives and require them to make enemies of each other. Indeed, it is their very otherness which attracts them to one another: '"You are in a foreign country"' Rosaleen shouts at Gerry. '"Nobody invited you!"' They stood gaping at each other like startled enemies. Desire shot through her' (Anderson, 1984/1985, 91).

In this scene, Rosaleen's rebellion against the ideologies constraining the female body (she should remain a faithful Catholic wife) and her resistance to nationalism (she should certainly not be unfaithful with a British soldier) come together, her body providing the means with which to express her dissent from the male-authored nationalism weighing on her community. Anderson's novel portrays Rosaleen's attempts to stay alive, to stay human, in the face of a situation which seems calculated to crush the human spirit. Like the young heroines of Elizabeth Bowen, Edna O'Brien and Jennifer Johnston, Rosaleen's resistance to the values of her community is strengthened by reaching out to the other.

By the end of *To Stay Alive*, Rosaleen has decided she will stay in Belfast and become a symbol of resistance to the violent nationalisms of her environment. She is determined to cut any lingering sectarianism out of her life, and here the theme of the suppressed body comes into focus again. While Dan is being interrogated by the British Army, Rosaleen is sexually assaulted by British soldiers, the female equivalent of the physical abuse Dan is undergoing at the hands of the British. The shock of this assault proves a turning point in Rosaleen's development. She stays besieged inside her house and, as she crouches naked by the fire, she comes to realize that the violence in her country arises out of holding the body cheaply. Indeed the whole novel has been punctuated by episodes where the body is subjugated and humiliated: the prisoners on the 'dirty protest', a gang rape which leaves the female victim with a 'wet slick of blood curling from the punctured womb' (Anderson, 1984/1985, 47), Leo's punishment beating for consorting with a married woman, Dan being searched by the Army ('Dan's body was bent forward, rump jutting out like a female baboon inviting sexual entry', Anderson, 1984/1985, 162). Armies, politicians and anyone who preaches violence show contempt, Rosaleen now realizes, for the body: 'All men were wrong who held bodies in cheap esteem. Pornographers. Politicians. Armies. Even priests. Health of the soul does not depend on mortification of the flesh' (Anderson, 1984, 186). She resolves never again to despise it.

In this scene, Rosaleen's re-evaluation of the body leads to a desire, to quote Kristeva in 'Women's Time', to throw off the entire 'weight of what is sacrificial in the social contract' from her shoulders, to seek 'a more flexible and free discourse, one able to name what has thus far never been an object of circulation in the community: the enigmas of the body, the dreams, secret joys, shames, hatreds of the second sex' (Kristeva, 1986, 207). As in Kristeva's analysis, Rosaleen's re-evaluation of the claims of the body has the potential to subvert the deadly patriarchal and authoritarian ideologies by which her life is constrained. Strengthened by her encounter with the other, Rosaleen reclaims power over her body and over her life: 'She decided once and for all to cut out her own lingering instinctive loyalty to the Provisionals' (Anderson, 1984/1985, 186).

Rosaleen's growth is matched by that of her husband, Dan, who returns from his brutal interrogation by the British determined, despite the pressures on him as a Catholic male living in West Belfast, 'to quarrel with guns' (Anderson, 1984, 195). Together Rosaleen and Dan will stay in Northern Ireland, raise their son and find a different way to live. Though the novel ends on a note of hope, in the light of all that has gone before, the reader cannot help feeling that Rosaleen and Dan have a terrible struggle ahead of them in their search for more fluid identities than their community allows them. As Jayne Steel points out, critics have been divided as to how to interpret the novel's ending (Steel, 2004, 63). Padraig O'Malley believes the ending suggests there will be no way out for Rosaleen, while Christine St Peter argues that 'Rosaleen's fierce desire to stay alive in face of so much death [...] marks an heroic struggle against the false forms of heroism current in Belfast society' (St Peter, 2000, 114). Steel herself concurs with this latter verdict: '*To Stay Alive* leaves the reader with a sense that Irish women will never wholly capitulate to patriarchy' (Steel, 2004, 63). Certainly *To Stay Alive* is a powerful account of one woman's determination to evade the constraints of class, gender and nationalism which combine to stifle individual development in Northern Ireland. Rosaleen's encounter with the other underlines her resistance to the brand of nationalism prevalent in her community, while at the same time strengthening that resistance.

Dialog from the Margins: Give Them Stones (1987)

Mary Beckett's powerful novel, *Give Them Stones*, presents a woman whose initial embrace of the nationalism of her Catholic working-class community gives way to the more skeptical position on the margins that Kristeva finds typical of women.

The novel opens with a turning point in Martha's endorsement of her community's nationalism when a young boy is knee-capped by the IRA outside her bakery. It then flashes back to the past in order to trace Martha's growing disenchantment with the ideologies which rule her community.

As a working-class Catholic, Martha is, like Linda Anderson's heroine, marginalized in a Protestant state. While Martha's mother and grandmother work in the linen mills, her father, like many Northern Irish Catholic males, is unable to find work and so is responsible for child care in the home. As a child Martha is inspired by her father's talk of freedom:

> I loved listening to how Ireland was going to be free. I'd look off down Belfast Lough with the ships in it and the shipyard with the gantries and over to the little hills in Co. Down and Bangor with the yachts in front of it and I'd think wouldn't it be lovely if it really was our own country that we could be proud in, instead of being kept in cramped little streets with no jobs for the men and sneered at by the people who deprived us. It was as if we were all in prison looking out at a beautiful world we'd never walk free in. (Beckett, 1987, 17–18)

But Martha is also associated with the labor movement: she was born, as her Uncle Joe recalls, during the General Strike of 1926 and she endorses her family's allegiance to the workers. This allegiance partly cuts across national boundaries: her uncle supports the strike by British workers. Although Martha's support for her family's nationalism and her support for its socialism seem almost equally balanced at the beginning of the novel, by the end, as Megan Sullivan has shown, her nationalism has given way to her socialist sympathies (Kirkpatrick, 2000, 227–49). Even at this early stage, Martha's dislike of military violence is made clear: though she enjoys listening to her father's tales of Wolfe Tone addressing the United Irishmen on Cave Hill about the necessity of freedom, she dislikes 'the stories about tribes attacking or being besieged' (Beckett, 1987, 17). This scene foreshadows her later turning against IRA violence.

A colonial education system only serves to alienate Martha from her environment and causes her to turn in on herself. She refuses a scholarship to secondary school because she has already become disenchanted with school. The novel suggests that the colonial education Martha receives is largely to blame for her disenchantment. Catholic schools receive less funding than Protestant schools and the books they read are all about England and English life where Catholics are invisible. The pressure on the teachers in Catholic schools to get their pupils to succeed against the odds leads to cruelty: Martha is traumatized by her memory of the headmistress, Miss Killeen, slapping Lizzie McAteer. A colonial education system, as well as her family's lack of support, has contributed to Martha's prematurely closed mind. She leaves school at fourteen and goes to work in the mill like her mother and grandmother before her. Her more spirited younger sister, Mary Brigid, who accepts the offer of secondary education, becomes a teacher and thus escapes the grinding poverty of Martha's working-class life.

During the war, as Belfast is bombed and her father interned, Martha spends time in the country with two aunts. Bessie and Maggie, who support themselves by managing a small farm, are important examples for Martha of autonomous females. They teach her to bake bread, a skill which will be vital to her later independence. In the countryside Martha sees Protestants and Catholics getting on together in a way which would be inconceivable in the city. In addition, her aunts discourage her from making anti-Protestant remarks. The potential is here for Martha to open her mind to dialog with the other. However Martha remains loyal to the Catholic community, avid for Ireland's freedom and hostile to the British. Nevertheless her two aunts are important figures on her road to self-identity, not only because of the bread-making skills they instill in her but because, in bequeathing to her their small property which she converts on their deaths into cash, they contribute to her ability to become financially self-sufficient.

In some ways, though, this stay in the country increases Martha's sense of isolation, for she feels abandoned by her family. Her mother is too exhausted from coping with the demands of daily life to express the affection Martha craves. Her father, who was responsible for the warmth in the family home, is taken away from her by internment. Later, having contracted TB, he spends time in hospital and dies having failed to recognize Martha. Martha develops a determination, endorsed by her family, to stand on her own two feet and not be beholden to anyone. She marries Dermot Hughes, a van driver, not out of love, but from material aspirations: his house has a gas cooker. Using this she starts to earn a living for herself and her family by baking bread. To this end, she spends her aunts' legacy on a bakehouse. Like Helen Cuffe in Jennifer Johnston's novel, *The Railway Station Man*, Martha is moving towards establishing a room of her own, disentangling herself from the social constructs of her environment and cultivating her own voice.

When the civil rights marches begin, Martha becomes excited by them and by the reforming of the IRA, hoping that at last her dream of a united Ireland will be realized. When the IRA bombing campaigns start up, at first Martha is in sympathy with the bombers so long as they target only shops and factories and cost the British money in compensation. Under pressure from the local IRA, she refuses to serve British soldiers any longer. However, though she dislikes the soldiers' rude manners, her refusal to serve them is also partly motivated by the desire to protect them from threatened IRA retaliation. Already Martha is beginning to challenge not only British Army violence, but also that of the IRA. As that violence increases, Martha further questions nationalist rhetoric: 'The IRA talked about "accidents of war" but it sounded too glib and I felt ashamed, sometimes horrified' (Beckett, 1987, 124). She is beginning to position herself in opposition to the nationalism with which she has grown up.

Martha creates a parallel world apart from the violence in her bakehouse, concentrating on baking bread to such an extent that when a British soldier asks her whether she is a republican, her response is: 'I was going to be a heroine but instead I said, "I am a home baker"' (Beckett, 1987, 123). She rejects a male-authored nationalist identity in favor of the female world of home baking. Megan Sullivan sees this as a crucial stage in Martha's movement away from her former allegiance to nationalism: 'By claiming her status as a female wage earner, Martha complicates a nationalist narrative, while simultaneously insisting upon attention to gender-based material conditions' (Kirkpatrick, 2000, 227).

Her bakehouse has become more than an economic necessity; it is Martha's world, a room of her own where she can express her individuality and creativity away from the violence outside. It has become more important to her than her republican sympathies: 'If I am not baking bread I am nobody and nothing' she says (Beckett, 1987, 147). Refusing labels imposed on her by either side, she reserves the right to define her own identity. Like Helen Cuffe in her studio, in her bakehouse, Martha has created a woman's space apart from the ideologies that are dividing her society in two.

> But when I'd get a good run of baking on the way in the mornings and nobody around but myself and the warmth from the stove and the smell of bread all through my domain, I'd find myself so happy my mind would say, "How lovely is Thy dwelling place, Lord God of Hosts" [...] It gave over my place of work to God so that my bits of creation would join in with his. (Beckett, 1987, 113)

Like Helen in *The Railway Station Man*, Martha enters into a semiotic trance as she bakes, helped by the music she plays on the record player her sister has given her.

Not surprisingly, since it provides a space of resistance to the ideologies which constrain her community, Martha's bakehouse is attacked by both sides. Ignoring her self-definition as a home baker, the British Army insists that because her brother is a republican, she also must be an IRA supporter. They raid her bakery, disrupting for a while her ability to bake bread for her community. Similarly, after her refusal to contribute any more protection money to the Provos' funds, the IRA retaliates by knee-capping a young boy outside her bakery. Bringing back memories of Lizzie McAteer's beating at the hands of Miss Killeen, this is a turning-point in Martha's attitude to the IRA. She realizes that she cannot condone cruelty, even in pursuit of a united Ireland. She recognizes what is other in herself to the nationalist struggle: she cannot believe in a struggle which ignores the rights of the individual. This is, in essence Kristeva's own quarrel with political ideologies, namely that by speaking in generalities, they fail to honor the individual. In an interview, she has said: 'My reproach to some political discourses with which I am disillusioned is that they don't consider the individual as a value' (Kristeva, 1997, 347). Abandoning her usual aversion to risk-taking, Martha makes a stand against nationalist violence with the result that the Provos burn down her house and shop. Martha's move away from a nationalist, male-dominated identity is not recognized either by the British Army or by the IRA.

The novel ends with Martha moving into a new house furnishing it, ironically, by means of compensation given to her by the British secured through advice from the local Sinn Féin center. She has learned to negotiate her way between the various ideologies which threaten her independence. Her world will be preserved through some astute manipulation of the patriarchies on both sides: she decides to open a new bakery and she envisages training up some young girl 'so that it would go on when I was too old' (Beckett, 1987, 152).

Like Johnston's heroine, Helen Cuffe, Martha is intent on creating her own space, a room of her own outside the competing ideologies of her nation, where she can develop her creativity, in this case her bread making, unimpeded. However, like Johnston's novel, *Give Them Stones* does not simply proclaim the virtues of withdrawal: the position Martha evolves for herself is a Kristevan one, on the margins of her society yet in dialog with it. Martha's mothering of her sons has been a failure but in the course of her preoccupation with survival she has transferred her mothering skills outward into nurturing her community. Jayne Steel describes Martha's bakery as 'a female domain that is both a public space (the shop) and a private, domestic space (the home)' (Steel, 2004, 64). For Martha, baking bread is more than a means of earning a living. It is a way of reaching out to the women of her community as the bakehouse draws the neighborhood to her shop: 'they were kind to me and [...] called me "Martha love" [...] they filled the need I had for neighbours' (Beckett, 1987, 102). During the rent strikes of 1969 Martha gives away bread free.

For the stones thrown in violence on the streets outside, Martha substitutes nurturing bread, in much the same way as the women whom she so much admires broke the British Army curfew to bring bread to the besieged houses in the Lower Falls Road. Beckett's novel continually associates bread-making with women who resist male-dominated ideologies and in the process become empowered: the women of the Falls Road, Martha's aunts who refuse the binary oppositions on which Northern Irish identity is predicated and, finally, Martha herself. Fulfilling Kristeva's notion of women's dialectic movement between the public and the private, Martha's warm nurturing world remains as a counterpoint to the male violence on the streets outside.

Give Them Stones is a remarkable account of one woman's resistance to the ideological conflicts which rule her environment. From unpromising beginnings, Martha has found a way to express her individuality and creativity and in doing so she nurtures a whole community. Her room is not some sentimentalized private sphere cut off from the violence outside: Martha's bread making draws in and nourishes an entire community. Despite the dourness and bitter pride which almost wreck her personal life, Martha illustrates Kristeva's notion of women in a nation using their position on the margins to positive effect.

Oscillating between the semiotic and the symbolic:
One by One in the Darkness (1996)

Deirdre Madden's novel, *One by One in the Darkness*, set in rural Northern Ireland, takes as its subject the growth to maturity of the three Catholic Quinn sisters: Helen, a Belfast lawyer, Cate, a fashion writer in London and Sally, a primary school teacher who has remained at home with their mother. Always close, despite their very different personalities, the sisters draw even more on the emotional bond between them after the sectarian murder of their father in a case of mistaken identity: 'fear was like a wire which connected them with each other and isolated them from everyone else' (Madden, 1996/1997, 9).

This isolation from the life of their nation began early on when the sisters realized that, as Catholics, they were not included in the dominant political identity of Northern Ireland:

> [...] they knew that their lives, so complete in themselves, were off centre in relation to the society beyond those few fields and houses. They recognized this most acutely every July, when they were often taken to the Antrim coast for the day, and as they went

through Ballymena and Broughshane, they would see all the Union Jacks flying at the houses, and the red, white and blue bunting across the streets. They thought that the Orange arches which spanned the roads in the towns were ugly, and creepy, too [...] They knew that they weren't supposed to understand what these things meant; and they knew, too, without having to be told that the motto painted on the arches: 'Welcome here, Brethren!' didn't include the Quinn family. (Madden, 1996/1997, 75)

In one sense the novel is a straightforward depiction of the effects of this marginalization and, later, of their father's murder, on the lives of the three sisters. The novel is set against the rise of the civil rights movement, the advent of the British army and the growing violence in the North and it registers an obvious protest against the marginalization of Catholics within the state. Yet the novel also registers a more subtle protest by the way in which, despite the seemingly flat, realist narrative tone, it inscribes the semiotic in various ways. In this respect *One by One in the Darkness* lends itself to a Kristevan reading, as Jayne Steel has shown in one of the few instances of an application of Kristevan theory to work by an Irish woman writer (Steel, 2004, 55–66). The following discussion of Madden's novel is indebted to and extends Steel's analysis.

From the start, the very structure of the novel, flashing between present and past in alternate chapters, registers a protest against linear time as the novel sways between the 1960s and the 1990s. The novel opens with what is ostensibly a realistic description of Cate's home but by the end of the first paragraph a hidden, uncanny dimension has been suggested:

Home was a huge sky; it was flat fields of poor land fringed with hawthorn and alder. It was birds in flight; it was columns of midges like smoke in a summer dusk. It was grey water; it was a mad wind; it was a solid stone house where the silence was uncanny. (Madden, 1996/1997, 1)

This description is repeated at the end of the novel, by which time the reader has learned the reason for the uncanny silence, namely the murder of the sisters' father at the hands of loyalist paramilitaries. However this uncanny dimension runs right through the novel in the dreams of the female characters by which they register their protest against the constraints of the political circumstances in which they are trapped.

Dreams, for Kristeva, are a space outside linear time where the unspeakable may be represented. As Anne-Marie Smith explains: 'the unrepresentable may find representation in a type of dreamwork which makes visible and, in the account of the dream, brings into language images and emotion which otherwise have no access to the visible or to language' (Smith, 1998, 59). In *One by One in the Darkness*, the dreams and visions of the female characters express more than they are able to articulate in language. The dreams of the sisters' mother, Emily, register her valuing of family life and her desire for reconciliation with her own mother, both things she finds difficult to articulate in words. They also register her lack of forgiveness for the murderer of her husband. Her daughter, Cate, as a child, loved imagining the leisured life going on behind the walls of Shane's Castle and her imaginings provided a counterpoint to the relative poverty of her own home. As a grown-up, Cate has a vision that one day a huge memorial will be erected to the memory of all the victims of violence in Northern Ireland. The structure she imagines embodies both formal elements (three walls covered with the victims' names) and more fluid, semiotic elements – the fourth wall will be a window open to the sky.

Cate's elder sister, Helen, distrusts words. She is particularly distrustful of media accounts of deaths resulting from the violence in Northern Ireland. In the case of Helen's father, the British tabloids implied, wrongly, that because his brother Brian was a member of Sinn Féin and because the murder took place in Brian's house, their father must somehow have been involved in paramilitary activity. Helen escapes both her anger over this calumny of their gentle, tolerant father and the grimness of her working life as a lawyer specializing in terrorist cases and working out of the Falls Road by listening to music, using its soothing semiotic rhythms to transport herself to another world. She also, like Cate, uses dreams for consolation. Before the tragedy of their father's murder, Helen, slipping 'into a fold in her mind somewhere between her dreams and her imagination' (Madden, 1996/1997, 178), was in the habit of using safe, comforting images of home to lull herself to sleep. Since her father's death, Helen's visions have changed. She no longer sees a safe, warm, living universe, blessed by God. Instead she imagines the moment of her father's death set against the backdrop of a huge, empty universe filled with 'the cold light of dead stars' (Madden, 1996/1997, 181). In the same way, her younger sister, Sally, experiences a waking dream of terror when she imagines a man walking into her classroom and gunning down the children in her charge. Neither Helen nor Sally can articulate their fears to their family. Their dreams represent what is unspeakable about their lives in Northern Ireland.

The female characters are drawn together also by their association with color which runs like a leitmotif through the novel. As if to register a protest against the grimness of their lives, Granny Kate and her granddaughter Cate have only brightly colored clothes in their wardrobes. 'I wouldn't wear black,' Granny Kate tells her granddaughter, 'not if all belonging to me was dead' (Madden, 1996/1997, 4). Granny Kate, the grandmother Cate most resembles, is particularly associated with color:

> When Granny Kate talked about the colour of her clothes, she never just used simple words like 'red', 'blue' or 'green'. Her cardigan was 'a soft blue, the colour of a thrush's egg'. She had a skirt that was 'a big strong purple, like an iris', and a coat that was 'reddy-brown, the colour of a brick'. She was wearing a new coat at Mass this morning, and Kate was keen to have a closer look at it, for she'd heard Granny describe it to Kate's mother during the week as being 'that lovely rich-green colour you get when a mallard turns its neck and the light hits it'. (Madden, 1996/1997, 10)

Granny Kate's love of color is inherited by her granddaughter. When Cate flies into Belfast, the 'cold expanse of grey water' that is Lough Neagh lies spread out below her, but what Cate registers is the bright splash of blue in the landscape formed by the sheep stained blue as a mark of ownership (Madden, 1996/1997, 4–5). As she walks in the fields after lunch, it is colors she particularly notices: 'After a day of showers the sun was hidden now in white clouds which it split and veined with light; pink and blue like the opal Cate wore on her right hand' (Madden,

1996/1997, 9). Cate's sisters, too, value color. As a child, rather than listen to the priest, Helen prefers to read through a book of colored pictures. And Sally's primary school classroom is a riot of bright colors.

At the end of 'About Chinese Women', Kristeva associates the semiotic with color:

> I think of Virginia Woolf, who sank wordlessly into the river, her pockets weighed down with stones. Haunted by voices, waves, lights, in love with colours – blue, green [...] Or Sylvia Plath, another of those women disillusioned with meanings and words, who took refuge in lights, rhythms, sounds. (Kristeva, 1986, 157)

In Madden's novel, their valuing of colors draws the female characters together, as if to value color is to register a protest against the conditions of their lives. One of the first things Cate does after their father's funeral is to have her apartment redecorated 'in pale colours which gave a greater sense of light and space' (Madden, 1996/1997, 91). She fills her apartment with flowers and goes walking amongst the crowds in the West End. Like the women named at the end of 'About Chinese Women' – Woolf, Tsvetaeva, Plath – in the midst of tragedy Cate craves 'noise and brightness and colour' (Madden, 1996/1997, 91). Similarly, after her husband's murder, Emily becomes obsessed with growing flowers, using her love of flowers and the color of flowers as a way of attaching herself to the cyclical rhythm of the seasons. In doing so, she registers a protest, not only against political violence, but also against the demands of linear time, the symbolic order itself:

> It made her bear time, because it hooked her into the circle of the seasons, and time would otherwise have been a horrible straight line, a straight, merciless journey at speed towards death. Instead of which, she had pulled Charlie back into the circle and back into her life, in a way which she wordlessly comprehended, and which offered to her the nearest approximation she would ever have to comfort or consolation. (Madden, 1996/1997, 106)

For Emily, time is like 'the ocean' (Madden, 1996/1997, 112), surging back and forth between the present and the past, rather like the structure of this novel.

Despite brief moments of consolation like these, *One by One in the Darkness* ends, like Madden's novel, *Hidden Symptoms*, also set in Northern Ireland, on a vision of utter bleakness with Helen's dream of a dark lonely universe. Nevertheless, the novel's semiotic dimension registers a slight, but unmistakable protest against the symbolic. In this reading *One by One in the Darkness* becomes, as Kristeva argues literature should be, a therapeutic space in which dissension against the symbolic may be registered, however tenuously, and the unspeakable named. It remains the case, though, that in this novel, unlike, say, the short stories of Mary Dorcey examined in chapter three, the revolutionary potential of the semiotic is not presented as making any discernible impact in the realm of public discourse.

The Foreign Other: Dora, or the Shifts of the Heart (1990)

In *One by One in the Darkness*, Kate Quinn moves to London, changes her name to Cate in an effort to shake off her Irish origins and discovers during the course of this just how much she is regarded as the foreign other in England where people interpret the murder of her father to mean that he must have been involved in paramilitary activity. Insecurity and a sense of impermanence belie the outward glamour of Cate's life in London and she attempts to counter these by having a baby which at least, she feels, will be 'something real' (Madden, 1996/1997, 93). Cate is clearly a literary descendant of that other country girl, Caithleen. In the third volume of Edna O'Brien's trilogy, *Girls in their Married Bliss*, Caithleen moves to England, changes her name to Kate but finds it impossible to disentangle herself from the memory of her mother and of her mother country. This is a recurrent theme in O'Brien's work: as we have seen, Ellen in *August is a Wicked Month* and Nell in *Time and Tide*, undergo a similar conflict. Dora, the heroine of Polly Devlin's novel, *Dora, or the Shifts of the Heart*, is another literary descendant of Edna O'Brien's country girls.

Like Edna O'Brien, Polly Devlin comes from a rural Catholic background, though from Northern Ireland. Although Devlin's novel was published in 1990, it is set in the 1970s with flashbacks to Dora's childhood in the 1940s and 1950s. It is thus close in atmosphere and time to *The Country Girls Trilogy*. *Dora* presents the experiences of the eponymous heroine, a rural Catholic from Northern Ireland who moves to England and thus encounters the foreign other. In England Dora who, like Madden's heroine, Cate, works in the glamorous world of fashion magazines, experiences all those feelings of insecurity and loneliness which are ascribed to the foreigner by Kristeva in *Strangers to Ourselves*. Devlin's novel is partly autobiographical since it draws for Dora's background on the author's own upbringing in County Tyrone as evoked in her haunting memoir, *All of Us There* (1983), and on her subsequent career as a journalist with *Vogue*.

Like Edna O'Brien's Cait, Devlin's heroine Dora is presented as the daughter of a joyless, self-denying mother who exhausts herself trying to protect her daughter from the effects of her husband's irresponsibility: gambling in the case of Dora's father. Like Caithleen, Dora is raised in a society which favors the male and her upbringing is a lesson in the vulnerability of females in Ireland during the 1940s and 1950s. Added to this is the punitive influence of the Catholic Church with its equation of womanhood with chastity, passivity and obedience, an ethos reinforced by the convent school which Dora, like Caithleen, attends.

At this stage, Caithleen's rebellion against her surroundings is largely influenced by her friendship with Baba, whereas Devlin's sixteen-year-old heroine, who is less passive and more pragmatic than Caithleen and in many ways amalgamates the voices of Caithleen and Baba, already feels alien to her Irish surroundings. Mirroring Caithleen's later change of name to Kate, Devlin's heroine alters her name from Nora to the more English-sounding Dora, wearing her new name as a disguise in a bid to free herself from the past. Nora is too old-fashioned, too country Irish; this new name she hopes will lift her 'above her earlier, defined, and limited identity, which, she felt, had been so hooked into her relationships with her family, her school mates, her teachers that she could never escape the prison of the shame of childhood' (Devlin, 1990/1992, 4). 'Shame' is a word which recurs in the account of Caithleen's youth and is similarly environmentally induced.

In *Strangers to Ourselves*, Kristeva poses the question whether one becomes a foreigner because one has already recognized that one feels foreign to the ethos of one's native country: 'should one recognise that one becomes a foreigner in another country because one is already a foreigner from within?' (Kristeva, 1991, 14). At nineteen, feeling foreign to her society's ethos and unwilling to duplicate her mother's thwarted life, Dora escapes 'the defeating swamp of damp, rural, vicious Ireland' (Devlin, 1990/1992, 130) to England where she intends to leave Nora behind, like some permanently paralyzed Sleeping Beauty. As Kristeva argues in 'A New Type of Intellectual: The Dissident': 'Exile is already in itself a form of *dissidence*, since it involves uprooting oneself from a family, a country or a language' (Kristeva, 1986, 298).

However, escape is only the beginning of the search for a new identity. In England Dora, like Cait and Ellen and Nell, has difficulty establishing a new identity strong enough to counter the Irish identity she has only partly outgrown: 'for years Nora lived in Dora's head' (Devlin, 1990/1992, 5). Looking in the mirror she dreads to see her own mother staring back at her. Scolding and complaint are habits learned from her mother which she has not managed to train herself out of: 'perhaps the patterns had been set too far behind for her to be able to change them' (Devlin, 1990/1992, 12). Like O'Brien's heroines, Dora learns that her mother is not so easily left behind and neither is her mother country.

Nevertheless she is determined to try to break the mold. Devlin's novel opens with Dora in the 1970s reviewing her life in a frantic attempt to avoid inflicting patterns of emotional repression and joylessness learned from her mother onto her own daughters. The narrator who, like Baba with Caithleen, often takes a wry view of Dora's goings-on, remarks: 'Dora sought to dismantle her life in order to try to build its future in another shape' (Devlin, 1990/1992, 14). In the course of this dismantling, Dora comes to realize that behavior she had taken to illustrate her mother's deliberate suppression of pleasure was often simply the result of exhaustion. 'She did her best' Dora acknowledges years later (Devlin, 1990/1992, 13). This ability to see the mother as a subject in her own right, with her own story is, as we have seen, very much a feature of Irish women's writing on the mother-daughter relationship in the 1990s. It is quite different from Kate's cry of hatred against her mother in *Girls in their Married Bliss* which leaves her as much emotionally entangled with her mother as ever (O'Brien, 1987, 476–7).

Devlin's novel is not only about the mother-daughter relationship but also about an Irish woman in exile. Dora, however, does not intend to remain an outsider for long. From the outset, she is determined to establish herself in England. As Kristeva writes in *Strangers to Ourselves*:

The foreigner has fled from that origin – family, blood, soil – and, even though it keeps pestering, enriching, hindering, exciting him, or giving him pain, and often all of it at once, the foreigner is its courageous and melancholy betrayer. His origin certainly haunts him, for better and for worse, but it is indeed *elsewhere* that he has set his hopes, that his struggles take place, that his life holds together today. (Kristeva, 1991, 29)

The novel delineates some of Dora's problems. As an Irish woman trying to pick her way through the English class system, Dora comes up against English hostility and English arrogance: 'what she never came to terms with was that they, this foreign race on whose soil she lived, were inherently patronising' (Devlin, 1990/1992, 65). She is unable to translate the complexity of Ireland to the English:

> She knew there was no point in trying to compress the long savagery of the history of Ireland under English rule into cursory conversations. Tragedy became petulance under such conditions. (Devlin, 1990/1992, 85)

To be a foreigner, Kristeva says in *Strangers to Ourselves*, is 'To be of no account to others. No one listens to you [...] Your speech has no past and will have no power over the future of the group: why should one listen to it? You do not have enough status – no 'social standing' – to make your speech useful' (Kristeva, 1991, 20). As an Irish woman living in England, Dora is unable to make her speech count. A reading of Bronwen Walter's study of Irish female emigrants to Britain, *Outsiders Inside: Whiteness, Place and Irish Women*, would suggest that Dora's case is not unusual. Walter's study emphasizes the invisibility of Irish women in England, both because of the lack of recognition of Irish cultural difference in British life and Irish anxieties about hostility: Walter found that many Irish women preferred to keep a low profile in England in order to avoid negative ethnic labeling (Walter, 2001, 211).

Dora's affair with Tony Flaxmeyer shows her that she has not left Nora as far behind as she had thought. Tony is another refugee in English life, a Jewish artist who was brought up in Ireland. When Tony introduces her to his Ireland, the gracious, easy, guilt-free Ireland of the Anglo-Irish, Dora is filled with class rage, rejecting the idea that the Anglo-Irish, who displaced her ancestors from their land, can have any share in the Irish identity. When Tony expects to sleep with her she is inhibited by the presence in the house of two women of her own class and background who, she is well aware, would instantly categorize her as a whore:

> When she set foot in Ireland, like it or lump it, the creature in the glass coffin stirred and opened one eye and watched. She was outside the reach of that vision in England but in Ireland she was subject to its survey. (Devlin, 1990/1992, 107)

Dora recognizes old-fashioned innocence when she sees it and the extent to which she can recognize it is a measure of the loss of innocence in herself. Dora's flight to England has resulted in her becoming an outsider in both countries. The Ireland she has returned to with Tony is a different country from that of her parents. To that country, her parents' country, she can no longer return; she has chosen to become a person who will no longer fit into their world: 'she cried for the journey she had made, the journeys she could no longer make' (Devlin, 1990/1992, 108–9). She has become what Kristeva terms the 'melancholy betrayer' of her homeland.

But if Dora is now an outsider in her own country, neither does she fit into English life. Money matters to Dora, as it does to Baba, but, despite her marriage to the wealthy Simon which would seem to root her firmly in upper middle-class English life, she continues to experience those feelings of loss and insecurity ascribed by Kristeva to the foreigner:

> Even the bricks and mortar of their centuries-old house seemed transient and she walked
> around its gardens feeling that the whole place was a separate state to which she did not
> have citizenship. (Devlin, 1990/1992, 40)

Though she is now in her mid thirties and has two children, Dora still feels exiled
in England and defensive about her origins: 'There was something gaping in her
life, some emptiness at the centre which was to do with her displacement' (Devlin,
1990/1992, 131). In Kristeva's account of the foreigner in *Strangers to Ourselves*
the foreigner compensates for this emptiness by insatiable party-going which
always leaves him dissatisfied. He devours food like a greedy child, as Dora sitting
in Stella's kitchen, sucks greedily on her spoon 'avid for more' (Devlin,
1990/1992, 48).

In Dora's case, she attempts to compensate for her feelings of insecurity and
rootlessness by cramming Simon's home with possessions. Every time she thinks
of Ireland she buys something else:

> If she could get off stage where would she be, she wondered. Back in old Ireland where
> she had no possessions? Back to being Nora again? She lifted the local gazette to see if
> there was an auction she could go to for the staunch of another acquisition. (Devlin,
> 1990/1992, 68)

Dora comes to fear that 'her mania for collecting is, at its base, a joyless search for
a tourniquet on her life' (Devlin, 1990/1992, 138). Only years later does Dora
make the link between her need to fill her life with possessions and the fact that, as
an Irish Catholic, she comes from a historically dispossessed people:

> The destitution of the peasantry rendered storage boxes superfluous. In other words there
> was nothing to store. By Christ, Dora thought, no wonder I fill coffers and carve my
> name on them. Destitution, restitution. With one bound Dora was incarcerated in
> acquisition. (Devlin, 1990/1992, 263)

Love is another way of filling the gap left by loss of her homeland. Like Kate in
Girls in their Married Bliss Dora, though married, embarks on a passionate love
affair with Theodore. Like Kate, Dora's Irish Catholic upbringing remains
ingrained in her psyche: unable to leave the punitive religion of her childhood
behind, she would prefer Simon to punish her for the affair rather than remain
silently and miserably tolerant. Instead she punishes herself by various accidents
which inflict minor physical injuries on herself. She even toys, like Kate, with the
idea of suicide as a way out of her predicament. Through the book Dora's thought
processes remain firmly Catholic: she wears her new name like a nun's habit, she
regards marriage as a sacrament and sees her husband as 'cloaked in a good grey
mist like a nun' (Devlin, 1990/1992, 36). Dora remains imperfectly translated into
English life, ashamed of her Irish country origins, yet ready to defend her nation
passionately against mistaken English assumptions, as Kate passionately defends
the need for roots against Baba's skepticism (O'Brien, 1987, 525–6). Again, a
reading of Bronwen Walter's study, *Outsiders Inside: Whiteness, Place and Irish
Women*, would suggest that Dora's case is not unusual. Walter comments on the
double identity possessed by Irish women in Britain. They feel simultaneously

inside and outside the mainstream, placed in England but at the same time displaced because of their continuing ties with Ireland, ties which often last into the second and third generation (Walter, 2001, 266).

Dora's double identity is clearly spelled out in one of the final scenes of the novel. Accompanying her friend, Elvira, a sister-in-law of Lord Tyrone, to Northern Ireland, on the ferry Dora meets an Irish man who rails against the titled Anglo-Irish and their collusion in the Anglicization of Ireland. He is head of a society which aims to restore to Ireland the titles of the ancient Gaelic noblemen who fled in 1607. While Dora understands the emotional landscape behind the man's endeavor better than she often understands 'what's behind the big ringing tones of England' (Devlin, 1990/1992, 267), she resists the temptation to give in to his emotional appeal by setting out the historical facts: the Earls who fled in 1607 abandoned their country; one of them, Hugh O'Neill, the hereditary King of Ireland, was educated in England and was more or less bankrupt by the time he was run to ground.

When Dora goes from lunch in Lord Tyrone's castle to visit her father, descendant of Hugh O'Neill's bodyguards historically displaced from their homes by the planters, she realizes that, unlike the man on the ferry, she has learned to mediate between these two different worlds:

> She had learnt to speak two languages, not the native one spoken in those fields of Roscommon, the old Gaelic tongue, but another kind of native one, with code words and language as different from the one she had learnt from Caroline and her ilk as Cyrillic from romance. One gave her the passwords and access to the world she entered at lunchtime, the other to that world she had left behind long ago. (Devlin, 1990/1992, 273)

Knowing two languages helps Dora avoid the limiting bitterness of the man on the ferry. For all her insecurities and uncertainty, Dora has learned to negotiate the boundary position between self and other, to translate between the two different cultures in which she moves.

Polly Devlin's novel arguably provides a more hopeful solution than does Edna O'Brien's trilogy to the problems of mother and mother country. It raises the question whether Dora's early experiences of cultural hybridism in Northern Ireland may have contributed to her eventual greater skill in moving between cultures. Whatever the case, by the end of the novel, Dora has achieved reconciliation with the memory of her mother and has discovered that not only does her strength lie precisely in her ability to translate between cultures, but also that her notion of Irish identity has become more fluid, incorporating as it now does even the Anglo-Irish. This is expressed in concrete terms by her adoption and raising of the son Tony Flaxmeyer later has by her English colleague, Henrietta.[7] The three children Dora is raising thus draw upon a combination of Catholic Irish, Jewish, English and Anglo-Irish ancestry. Her story bears out Kristeva's view that women may be especially skilled in translating between cultures and that what they learn thereby may contribute to the polyphonic nations which Kristeva sees as the future.

---

[7]   Suggested by Polly Devlin in private correspondence with the author.

A comparison may be drawn between Polly Devlin's novel and Anne Devlin's play, *After Easter*, first performed in 1994. Like *Dora*, *After Easter* portrays a Northern Irish woman who flees both a harsh mother and a troubled motherland but has difficulties settling in England. The time span of the play is roughly the same as the novel: like Dora, Greta left Northern Ireland in the 1970s and the action is set in the 1990s. Although Greta is married to an Englishman and has lived in England for fifteen years, the play opens with her undergoing a mental breakdown which, it gradually becomes clear, is related to her situation as an Irish woman living in England. For years, feeling herself to be in a hostile environment, Greta has suppressed her Irish identity out of fear. She tells her sisters: 'I wanted to be English [...] I ran as far away as I could get from Ireland' (Devlin, 1994/1996, 15). She tried to pass by copying English behavior, yet, like Dora, she was unable to establish a secure identity in England: 'I left Ireland in 1979, but I never arrived in England. I don't know where I went' (Devlin, 1994/1996, 16). Like Dora, Greta, though a lapsed Catholic, has never abandoned her Catholic thought processes and now she feels Ireland calling her back in the form of a vision variously identified as the Virgin Mary, Mother Ireland and a Banshee.

Greta's crisis immediately follows the birth of her third child, and Walter's study, *Outsiders Inside*, reveals that many Irish-born women migrants experience a phase of intense longing for their birthplace when they have children of their own. Memories of their home country resurface and they long to pass these on to their children or even to revisit Ireland with their children (Walter, 2001, 201). In Devlin's play, Greta rejects both the fierce nationalism of her middle sister, Aoife, who has remained in Northern Ireland, and the cosmopolitanism of her younger sister, Helen, who is permanently rootless. Instead, after a visit back to Northern Ireland and a partial reconciliation with her mother, Greta opts, like Dora, to translate between cultures. She will remain in England because her children are English, but she will no longer suppress her Irish identity. She will have 'two separate windows, each with a different view' (Devlin, 1994/1996, 25). The final scene of the play presents Greta in the traditional role of the Irish storyteller, recounting stories about origins to her child.

In *Outsiders Inside*, Walter comments: 'Diasporic relationships involve not simply dual allegiances between two sets of homes, but an active remaking of identities which are continuously in flux' (Walter, 2001, 213). As Irish women in England, tied to England by their rearing of English children, both Greta and Dora have constantly to rethink the balance between Irishness and Englishness in their identities, a complicated process which ensures that they remain Kristevan subjects-in-process.

So far, the writing dealt with in this chapter recounts women's struggles to destabilize only one of the dominant narratives of Northern Ireland, namely the Catholic nationalist narrative. The Protestant community is a significant gap in these texts as, according to Christine St Peter, it is a gap generally in women's fiction writing on the North (St Peter, 2000, 121).[8] The following two novels set in Northern Ireland do, to some extent, remedy this absence by portraying interactions between women from both communities.

---

[8] Exceptions to this would include the novels of Janet McNeill and the plays of Christina Reid.

The Mother-Daughter Relationship: Mother of Pearl (1996)

In chapter four of this study, we saw how, in 'Stabat Mater', Julia Kristeva points out that Christianity's idealization of the Virgin Mary has impeded our understanding of motherhood. Since her arguments have a direct bearing on our reading of Mary Morrissy's novel, *Mother of Pearl*, it may be convenient to summarize them here. In 'Stabat Mater', drawing on the work of Marina Warner, Kristeva argues that the Virgin Mary has been used to oppress women by setting before them an impossible ideal of a woman who is at once virgin and mother. The cult of the Virgin Mary, as Warner has argued, makes all other women feel inferior and carnal. In effect, it turns them all into Eve. Kristeva suggests that the West's elaborate construct of the Virgin Mary is essentially 'a masculine appropriation of the Maternal', a fantasy which masks a narcissistic longing to return to a relationship with the lost, idealized mother (Kristeva, 1997, 310). However, Kristeva also points out that, as the Virgin Mary wanes in influence, we in the West are being left without a satisfactory discourse on motherhood. In fact we are caught in a double bind between accepting the idealizations of motherhood inherent in the Virgin Mary cult and rejecting motherhood entirely, as some radical feminists have done. But this latter course is no solution since it leaves out of account women's continued desire to have children. We need to listen, Kristeva argues, to what mothers are saying (Kristeva, 1997, 326). In this way it may be possible to uncover what the cult of the Virgin ignores or represses in women's experience of motherhood. This is in effect what Mary Morrissy's novel aims to do – to get behind the Catholic construct of motherhood and uncover what has been suppressed in women's experience, namely the semiotic maternal body, what Kristeva terms 'the immeasurable, unconfinable maternal body' (Kristeva, 1997, 322).

Mother of Pearl, part myth and fable, is set against a generalized Irish background with many features – shipbuilding, tribal marches, biblical fundamentalism, the rise of sectarian violence, army patrols – which suggest Northern Ireland. In his study, *The Contemporary Irish Novel*, Linden Peach puts forward the persuasive argument that the Northern setting of the novel is not so much geographical as ideological (Peach, 2004, 156). The effects of this ideology are gendered. Whereas the men's lives are cut short by violence – Mel Spain is the victim of a sectarian killing, Pearl's husband, Jeff, is victim of another random shooting – for the women it is the Catholic construct of motherhood which overshadows their lives. Catholicism pervades the novel, from the title, 'Mother of Pearl', one of the names for Mary in the litany, to the many biblical allusions in the text (Lot's wife, barren women, Samson's judgment on the two mothers, Moses' adoption by Pharaoh's daughter, Elizabeth, the Annunciation) and the biblical vocabulary ('tabernacle', 'swaddling', 'benedictional grace').

The first idea that the novel demolishes in an effort to uncover the reality behind the myth of motherhood is that the mothering instinct is innate and that mothers naturally protect their children. Irene Rivers is a Catholic from the South. The mothering she receives from her own mother, Ellen, has been shaped by Ellen's environment. Famine, forced ejection from her childhood home, poverty and marriage to a violent husband have 'calcified' Ellen Rivers' emotions

(Morrissy, 1996/1997, 5). When Irene is discovered to have TB, a product of poverty and a damp, unhealthy environment, Ellen, conscious of the social stigma attached to the disease, treats her daughter as the abject, to be expelled from the family home and never spoken about again. Ellen is a brutal mother but we are shown the reasons and Irene herself acknowledges the environmental factors which have determined her mother's mothering when she fantasizes about being visited by a newly prosperous mother eager to bring her back home. Coming into the money is 'the only circumstance Irene could imagine which would justify this new expansiveness' (Morrissy, 1996/1997, 17). In the face of a motherhood shaped and thwarted by poverty, Catholic idealizations about motherhood ring hollow in this novel.

The idea that the mothering instinct is innate is likewise deconstructed through the portrait of Rita Golden, Pearl's natural mother, who lives in the North. Rita is only eighteen when she falls pregnant and she resents her unborn baby for robbing her of her girlish identity:

> Rita Golden was lost. Her own name seemed strange to her, like a faint tinselly echo, or a glittering promise withdrawn. Rita Golden had no history. No sooner had she taken flight, a shaky fledgling on a short, tentative foray from the nest, than she had been preyed upon. She no longer knew herself, a married woman, a mother-to-be. Rita Golden, or the notion of her, was fading away. (Morrissy, 1996/1997, 103)

Rita fears the unborn child in her body. So far from experiencing pregnancy in Kristevan terms, as a time of reaching out to the other, Rita sees the baby inside her as the enemy, 'something separate and wilful' (Morrissy, 1996/1997, 104).

Pearl is born prematurely and, lacking confidence in her mothering ability, Rita fears to touch her child. As for the maternal love displayed by the other mothers in the hospital: 'she couldn't understand it; it both baffled and irritated her, this love-sickness' (Morrissy, 1996/1997, 120). Her lack of mothering instinct is an ironic commentary on the figure of the teenage Virgin Mary. Indeed, Rita's friend, Imelda, refers to the birth as a virgin birth: 'I mean, it was your first time, wasn't it?' (Morrissy, 1996/1997, 118). The three weeks when she is obliged to leave her premature baby behind in the hospital seem to Rita like 'a reprieve' (Morrissy, 1996/1997, 121). Rita's lack of mothering results in the grown-up Pearl being unable to mother: 'the sin of the mother' is visited upon her child, though not in the way Rita has envisaged (Morrissy, 1996/1997, 133). Even with her second daughter, Stella, Rita behaves more like an elder sister than a mother, attempting to recapture the days of a girlhood lost too soon.

By contrast, there is an instant physical and emotional bond between Pearl and Irene who abducts her: 'Her fontanelle fluttered in time to Irene's racing pulse. They were as one' (Morrissy, 1996/1997, 70). Irene is a calm and confident mother whose mothering Pearl will dimly remember and yearn for long after she has been returned to her natural mother, Rita. Even Rita, when she learns of the abduction, recognizes that 'someone had wanted her baby more than she had' (Morrissy, 1996/1997, 126). The ideology of motherhood enshrined in the discourses of both the Protestant and the Roman Catholic churches in Northern Ireland and which assumes all women possess a mothering instinct is shown to bear little relation to the emotional lives of these particular mothers, Ellen and Rita.

Morrissy's novel subverts Catholic representations of Mary. Irene is a virgin mother, but the irony behind this is that, though technically a virgin, she is practiced in giving sexual relief to men. In a parodic echo of the cult of the Virgin Mary, Irene in the sanitorium becomes a focus of men's desires and aspirations and she regards it as her vocation to tend to them 'with the helpless fondness of a mother for her absent, roving sons' (Morrissy, 1996/1997, 24). Her view of herself wobbles a little when Davy Bly accuses her of acting like a whore – the Virgin Mary is in danger of turning into Mary Magdalene – but it is restored by her marriage to Stanley Godwin. Stanley, a Northerner, has worshiped his mother all his life with the result that he is sexually impotent. When his mother dies in the sanitorium, he transfers this worship to Irene who remains therefore a virgin. For Stanley, Irene is 'the giver of life'; she closes his mother's eyes with 'a benedictional grace' (Morrissy, 1996/1997, 32). We may recall here Kristeva's positing in 'Stabat Mater' of the Virgin Mary as one who enables men to overcome their fear of death: 'Mary defying death is the theme that has been conveyed to us by the numerous variations of the *Stabat Mater* [...] Man overcomes the unthinkable of death by postulating maternal love in its place' (Kristeva, 1997, 324–5). So, after his mother's death, Stanley sees Irene as taking her place and offering him the possibility of 'new life' (Morrissy, 1996/1997, 35).

Yet if Stanley longs for a new family, he marries Irene knowing that what he desires is impossible: she cannot, because of his impotence, become a mother herself. If Irene is abject in her first family because of TB, she is abject in Stanley's Northern community both because she is from the South and because she is childless (ironically, the excuse Ellen gave her husband for sending Irene away was that their daughter was pregnant). In this society the childless married woman is as abject as the unmarried mother: 'She was an unknown quantity among them and she knew that the only way she could counter that was to bear a child, whom they could claim as one of their own' (Morrissy, 1996/1997, 40). Whereas Stanley desires a child to carry on his name, Irene's desperation for a child is not so much innate as a product of her society's sectarianism and social expectations. Pressurized by the neighbors, she invents an imaginary child and for a while, until Stanley loses faith, she, Stanley and this imaginary child, whom Stanley names Pearl after his mother, form a Holy Family. The loss of Stanley's belief in their child fills Irene with despair until she decides, in a reversal of the Old Testament text, that a child has been fashioned out of the ribs she had removed in the sanitorium as part of her TB treatment. She believes that the child, 'fruit of Eve's ribs' (Morrissy, 1996/1997, 55), is waiting for her unclaimed in a hospital ward. Lodging with Mrs Blessed ('Plenty of room at the inn'; Morrissy, 1996/1997, 56) across the river which divides the north side of the city from the south, Irene awaits her opportunity to steal Rita's baby.

Rita's baby, initially named Hazel Mary by Rita after Hail Mary, becomes a second Pearl and a child of redemption for Stanley and Irene. Her arrival rescues Irene from her barrenness and turns the Godwins into a Holy Family again; by contrast, 'the holy family' (Morrissy, 1996/1997, 125) Rita had hoped to become part of is destroyed by this act of Irene. Rita blames her own lack of maternal instinct for her baby's disappearance and her peace of mind is only restored during a church service honoring Mary. As the words of the litany pass through her head,

Rita feels 'blessed and released' (Morrissy, 1996/1997, 139), illustrating the way in which, despite Kristeva's insistence on the decline of the cult of the Virgin Mary in the West as well as her assertion that women's identification with the Virgin is always masochistic, Mary continues to be a consoling and liberating figure for some women.[9]

Despite Pearl's arrival, Irene's holy family is under threat from the start. She denies her own immaculate conception by claiming that a former inmate of the TB sanatorium, Charlie Piper, is Pearl's father. This drives Stanley into such a frenzy of sexual jealousy that he rapes Irene. Thereafter the holy family is re-established and Pearl lives contentedly with Irene and Stanley until, four years later, Charlie Piper turns up and recognizes her to be the abducted Baby Spain. He notifies the authorities, Pearl is removed from the Godwins and Irene is sent to prison. The holy family is broken up.

Pearl's natural father, Mel Spain, has been killed in a sectarian attack and Pearl's return across to the south side of the river is interpreted by Rita as some kind of peace offering from the enemy who killed her husband. Rita renames Pearl Mary but cannot suppress the feeling that this newly found child, whom at first she is so reluctant to meet, is not the Hazel Mary she gave birth to but a stranger. In the same way, Rita is not the mother Pearl/Mary is looking for. In 'Stabat Mater', one of the criticisms Kristeva brings to bear against the Virgin Mary myth is that it leaves out any account of the mother-daughter relationship. She speaks of: 'the war between mother and daughter, a war masterfully but too quickly settled by promoting Mary as universal and particular, but never singular – as "alone of her sex"' (Kristeva, 1997, 328). In Morrissy's novel, presentation of the tensions between mothers and daughters – between Ellen and Irene, between Rita and Pearl/Mary and Rita and Stella – is one of the ways she unravels myths about motherhood. As Pearl/Mary grows up, the mothering she receives from her biological mother, Rita, remains unsatisfactory and the memory of her other mother pulses, like the semiotic, against her daily life providing her with odd, fragmented memories of a lost child whom she names Jewel. She imagines Jewel living on the north side of the city, a late and much-longed-for child with an anxious, loving mother whose endearments provide a sharp contrast to Rita's off-handedness. This dream world presses against the symbolic, allowing Pearl/Mary momentary glimpses into a lost world and a different kind of mothering:

> I was allowed only brief glimpses before I would wake from the dream of her life and find little seams in the air as if the skin of a new world had for a moment been peeled back and then hurriedly sewn up again leaving behind only the transparent incisions. (Morrissy, 1996/1997, 189)

Predictably Jeff, the man Pearl/Mary chooses to marry, comes, like her adoptive parents, from the north side of the river. Taken by him to visit his family, she feels an immense sense of homecoming. Everything about their home gives her a sense of familiarity whereas in Rita's house she has always felt like an intruder. After her marriage, Pearl/Mary unexpectedly finds herself pregnant. For Kristeva

---

[9] For more on the Virgin Mary as an empowering figure for women, see my *Women's Spirituality in the Twentieth Century*, 2004, 17–19.

in 'Stabat Mater' pregnancy is a time out of time, a return of the repressed and a time when a woman moves more closely in touch with the semiotic. In the same way, in pregnancy, Pearl/Mary's memories of Jewel begin to surface again:

> She rose from the ashes of the north city, and travelling by night, she crossed the bridge and became a living, breathing child, clamouring for my attention [...] I was being revisited by the dream of a child I had created so long ago that I was amazed she still remembered me. I had left her behind, a little girl, *my* little girl, and now she was claiming me back. (Morrissy, 1996/1997, 213–14)

Now Pearl/Mary is not only a daughter waiting for her mother to return but also mother to the lost little girl inside herself. She becomes unwilling to mother the child in her womb because she refuses to replace the lost little girl who clamors for a mother's attention: 'She was my firstborn, my only child. No other baby could be allowed to take her place' (Morrissy, 1996/1997, 215). In an act which makes perfect sense psychologically (unmothered herself she does not have the resources to mother), Pearl/Mary aborts her unborn child. In 'Stabat Mater', Kristeva argues that pregnancy returns a woman to her mother, but Pearl/Mary has no mother to return to. What Kristeva terms in 'Stabat Mater', 'the fantasy that is nurtured by the adult, man or woman, of a lost territory' (Kristeva, 1997, 308), namely the idealization of the relationship with the archaic mother, is complicated in Pearl/Mary's case because she really has lost the early, nurturing mother: 'someone whose presence I have never known. And it seemed more real to me than all the presences' (Morrissy, 1996/1997, 218). Endlessly replaying this lack in her head, Pearl/Mary is doomed for ever to be the daughter waiting for her mother to return while she tries in vain to mother the lost little girl inside herself.

As the grown-up Pearl/Mary longs to be back in her lost Eden with the Adam and Eve she can only dimly remember, so Irene, now back in the South, waits for her daughter to be found:

> The knowledge that she lives and breathes is enough to sustain Irene. Pearl is out in the world and as long as Irene lives, she is not lost but merely waiting to be found again. (Morrissy, 1996/1997, 223)

On some mythical level, since they never meet again in the novel, Irene and Pearl/Mary, through their yearning for one another, overcome the sectarian divide of their society. Names are never arbitrary in this novel. In Greek mythology Irene was the goddess of peace and Pearl, too, is seen by Rita as coming from enemy territory, from the enemy who killed Mel, as 'some gruesome kind of peace offering' (Morrissy, 1996/1997, 160). Rita's inadequate mother love is bolstered by the politics of her environment since she is prejudiced against all people from the north side of the city: '"They eat their young over there," my mother used to say' (Morrissy, 1996/1997, 167). Rita never comes to terms with the fact that Pearl/Mary returns to her from enemy territory. She remains, as Pearl/Mary acknowledges, 'exasperated by my difference' (Morrissy, 1996/1997, 217).

By contrast, the bond between Irene and Pearl is portrayed as cutting across the sectarian divisions on which this society is founded. The stress on mothers and daughters in Morrissy's novel disrupts the mother-son iconography central to

Catholicism and, in portraying the mutual yearning between Irene and Pearl, presents the love of mother for daughter and daughter for mother as an outlaw love which cannot be contained within the symbolic order.

The Sacred: Bridie Steen (1949)

As we saw in the previous chapter, for Kristeva, the sacred is located, exactly as women are located, on the borders between nature and culture. In this context I would like to look at Anne Crone's novel, *Bridie Steen*, published in 1949 and set in rural Fermanagh.

The eponymous heroine, Bridie Steen, possesses a hybrid identity which troubles her since it breaks the fundamental duality on which her society is based:

> There were two kinds of people, Catholics and Protestants. They were people who lived close to one another, worked together, whose children learned and played together. Yet, naturally, there flowed between them a river of darkness of which the current could bear neither bridge nor boat. (Crone, 1949, 5)

Bridie is the daughter of a Catholic mother and a Protestant father. Orphaned early on and rejected by her father's family who disapproved of the mixed marriage, she is raised by her mother's sister, Aunt Rose Anne, in strict adherence to the Catholic faith. Aunt Rose Anne, a bigot, teaches Bridie to distrust all Protestants. Though an obedient Catholic, during her harsh upbringing Bridie unconsciously derives more solace from her love of nature than from her religion. Like Orla in *The Dancers Dancing*, Bridie lives on the Kristevan border between nature and culture. Nature is a central theme in the novel and there are many beautiful descriptions of the countryside as seen through Bridie's eyes. The book begins and ends with the bog where Bridie was raised, opening with the words: 'The bog was beautiful, or so it always seemed to Bridie in the days when she played house in little sheltered nooks behind the turf-stacks. She held dominion over it' (Crone, 1949, 1). The bog is Bridie's natural home; it provides a refuge from the harsh and intolerant Aunt Rose Anne, and Bridie shares her love of it with her gentle Uncle James. After the latter's death nature, rather than the Catholicism in which she has been raised, provides her with spiritual consolation. Unconsciously, away from the sectarian divisions of her culture, Bridie has carved out her own sacred space which gives her a freedom unobtainable in the orthodox religions of her society. In Crone's novel, nature is essentialized as a wild, primitive place outside social constructs, a view of nature that, although disputed by recent ecofeminist theories of the landscape, is, as we saw in chapter six, consonant with that of Kristeva.

From the age of fourteen Bridie works as maid for the tolerant Protestant Miss Anderson in whose house she feels more at home than she ever did with her aunt. At eighteen, however, she is summoned to live with her grandmother. Alicia Musgrave, though not much given to church attendance, is as dogmatic in her Protestantism as Aunt Rose Anne is in her Catholicism. Once again nature provides spiritual comfort for Bridie away from the harshness of humans. By the lough she feels a sense of homecoming and peace:

> The lough was comforting. It did not change. Like the bog, it knew her. The stillness of
> the morning air, the grey shimmer of the waters, the liquid purity of the light which, with
> each passing minute, seemed perceptibly to brighten, combined to bathe her mind and
> senses in a dream-like peace. (Crone, 1949, 146)

This is the timeless, personified nature of the Romantic poets presented as
untouched by human hand.

Gradually Bridie learns to love her imperious and possessive grandmother but
resists efforts to get to her to convert to the Protestant religion. When Alicia's
nephew, William Musgrave, falls in love with Bridie, her grandmother encourages
the match hoping that Bridie will 'turn'. After many vicissitudes, Bridie finally
agrees to trust William's judgment on religion, in large part because his faith is not
shaped by the sectarian divide which dominates their society but incorporates
recognition of the spirit at work in nature. He tells her: "'My God is wider and
bigger than theirs. He is more out in the fields and with people everywhere, and not
so much in churches or in chapels'" (Crone, 1949, 302). When Bridie agrees to
marry William on the understanding that she will also adopt his religion, her dying
grandmother gives the couple her blessing. However after Alicia's death, visits
from her Aunt Rose Anne and from the local Catholic priest unnerve Bridie.
Unable to shake off the indoctrination of her Catholic upbringing, she fears she is
risking hell by marrying William. Searching for peace for her soul, she flees her
grandmother's house. At first she heads for the convent where her Aunt Rose Anne
lives, then she remembers the bog where she and Uncle James used to walk and
find peace together. She meets her death walking alone there in the dark.

It is left to William, in a lament over Bridie's body which recalls Mary
McNamara's cry at the end of *Down by the River*, to sum up the message of the
novel. He sees Bridie as a child of nature destroyed by the sectarian divisions of
her society:

> We have broken her, torn her in two, made her suffer so that she could not live naturally,
> she who was so natural, so pure, so free. In her heart she was whole, in her heart she
> loved God, who is here above all our senseless differences. (Crone, 1949, 328)

The Catholic and Protestant men who have been helping William search for Bridie
hear his cry but the novel holds out little hope of change:

> The men stood rooted to the ground, compassionate, motionless, humble, acknowledging
> by their wet eyes that what he said was true. But helpless, each in his station doomed to
> play the part destiny and the social order had ordained for him. (Crone, 1949, 328)

In *Bridie Steen*, the land is placed in direct opposition to the religious conflicts
dividing the nation, and Bridie, a child of nature, represents Ireland torn apart by
the sectarian divide. In the previous chapter we looked at Kristeva's argument, in
Revolt, She Said, that new forms of spirituality are a necessary defense against
institutionalism and political dogmatism. Here, though she is barely able to
articulate her rebellion, Bridie attempts such a defense but her efforts to carve out a
private sacred space are defeated by the religious dogmas of her divided society.

Towards the end of her essay on 'Fiction in conflict: Northern Ireland's prodigal novelists' (Bell, 1995, 128–48), Eve Patten points to ways in which certain novelists from the North are beginning to use postmodern techniques in order to challenge the division between public and private. Only two of our novels, *One by One in the Darkness* and *Mother of Pearl*, could truly be called postmodern in their techniques; however, a Kristevan reading of fiction by Northern Irish women, demonstrating as it does the interpenetration of the political and the private, allows even realist novels such as *To Stay Alive*, *Give Them Stones*, *Dora* and *Bridie Steen* to fall into this category of posing a challenge to the division between the public and the private world. Home is a dominant motif in these women's writing: the loss of home (*One by One in the Darkness*, *Mother of Pearl*), the struggle to create a safe domestic space (*Give Them Stones*), the awareness that home may lie in some in-between space (*Dora*, *After Easter*) or even outside the domestic altogether, in nature (*Bridie Steen*). A Kristevan reading shows that even where women's writing is predominantly occupied with the private sphere of personal feeling, it displays an awareness that the private world is in fact shaped by the political. This awareness is shown as informing their heroines' struggle to remodel their lives, a struggle which in turn implies a critique of the ideological structures in which they are obliged to live. As has been said many times, politicizing the private can in fact provide a politically empowering agenda for women.

Patten's point about the political possibilities inherent in postmodernism is taken up by Elmer Kennedy-Andrews in *Fiction and the Northern Ireland Troubles since 1969: (de-)constructing the North* where he argues that:

> In a Northern Ireland context, post-modernism offers the possibility of deconstructing the perennial categories of Catholic and Protestant, Unionist and Nationalist; exposing the difference and *différance* within identity; exploring new horizons of identity altogether. (Kennedy-Andrews, 2003, 19)

Despite the fact that they are not all postmodernist in their technique, all six novels examined in this chapter bear out Kennedy-Andrews' observation: reading them through the lens of Kristevan theory highlights the heroines' struggles to formulate new identities for themselves as they negotiate their way through the various political and religious constructs that weigh on their lives. In the collision between their evolving selves and their society's imposed identities, these women deconstruct the binaries on which life in the North is predicated and learn to live with difference. All six novels may be read in the light of Kristeva's endorsement of a politics which pays attention to individual difference. Acknowledging their outsider status, Rosaleen and Martha struggle to resist the dogmatic nationalism of their environment while Dora, the foreigner, learns to translate between cultures. In *One by One in the Darkness* the female characters' semiotic world of dreams, music and color presses against the symbolic, registering a protest against the conditions of their lives, while in *Mother of Pearl* the semiotic bond between mother and daughter reaches across the sectarian divide. In *Bridie Steen* the young heroine's hybrid identity disturbs the symbolic order, but her attempt to secure a private sacred space is defeated by the ideological rigidities of her society.

A Kristevan reading highlights the way in which these novels portray Northern Irish women as dissidents who employ a variety of strategies to re-formulate their identities. In the course of this re-formulation, confusion, self-division, uncertainty and boundary-crossing become positive values when set against a political context of extreme ideological rigidity. This in itself forms a critique of the kind of intransigence which too often has been all that is on offer in Northern Ireland.

Conclusion

In my introduction I suggested that there were compelling reasons to look again at Irish women's fiction of the twentieth century. This study has, I hope, highlighted the richness and diversity of Irish women writers' engagement with the idea of the nation and the constraints it places on their heroines. Reading their fiction through the lens of recent feminist literary theory allows us to appreciate the sophistication of this body of writing and challenges any attempt to relegate Irish women writers to a sub-category within Irish literature. As Eavan Boland said in an interview in 1998: 'there seems to be no difficulty in being perceived as a woman poet. The trouble appears to lie in being fully accepted as an Irish poet' (Boland, 1998, 12). Dialog from the margins should not be an argument in favor of marginalization. The fact that much Irish writing by women, both North and South of the border, is centered in domestic life has often rendered it invisible in the canon of Irish literature. A study of such writing through a Kristevan lens highlights the extent to which these writers interrogate the ideologies which weigh on private lives and, through that interrogation, connect with the public discourse of the nation. By demonstrating that it is possible to put Irish women writers at the heart of Irish writing on the nation I hope to have shown that the canon of Irish literature needs remapping and that the perennial assessments of writers like Edna O'Brien or Jennifer Johnston as minor figures need revising.

Irish women writers engage centrally with the nation in their works but often on very different terms from male writers, with the result that the nation itself begins to look rather different when examined from a female point of view. In Irish women's writing the focus shifts from the father-son relationship to mothers and daughters. Exile (both within and outside the nation) becomes a prominent topic, as does the subject of the body and female sexuality. Irish women writers do engage with the theme of the land but it is an engagement which interrogates nationalist ideas of ownership and control. These writers have complex attitudes to religion, too. Some of our texts, notably *The Ante Room*, *That Lady* and perhaps *The Land of Spices*, illustrate Myrtle Hill's argument that the centrality of the Catholic faith to Irish women's sense of self during this period has been underestimated by commentators eager to dwell on the oppressive nature of Catholicism. By contrast, novels such as *The Dancers Dancing* and *Bridie Steen*, portray women exploring alternative ideas about the sacred.

A study such as this, bringing together women's writing from the North as well as from the Republic, provides an opportunity to assess the way in which Irish women writers across the binaries (North/South, Catholic/Protestant, nationalist/unionist) are concerned with similar themes. Young girls from both sides of the border find their lives constrained in similar ways. Both Caithleen Brady, Edna O'Brien's heroine from the Republic, and Rosaleen from the North resist their nation's conflation of itself with the female body and motherhood. Both Lois and Nancy, the Anglo-Irish heroines of Elizabeth Bowen and Jennifer Johnston respectively, are as much engaged in resisting the assumptions of their tribe about gender and nation as is Rosaleen, Linda Anderson's working-class heroine from the Catholic North. Lois, Nancy and Rosaleen find themselves unable to accept the identity prepared for them by their class and their gender and reach out to what is other in their environment: nationalist rebels in the case of Lois and Nancy, an English soldier in Rosaleen's case.

Themes cross time as well as borders. In Kate O'Brien's novel, *The Land of Spices*, Reverend Helen Archer experiences a moment of kinship with her young pupil, Anna Murphy, and helps to ensure that Anna's future will develop along larger lines than that envisaged by her family. Her insistence that Anna's future must remain open-ended contrasts both with the Murphys' desire for her to choose a career and with the views of the nationalist nun, Mother Mary Andrew, who believes that the Reverend Mother is taking so much care over Anna's future only because she expects to recruit Anna to the religious life. In *One by One in the Darkness*, published over fifty years later, there is a similar conflict in Helen Quinn's convent school between the views of the nationalist nun, Sister Philomena, and the head of the school, Sister Benedict. Like Helen Archer, Sister Benedict takes a special interest in her pupil and tries to preserve the open-endedness of her future by discouraging Helen from remaining in Northern Ireland. She argues that for Helen to stay in the North out of reasons of idealism and self-sacrifice is tantamount to throwing her life away. Helen, however, sides with Sister Philomena who insists that Northern Ireland needs its educated Catholics. Unlike Kate O'Brien's Reverend Mother who endeavors to preserve a spirit of detachment in her dealings with Anna, Sister Benedict's arguments partly arise out of regrets over the turn her own life has taken. Sensing this, Helen resists her. She does indeed become a successful lawyer but the psychological price in terms of Helen's personal happiness is, as Sister Benedict indicated it would be, too high. Helen turns into an austere, icily self-contained, workaholic. The contrast between the opening out of Anna's life at the end of *The Land of Spices* and the narrowing of Helen's (she goes from her argument with Sister Benedict to writing a history essay on the Partition of Northern Ireland) vividly illustrates the political constraints weighing on a young Catholic woman's life in this period. In fact the comparison arguably shows that the constraints on Helen's life are even more oppressive than those on a young woman like Anna from an earlier generation.

The lives of older women display similarities too. Johnston's novel, *The Railway Station Man*, and Anne Devlin's play, *After Easter*, portray women who, for different reasons, have submerged their identity in marriage. Both novel and play deal with the theme of women finally taking control of their lives. Violence impinges in similar ways on women's lives on both sides of the border. Both the Protestant Helen Cuffe in the Republic and Martha, Mary Beckett's Northern Catholic heroine, find themselves rebuilding their worlds after they have been torn apart by violent acts carried out in the name of the Irish nation. Both women create a private space which allows them to express their creativity outside the political ideologies which rule their environment, evolving a position for themselves on the margins of their society yet in dialog with it. In Miranda's Anglo-Irish narrative,

Fool's Sanctuary, the semiotic pulsing against the symbolic registers a protest against nationalist violence in the early part of the twentieth century as the dreams of the Catholic Quinn sisters in Deirdre Madden's Northern narrative, *One by One in the Darkness*, do against the Troubles in the latter part of the century.

Women's writing from both North and South of the border thus provides a therapeutic space where female protest is registered against violence done in the name of politics: neither Helen in *The Railway Station Man*, nor the three Quinn sisters in *One by One in the Darkness* find themselves able to forgive those who perpetrate violence in the North. Heroines from both sides of the political divide resist the grand narratives of nationhood and attempt to refashion for themselves new and less constraining identities. All these factors suggest that Irish women's writing may indeed constitute the 'third force' described by John Wilson Foster as capable of destabilizing the binaries on which Irish identity has long been built (Foster, 1991, 246).

The above examples draw together works from all decades of the twentieth century with the result that the effort to pinpoint milestones in Irish women's writing becomes problematic. Themes such as reaching out to the other, the semiotic, and translating between cultures feature as much in writers from the earlier part of the century as they do in writers from the later part, though it is true that from the 1980s onwards Irish women writers have been published in larger numbers and therefore these themes have become more visible. The history of Irish women's fiction in the twentieth century is not necessarily one of straightforward progress, but rather of themes being reworked down the decades. As we have seen, in some cases, particularly in literature from Northern Ireland, the constraints on women's lives in the later part of the century may be even greater than in the earlier.

Perhaps only in the area of mother-daughter relations and the portrayal of the mother can we discern anything that could be called progress. Again this theme crosses binary divisions. In the work of writers both North and South of the border (Edna O'Brien and Jennifer Johnston from the Republic, and Polly Devlin and Deirdre Madden from the North), heroines show a desire to flee their mothers and their mother countries. On both sides of the political divide this theme becomes more optimistic in the 1990s when the hostile mother-daughter relationship in earlier writing is replaced by a sense that the mother is important for the daughter's sense of identity. There is a striving towards reconciliation with the mother and the mother country. In many cases these later novels demonstrate an opening out of women's lives. The heroines of Clairr O'Connor, Kate O'Riordan and Polly Devlin do not repeat the dependent, domestic bound lives of their mothers. In many instances (the eponymous heroine of *Dora*, Nell in *The Memory Stones*, Deirdre in *Belonging*, Greta in Anne Devlin's play, *After Easter*), these daughters reject their mothers' exclusive identification with one nation by learning to translate successfully between cultures.

Irish women writers present heroines who register a severe protest against being a woman (Lois in *The Last September*, Cait in *The Country Girls*) or who wish to escape to some unmapped place, away from constraints of Irish nationalism – Lois in *The Last September* who wishes to be in 'some ideal no-place' (Bowen, 1929/1987, 89); Betty in *Down by the River* who yearns for 'some lost unmapped region' (O'Brien, 1996/1997, 163). More often, though, there is a sense, on the part of these characters, of wishing to engage in the nation, to act as a go-between in Kristeva's sense. A Kristevan reading of Irish women's fiction reveals how the rigidities and exclusions of national political discourse may be resisted or evaded by women and how the central characters in these works often strive for new, more liberatory ways of living. They may not always achieve a solution, they may be defeated in their attempts to reconcile their nation and their gender, but in the course of their struggles a glimpse of the future potential for the Irish nation and its women is perceived. Oscillating between the public and private spheres these women, in their search for identities more satisfactory than those on offer, urge a re-evaluation of both Irish women and the Irish nation.

Much remains to be done. I hope I have made the case that the many works by Irish women writers currently out of print (Evelyn Conlon's *Stars in the Daytime*, Mary Dorcey's *A Noise from the Woodshed*, Mary Leland's *Approaching Priests*, Mary Beckett's *Give Them Stones*, Polly Devlin's *Dora*, to name but five), do not on that account deserve to be lost to scholarly debate. It is one of the perennial frustrations of teaching and researching Irish women's fiction that so many crucial texts go so quickly out of print. More work of reclamation remains to be done. Short stories have been touched on in this study but Irish women's short story writing merits a book of its own. Such a study, examining the women's short story tradition on its own terms, might well alter our rather calcified view of the Irish short story itself.

The engagement with history in recent writing by Irish women also merits study. Far from being merely costume drama, such writing, as Patricia Coughlan demonstrates in her perceptive reading of Anne Enright's novel, *The Pleasure of Eliza Lynch*, often provides an opportunity to explore issues of nation and gender in a context outside the usual field of the Irish literary tradition (Donoghue, 2005, 349–73). Emma Donoghue's ventures into history in her novels, *Slammerkin* (2000) and *Life Mask* (2004), as well as in her short story collection, *The Woman who Gave Birth to Rabbits* (2002), deserve investigation in this context.

There is space too for discussion of the way in which Irish women's writing has portrayed the father. If the mother-daughter relationship has been under-discussed, the same could be said of the father-daughter relationship. Fathers may be weak (Portia's father in *The Death of the Heart*), or drunk and violent (Mr Brady in *The Country Girls*), but they are also portrayed as engaged in boundary-crossing (Miranda's father in *Fool's Sanctuary*, Michael Quinn in *One by One in the Darkness*). In *Down by the River*, Edna O'Brien takes particular care to counter her portrayal of a patriarchal nation-state with males who are tolerant of diversity (Luke, Cathal, L'Estrange). In *The Railway Station Man*, Damian, Catholic and working-class, crosses several boundaries in his friendships with Helen (Protestant and middle class) and with Roger, the Englishman. The time is ripe for a consideration of the portrayal of masculinity in Irish women's fiction.

In comparison with other countries, the establishment of a distinctly female tradition of Irish writing has been slow to gain acceptance and recognition. But when I discern resonances of Edna O'Brien's *Country Girls* in Polly Devlin's novel, *Dora*; when I read Éilís Ní Dhuibhne's short story, 'The Banana Boat', published in 2000, and see her intertextual use of Mary Lavin's short story, 'The

Widow's Son'; or when I read Paula Meehan's poem, 'It is all I ever wanted', also published in 2000, dedicated to Eavan Boland and picking up on Boland's image of a woman writing at a desk by a window in the center of Dublin, I have faith that slowly there is beginning to emerge a recognizable women's tradition of Irish writing.

Bibliography

Anderson, L. (1984/1985), *To Stay Alive*, Futura, London.

Anderson, L. (1990), *Plotting Change: Contemporary Women's Fiction*, Edward Arnold, London.

Aretxaga, A. (1997), *Shattering Silence: Women, Nationalism, and Political Subjectivity in Northern Ireland*, Princeton University Press, Princeton.

Balakrishman, G. (ed.), (1996), *Mapping the Nation*, Verso, London and New York.

Barrington, M. (1939/1990), *My Cousin Justin*, Blackstaff, Belfast.

Baudrillard, J. (2001), *Jean Baudrillard: Selected Writings*, ed. M. Pastor, Polity Press, Oxford.

Beaumont, C. (1999), 'Gender, citizenship and the state in Ireland, 1922–1990' in *Ireland in Proximity: History, Gender, Space*, Routledge, London and New York, pp. 94–108.

Becker-Leckrone, M. (2005), *Julia Kristeva and Literary Theory*, Palgrave, Basingstoke and New York.

Beckett, M. (1987), *Give Them Stones*, Bloomsbury, London.

Bell, I.A. (ed.), (1995), *Peripheral Visions: Images of Nationhood in Contemporary British Fiction*, University of Wales Press, Cardiff.

Benjamin, J. (1990), *The Bonds of Love: Psychoanalysis, feminism, and the problem of domination*, Virago, London.

Bennett, A. and Royle, N. (1995), *Elizabeth Bowen and the Dissolution of the Novel: Still Lives*, Macmillan, Basingstoke.

Berry, P. and Bishop, A. (eds) (1985), *Testament of a Generation: The Journalism of Vera Brittain and Winifred Holtby*, Virago, London.

Boland, E. (1995), *Collected Poems*, Carcanet Press, Manchester.

—— (1995/1996), *Object Lessons: The Life of the Woman and the Poet in Our Time*, Vintage, London.

—— (1998), 'Interview', *The Irish Times*, September.

Bourke, A. (2004), *Maeve Brennan: Homesick at* The New Yorker, Jonathan Cape, London.

Bowen, E. (1929/1987), *The Last September*, Penguin, Harmondsworth.

—— (1935/1976), *The House in Paris*, Penguin, Harmondsworth.

—— (1938/1989), *The Death of the Heart*, Penguin, Harmondsworth.

—— (1968/1992), *Eva Trout*, Penguin, Harmondsworth.

—— (1984), *Bowen's Court and Seven Winters*, Virago, London.

—— (1986/1999), *The Mulberry Tree: Writings of Elizabeth Bowen*, ed. H. Lee, Vintage, London.

Boylan, C. (1983/1998), *Holy Pictures*, Abacus, London.

Bradley, A. and Valiulis, M. (eds), (1997), *Gender and Sexuality in Modern Ireland*, University of Massachusetts Press, Amherst.

Brennan, M. (1999), *The Springs of Affection*, Flamingo, London.

—— (2000), *The Rose Garden*, Counterpoint, Washington.

—— (2001), *The Visitor*, Atlantic Books, London.

Brown, T. (1981/2004), *Ireland: A Social and Cultural History 1922–2002*, Harper Perennial, London.

Butler, J. (1990), *Gender Trouble: Feminism and the Subversion of Identity*, Routledge, New York and London.

Butler, J. (1993), 'The Body Politics of Julia Kristeva', in *Ethics, Politics and Difference in Julia Kristeva's Writing*, ed. K. Oliver, Routledge, New York and London, pp. 164–78.

Cairns, D. and Richards, S. (1988), *Writing Ireland*, Manchester University Press, Manchester.

Chanter, T. (1993), 'Kristeva's Politics of Change: Tracking Essentialism with the help of a Sex/Gender Map', in *Ethics, Politics and Difference in Julia Kristeva's Writing*, ed. K. Oliver, Routledge, London, pp. 179–95.

Cixous, H. and Clément, C. (1996), *The Newly Born Woman*, Tauris and Co., London.

Clark, S. and Hulley, K. (1991), 'An Interview with Julia Kristeva: Cultural Strangeness and the Subject in Crisis' *Discourse* 13.

Clear, C. (2000), *Women of the House: Women's Household Work in Ireland 1922–1961*, Irish Academic Press, Dublin.

Clément, C. and Kristeva, J. (2001), *The Feminine and the Sacred*, Columbia University Press and Palgrave, New York and Basinsgtoke.

Conlon, E. (1989), *Stars in the Daytime*, Attic Press, Dublin.

—— (1993), *Taking Scarlet as a Real Colour*, Blackstaff Press, Belfast.

Connolly, L. (2003), *The Irish Women's Movement: From Revolution to Devolution*, Lilliput Press, Dublin.

Corcoran, N. (1997), *After Joyce and Yeats: Reading Modern Irish Fiction*, OUP, Oxford.

—— (2001), 'Discovery of a Lack: History and Ellipsis in Elizabeth Bowen's *The Last September*' *Irish University Review*, 31 (2), 315–333.

Costello, M. (1992), *Titanic Town: Memoirs of a Belfast Girlhood*, Methuen, London.

Coughlan, P. (2005), '"Without a Blink of Her Lovely Eye": *The Pleasure of Eliza Lynch* and Visionary Scepticism' *Irish University Review*, 35 (2), 349–73.

Coulter, C. (1993), *The Hidden Tradition: Feminism, Women and Nationalism in Ireland*, Cork University Press, Cork.

—— (1998), 'Feminism and Nationalism in Ireland', in *Rethinking Northern Ireland: Culture, Ideology, and Colonialism*, ed. D. Miller, Longman, London and New York, 160–77.

Crone, A. (1949), *Bridie Steen*, William Heinemann, London.

Cullen, M. (ed.) (1987), *Girls Don't Do Honours: Irish Women in Education in the Nineteenth and Twentieth Centuries*, Web, Dublin.

Cullen, M. and Luddy, M. (eds), (2001), *Female Activists: Irish Women and Change 1900–1960*, The Woodfield Press, Dublin.

Curtin, C. Jackson, P. and O'Connor, B. (eds), (1987), *Gender in Irish Society*, Galway University Press, Galway.

Davidson, C. N. and Broner, E.M. (eds), (1980), *The Lost Tradition. Mothers and Daughters in Literature*, Frederick Ungar, New York.

Deane, S. (ed.), (1991), *The Field Day Anthology of Irish Writing*, Vol. III, Field Day Publications, Derry.

Devlin, A (1986/1987), *The Way-Paver*, Faber, London.

—— (1986/1990), *Ourselves Alone*, Faber, London.

—— (1994/1996), *After Easter*, Faber, London.

Devlin, P. (1983), *All of Us There*, Weidenfeld and Nicolson, London.

—— (1990/1992), *Dora, or the Shifts of the Heart*, Arrow Books, London.

Donoghue, E. (1994/1995), *Stir-fry*, Penguin, Harmondsworth.

—— (1995/1996), *Hood*, Penguin, Harmondsworth.

—— (2000), *Slammerkin*, Virago, London.

—— (2002), *The Woman Who Gave Birth to Rabbits*, Virago, London.

—— (2004), *Life Mask*, Virago, London.

Dorcey, M. (1989), *A Noise from the Woodshed*, Onlywomen Press, London.

—— (2001), *Like Joy in Season, Like Sorrow*, Salmon Publishing, Co. Clare.

Duffaud, B. (1993), *A Wreath upon the Dead*, Poolbeg, Dublin.

Eckley, G. (1974), *Edna O'Brien*, Bucknall University Press, Lewisburg.

Edelstein, M. (1993), 'Toward a Feminist Postmodern Poléthique: Kristeva on Ethics and Politics', in *Ethics, Politics, and Difference in Julia Kristeva's Writing*, ed. K. Oliver, Routledge, New York and London, pp. 196–214.

Ellmann, M. (2003), *Elizabeth Bowen: The Shadow Across the Page*, Edinburgh University Press, Edinburgh.

Enright, A. (2004), *Making Babies: Stumbling into Motherhood*, Jonathan Cape, London.

Evason, E. (1991), *Against the Grain: The Contemporary Women's Movement in Northern Ireland*, Attic Press, Dublin.

Fallon, B. (1998), *An Age of Innocence: Irish Culture 1930–1960*, Gill & Macmillan, Dublin.

Fearon, K. (1999), *Women's Work: The Story of the Northern Ireland Women's Coalition*, The Blackstaff Press, Belfast.

Ferguson, K. (1994/1995), *The Maid's Tale*, Poolbeg, Dublin.

The Field Day Anthology of Irish Writing, Vol. V, *Irish Women's Writing and Traditions*, (2002), (eds), Bourke, Kilfeather, Luddy, MacCurtain, Meaney, Ni Donnchadha, O'Dowd and Wills, Cork University Press, Cork.

Foster, J.W. (1991), *Colonial Consequences: Essays in Irish Literature and Culture*, The Lilliput Press, Dublin.

—— (ed.), (1997), *Nature in Ireland: A Scientific and Cultural History*, The Lilliput Press, Dublin.

Freud, S. (1955), *The Complete Psychological Works* ed. and translated by James Strachey in collaboration with Anna Freud, Hogarth, London.

Giorgio, A, (ed.), (2002), *Writing Mothers and Daughters: Renegotiating the Mother in Western European Narratives by Women,* Benglahn Books, New York and Oxford.

Graham, A. (1996), '"The Lovely Substance of the Mother": Food, Gender and Nation in the Work of Edna O'Brien', *Irish Studies Review*, 15, 16–20.

Graham, C. (2003), 'Subalternity and Gender: Problems of Postcolonial Irishness', in C. Connolly (ed.), *Theorizing Ireland*, Palgrave, Basingstoke and New York, pp. 150–59.

Grant, P. (2001), *Literature, Rhetoric and Violence in Northern Ireland, 1968–98*, Palgrave, London.

Gray, K.M. (1994), 'The Attic Lips: Feminist Pamphleteering for the New Ireland', *Eire-Ireland*, Vol. 29 (1), 105–22.

Gubermann, R.M. (1996), *Julia Kristeva: Interviews*, Columbia University Press, New York.

Harrison, J. (1903/1922), *Prolegomena to the Study of Greek Religion*, Cambridge University Press, Cambridge.

Harte, L. and Parker, M. (eds), (2000), *Contemporary Irish Fiction: Themes, Tropes, Theories*, Macmillan Press, Basingstoke.

Hayes, A. and Urquhart, D. (eds), (2001), *The Irish Woman's History Reader*, Routledge, London and New York.

Heaney, J. (1998), '"No Sanctuary from Hatred": A Re-appraisal of Mary Lavin's Outsiders' *Irish University Review*, Vol. 28 (2), 294–307.

Herr, C. (1990), 'The Erotics of Irishness' *Critical Inquiry*, vol. 17 (1), 1–34.

Hill, M. (2003), *Women in Ireland: A Century of Change*, Blackstaff Press, Belfast.

Hoff, J. and Coulter, M. (eds), (1995), *Irish Women's Voices: Past and Present*, *Journal of Women's History*, vol. 6 (4), vol. 7 (1).

Hoult, N. (1930), *Poor Women*, William Heinemann, London.

Imhof, R. (2002), *The Modern Irish Novel: Irish Novelists after 1945*, Wolfhound Press, Dublin.

Ingman, H. (1998), *Women's Fiction Between the Wars: Mothers, Daughters and Writing*, Edinburgh University Press, Edinburgh.

—— (2004), *Women's Spirituality in the Twentieth Century: An Exploration through Fiction*, Peter Lang, Bern.

Innes, C.L. (1993), *Woman and Nation in Irish Literature and Society 1880–1935*, Harvester Wheatsheaf, New York and London.

Irigaray, L. (1991), *The Irigaray Reader*, ed. M. Whitford, Basil Blackwell, Oxford.

Jardine, A. (1986), 'Opaque Texts and Transparent Contexts: The Political Difference of Julia Kristeva', in *The Poetics of Gender*, ed. N.K. Miller, Columbia University Press, New York, pp. 96–116.

Jeffers, J. M. (2002), *The Irish Novel at the End of the Twentieth Century: Gender, Bodies and Power*, Palgrave, New York and Basingstoke.

Johnston, J. (1977/1991), *Shadows on Our Skin*, Penguin, Harmondsworth.

—— (1979/1984), *The Old Jest*, Fontana, London.

—— (1981/1982), *The Christmas Tree*, Fontana, London.

—— (1984/1989), *The Railway Station Man*, Penguin, Harmondsworth.

—— (1987/1988), *Fool's Sanctuary*, Penguin, Harmondsworth.

—— (1991/1992), *The Invisible Worm*, Penguin, Harmondsworth.

——(1995/1996), *The Illusionist*, Minerva, London.

—— (1998/1999), *Two Moons*, Review, London.

—— (2000), *The Gingerbread Woman*, Review, London.

—— (2005), *Grace and Truth*, Review, London.

Joy, M., O'Grady, K., Poxon, J. (eds), 2002, *French Feminists on Religion: A Reader*, Routledge, London and New York.

Keane, M. (1937/1984), *The Rising* Tide, Virago, London.

—— (1951/1988), *Loving Without Tears*, Virago, London.

—— (1981), *Good Behaviour*, Virago, London.

—— (1988), *Loving and Giving*, André Deutsch, London.

Kearney, R. (1988), *Transitions: Narratives in Modern Irish Culture*, Manchester University Press, Manchester.

—— (ed.), (1988), *Across the Frontiers: Ireland in the 1990s*, Wolfhound Press, Dublin.

—— (1997), *Postnationalist Ireland: Politics, Culture, Philosophy*, Routledge, New York.

Kelly, M. (1985/1991), *Necessary Treasons*, The Blackstaff Press, Belfast.

—— (1989), *Florrie's Girls*, Michael Joseph, London.

—— (1990/1991), *Orange Horses*, The Blackstaff Press, Belfast.

Kenneally, M. (ed.), (1988), *Cultural Contexts and Literary Idioms in Contemporary Irish Literature*, Colin Smythe, Gerrards Cross.

Kennedy-Andrews, E. (2003), *Fiction and the Northern Ireland Troubles since 1969: (de-)constructing the North*, Four Courts Press, Dublin.

Kiberd, D. (1995/1996), *Inventing Ireland: The Literature of the Modern Nation*, Vintage, London.

Kim, C.W.M., St Ville, S. M., Simonaitis, S. M. (eds) (1993), *Transfigurations: Theology and the French Feminists*, Fortress Press, Minneapolis.

Kirby, P., Gibbons, L. and Cronin, M. (eds), (2002), *Reinventing Ireland: Culture, Society and the Global Economy*, Pluto Press, London.

Kirkpatrick, K. (ed), 2000, *Border Crossings: Irish Women Writers and National Identities*, The University of Alabama Press, Alabama.

Kristeva, J. (1980), *Desire in Language: A Semiotic Approach to Literature and Language* ed. L.S. Roudiez, trans. Gora, Jardine, Roudiez, Columbia University Press, New York.

Kristeva, J. (1982) *Powers of Horror: an Essay on Abjection*, Columbia University Press, New York.

—— (1985), *Au commencement était l'amour. Psychoanalyse et foi*, Hachette, Paris.

(1984), 'Julia Kristeva in Conversation with Rosaline Coward' *Desire*, *ICA Documents*, 22–7.

—— (1985), *Au commencement était l'amour. Psychoanalyse et foi*, Hachette, Paris.

—— (1986), *The Kristeva Reader*, ed. T. Moi, Basil Blackwell, Oxford.

—— (1991), *Strangers to Ourselves*, trans. L.S. Roudiez, Columbia University Press, New York.

—— (1993), *Nations Without Nationalism*, trans. L.S. Roudiez, Columbia University Press, New York.

—— (1995), *New Maladies of the Soul* trans. Ross Guberman, Columbia University Press, New York.

—— (1997), *The Portable Kristeva*, ed. K. Oliver, Columbia University Press, New York.

—— (1999), *Le génie féminin: la vie, la folie, les mots. Tome premier. Hannah Arendt*, Fayard, Paris.

—— (2000a), *Le génie féminin: la vie, la folie, les mots. Tome second. Melanie Klein*, Fayard, Paris.

—— (2000b), *The Sense and Non-sense of Revolt: The Powers and Limits of Psychoanalysis*, trans. J. Herman, Columbia University Press, New York.

—— (2001), *The Feminine and the Sacred*, Columbia University Press, New York.

—— (2002a), *Le génie feminin: la vie, la folie, les mots. Tome troisième. Colette*, Fayard, Paris.

—— (2002b), *Intimate Revolt. The Powers and Limits of Psychoanalysis* vol. 2, trans. J. Herman, Columbia University Press, New York.

—— (2002c), *Revolt, She Said*, Semiotext(e), Los Angeles.

Kuykendall, E. (1989) 'Questions for Julia Kristeva's Ethics of Linguistics' *The Thinking Muse: Feminism and Modern French Philosophy*, ed. J. Allen and I. Young, Indiana University Press, Bloomington.

Lavin, M. (1945/1987), *The House in Clewe Street*, Virago, London.

—— (1950/1986), *Mary O'Grady*, Virago, London.

—— (1969), *Happiness and Other Stories*, Constable, London.

—— (1972), *A Memory and Other Stories*, Constable, London.

—— (1974), *The Stories of Mary Lavin. Volume II*, Constable, London.

—— (1977), *The Shrine and Other Stories*, Houghton Mifflin Company, Boston.

—— (1985), *A Family Likeness and Other Stories*, Constable, London.

—— (1999), *In a Café: Selected Stories*, Penguin, Harmondsworth.

Lee, H. (1981/1999), *Elizabeth Bowen*, Vintage, London.

Leland, M. (1985/86), *The Killeen*, Black Swan, London.

—— (1991), *Approaching Priests*, Sinclair-Stevenson, London.

Levenson, L. (1998), *The Four Seasons of Mary Lavin*, Marino Books, Dublin.

Levine, J. (1982), *Sisters: The Personal Story of an Irish Feminist*, Ward River Press, Dublin.

—— (1992), *A Season of Weddings*, New Island Books, Dublin.

—— (1994), 'From Cathleen to Anorexia: the Breakdown of Irelands' in *The Living Stream: Literature and Revisionism in Ireland*, Bloodaxe, Newcastle.

The Living Stream: Literature and Revisionism in Ireland, Bloodaxe, Newcastle.

Lynch, R.J. (1993), '"A Land of Strange, Throttled, Sacrificial Women": Domestic Violence in the Short Fiction of Edna O'Brien' *The Canadian Journal of Irish Studies*, vol. 19 (1), 36–48.

Lyons, F.S.L. (1979), *Culture and Anarchy in Ireland 1890-1939*, Clarendon Press, Oxford.

Macdona, A. (ed.), (2001), *From Newman to New Woman: UCD Women Remember*, New Island, Dublin.

Madden, D. (1986/1988), *Hidden Symptoms*, Faber, London.

—— (1992), *Remembering Light and Stone*, Faber, London.

—— (1996/1997), *One by One in the Darkness*, Faber, London.

Maley, W. (1999), 'Nationalism and revisionism: ambiviolences and dissensus', in *Ireland in Proximity: History, Gender, Space*, Routledge, London and New York, pp. 12–27.

Marks, E. and de Courtivron, I. (eds), (1981), *New French Feminisms: An Anthology*, Harvester Wheatsheaf, New York and London.

Mayer, T. (ed.), (2000), *Gender Ironies of Nationalism: Sexing the Nation*, Routledge, London and New York.

McAfee, N. (1993), 'Abject Strangers: Towards an Ethic of Respect', in *Ethics, Politics and Difference in Julia Kristeva's Writing*, ed. K. Oliver, Routledge, New York and London, pp. 116–34.

McKibbon, B. (1990), *The End of Nature*, Penguin, Harmondsworth.

McNeill, J. (1964), *The Maiden Dinosaur*, Geoffrey Bles, London.

McWilliams, M. (1993), 'The Church, the State and the Women's Movement in Northern Ireland', in A. Smyth (ed.), *Women's Studies Reader*, Attic Press, Dublin, 79–99.

Meaney, G. (1991), *Sex and Nation: Women in Irish Culture and Politics*, Attic Press, Dublin.

Merchant, C. (1982), *The Death of Nature: Women, Ecology and the Scientific Revolution,* Wildwood House, London.

Moi, T. (1990), *Sexual/Textual Politics: Feminist Literary Theory*, Routledge, London and New York.

Molloy, F. (1985), *No Mate for the Magpie*, Virago, London.

Morrissy, M. (1996/1997), *Mother of Pearl*, Vintage, London.

Murdoch, I. (1965/1984), *The Red and the Green*, Triad, London.

Murphy, O. (2002), *The Sway of Winter*, The Lilliput Press, Dublin.

Nandy, A. (1983), *The Intimate Enemy: Loss and Recovery of Self under Colonialism*, Oxford University Press, Oxford.

Nash, C. (1993), '"Embodying the Nation" – The West of Ireland Landscape and Irish Identity' in *Tourism in Ireland*, ed. M. Cronin and B. O'Connor, Cork University Press, Cork, pp. 86–112.

Nelson, D. (1982), *In Night's City*, Wolfhound Press, Dublin.

Ní Dhuibhne, É. (1990), *The Bray House*, Attic Press, Dublin.

—— (1999/2001), *The Dancers Dancing*, Review, London.

—— (2000/2001), *The Pale Gold of Alaska*, Review, London.

O'Brien Johnson, T. and Cairns, D. (eds), (1991), *Gender in Irish Writing*, Open University Press, Philadelphia.

O'Brien, E. (1965), *August is a Wicked Month*, Simon and Schuster, New York.

—— (1966), *Casualties of Peace*, Simon and Schuster, New York.

—— (1968), *The Love Object*, Jonathan Cape, London.

—— (1976/1978), *Mother Ireland*, Penguin, Harmondsworth.

—— (1977/1989) *Johnny I Hardly Knew You*, Weidenfield and Nicolson, London.

—— (1978), *Mrs Reinhardt and Other Stories*, Weidenfield and Nicolson, London.

—— (1985/2003), *A Fanatic Heart: Selected Stories*, Phoenix, London.

—— (1987/1988), *The Country Girls Trilogy and Epilogue*, Penguin, Harmondsworth.

—— (1992/1993), *Time and Tide*, Penguin, Harmondsworth.

—— (1994/1995), *House of Splendid Isolation*, Orion, London.

—— (1996/1997), *Down by the River*, Orion, London.

—— (1999/2000), *Wild Decembers*, Orion, London.

O'Brien, K. (1934/1988), *The Ante Room*, Virago, London.

—— (1936/1984), *Mary Lavelle*, Virago, London.

—— (1938), *Pray for the Wanderer*, Doubleday, Doran & Co., New York.

—— (1941/2000), *The Land of Spices*, Virago, London.

—— (1943/1990), *The Last of Summer*, Virago, London.

—— (1946/1985), *That Lady*, Virago, London.

—— (1951), *Teresa of Avila*, Max Parrish, London.

—— (1953), *The Flower of May,* William Heinemann, London.

—— (1958), *As Music and Splendour*, William Heinemann, London.

—— (1963/1994), *Presentation Parlour*, Poolbeg, Dublin.

O'Brien, K. Cruise (1991), *The Homesick Garden*, Poolbeg, Dublin.

O'Carroll, I. and Collins, E. (eds), (1995), *Lesbian and Gay Visions of Ireland*, Cassell, London and New York.

O'Connor, C. (1991), *Belonging*, Attic Press, Dublin.

O'Dowd, L. (1987), 'Church, State and Women: the Aftermath of Partition', in *Gender in Irish Society*, ed. C. Curtin, P. Jackson, B. O'Connor, Galway University Press, Galway.

O'Dowd, M. and Wichert, S. (eds), (1995), *Chattel, Servant or Citizen: Women's Status in Church, State and Society*, Institute of Irish Studies, Belfast.

O'Faolain, J. (1968), *We Might See Sights!*, Faber and Faber, London.

—— (1980), *No Country for Young Men*, Penguin, Harmondsworth.

O'Faolain, N. (1996), *Are You Somebody? The Life and Times of Nuala O'Faolain*, New Island Books, Dublin.

O'Mahony, P. and Delanty, G. (1998), *Rethinking Irish History: Nationalism, Identity and Ideology*, Macmillan Press, Basingstoke.

O'Riordan, K. (2003), *The Memory Stones*, Pocket Books, London and New York.

Oliver, K. (1993a), *Reading Kristeva: Unravelling the Double-bind*, Indiana University Press, Bloomington and Indianapolis.

——ed. (1993b), *Ethics, Politics and Difference in Julia Kristeva's Writing*, Routledge, London.

Owens, R. C. (1984), *Smashing Times: A History of the Irish Women's Suffrage Movement 1889–1922*, Attic Press, Dublin.

Parker, M. (2000), 'Shadows on a Glass: Self-Reflexivity in the Fiction of Deirdre Madden' *Irish University Review: A Journal of Irish Studies*, vol. 30 (1), 82–102.

Parkes, S. (2004), *A Danger to the Men? A History of Women in Trinity College Dublin 1904–2004,* The Lilliput Press, Dublin.

Peach, L. (1994), 'Contemporary Irish Women Writers and the Gendered Construction of Space' *Swansea Review*, 450–61.

Peach, L. (2004), *The Contemporary Irish Novel: Critical Readings*, Palgrave Macmillan, Basingstoke and New York.

Plumwood, V. (1993), *Feminism and the Mastery of Nature,* Routledge, New York and London.

Radford Ruether, R. (1992), *Gaia and God: An Ecofeminist Theology of Earth Healing*, SCM Press, London.

Rafroidi, P. and Brown, T. (eds), (1979), *The Irish Short Story: Studies of Irish Writers and their Work*, Colin Smythe, Gerrards Cross.

Rafroidi, P. and Harmon M. (eds), (1975), *The Irish Novel in Our Time*, Publications de l'Université de Lille III, Villeneuve-d'Ascq.

Ranchod-Nilssen, S. and Tétreault, M.A. (eds), (2000), *Women, States, and Nationalism: At Home in the Nation?*, Routledge, London and New York.

Reid, C. (1997), *Plays:1*, Methuen, London.

Rich, A. (1976/1977), *Of Woman Born: Motherhood as Experience and Institution*, Virago, London.

—— (1987), 'Compulsory Heterosexuality and Lesbian Existence' (1980) in *Blood, Bread and Poetry: Selected Prose 1979–1985*, Virago, London.

Rooks-Hughes, L. (1996), 'The Family and the Female Body in the Novels of Edna O'Brien and Julia O'Faolain', *The Canadian Journal of Irish Studies*, 83–97.

Rose, C. (1975), *The Female Experience: The Story of the Woman Movement in Ireland*, Arlen House, Galway.

Rose, J. (1993), 'Julia Kristeva: Take Two', in *Ethics, Politics and Difference in Julia Kristeva's Writing*, ed. K. Oliver, Routledge, New York and London.

Rose, K. (1994), *Diverse Communities: The Evolution of Lesbian and Gay Politics in Ireland*, Cork University Press, Cork.

Roulston, C. and Davies, C. (eds), (2000), *Gender, Democracy and Inclusion in Northern Ireland*, Palgrave, Basingstoke and New York.

Ruddick, S. (1990), *Maternal Thinking: Towards a Politics of Peace*, The Women's Press, London.

Sales, R. (1997), *Women Divided: Gender, Religion and Politics in Northern Ireland*, Routledge, London and New York.

Savage, R. (ed.), (2003), *Ireland in the New Century: Politics, culture and identity*, Four Courts Press, Dublin.

Shannon, C. (1997), 'The Woman Writer as Historical Witness: Northern Ireland, 1968-1994. An Interdisciplinary Perspective', in M. Valiulis and M. O'Dowd (eds), *Women and Irish History*, Wolfhound Press, Dublin, 239–59.

Sharp, J. (1996), 'Gendering Nationhood', in N. Duncan (ed.), *Bodyspace: Destabilizing Geographies of Gender and Sexuality*, Routledge, London and New York.

Showalter, E. (1977/1978), *A Literature of Their Own: British Women Novelists from Brontë to Lessing*, London, Virago.

Smith, A. (1996), *Julia Kristeva: Readings of Exile and Estrangement*, St. Martins Press, New York.

Smith, A-M. (1998), *Julia Kristeva: Speaking the Unspeakable*, Pluto, London.

Smyth, A. (1992), '"A Great Day for the Women of Ireland": The Meaning of Mary Robinson's Presidency for Irish Women' *The Canadian Journal of Irish Studies*, vol. 18 (1), 61–75.

—— (ed.), (1993), *Irish Women's Studies Reader*, Attic Press, Dublin.

Smyth, G. (1997), *The Novel and the Nation: Studies in the New Irish Fiction*, Pluto Press, London.

—— (2000), 'Shite and Sheep: An Ecocritical Perspective on Two Recent Irish Novels', *Irish University Review: A Journal of Irish Studies*, vol. 30 (1), 163–78.

Somerville, E. and Ross, V. (1938), *Sarah's Youth*, Longmans, Green and Co., London.

Soper, K. (1995), *What is Nature? Culture, Politics and the non-Human*, Blackwell, Oxford.

St Peter, C. (2000), *Changing Ireland: Strategies in Contemporary Women's Fiction*, Macmillan Press, Basingstoke and London.

Staly, T. (ed.), (1982), *Twentieth-Century Women Novelists*, Macmillan, London.

Stanton, D.C. (1986), 'Difference on Trial: A Critique of the Maternal Metaphor in Cixous, Irigaray, and Kristeva', in *The Poetics of Gender*, ed. N.K. Miller, Columbia University Press, New York.

Steel, J. (2004), 'Politicizing the private: women writing the Troubles', *Representing the Troubles: texts and images, 1970–2000* eds B. Cliff and E. Walshe, Four Courts Press, Dublin, pp. 55–66.

Stone, J. (1983), 'The Horrors of Power: A Critique of Kristeva', in *The Politics of Theory*, ed. F. Barker et al., University of Essex, Colchester, 38–48.

Sullivan, M. (2000), *New Voices in Irish Criticism*, ed. P.J. Mathews, Four Courts Press, Dublin.

Tweedy, H. (1992), *A Link in the Chain: The Story of the Irish Housewives' Association 1942–1992*, Attic Press, Dublin.

Valiulis, M. (1992), 'Defining Their Role in the New State: Irishwomen's Protest Against the Juries Act of 1927', *The Canadian Journal of Irish Studies*, vol. 18 (1), 43–60.

Valiulis, M. and O'Dowd, M. (eds), (1997), *Women and Irish History*, Wolfhound, Dublin.

Walshe, E. (ed.), (1993), *Ordinary People Dancing: Essays on Kate O'Brien*, Cork University Press, Cork.

—— (ed.), (1997), *Sex, Nation and Dissent in Irish Writing*, Cork University Press, Cork.

Walter, B. (2001), *Outsiders Inside: Whiteness, Place and Irish Women*, Routledge, New York and London.

Ward, M. (1989), *Unmanageable Revolutionaries: Women and Irish Nationalism*, Pluto Press, London.

—— (ed.), (1995), *In Their Own Voice: Women and Irish Nationalism*, Attic Press, Dublin.

—— (1997), *Hanna Sheehy Skeffington: A Life*, Attic Press, Dublin.

Warner, M. (1976/1985), *Alone of All Her Sex: The Myth and the Cult of the Virgin Mary*, Picador, London.

Weedon, C. (1992), *Feminist Practice and Poststructuralist Theory*, Basil Blackwell, Oxford.

Weekes, A.O. (1990), *Irish Women Writers: An Uncharted Tradition*, University Press of Kentucky, Lexington.

Winthrop, F. [Rosamond Jacob], (1920), *Callaghan*, Martin Lester, Dublin.

Woods, U. (1984), *The Dark Hole Days*, The Blackstaff Press, Belfast.

Yuval-Davis, N. (1997), *Gender and Nation*, Sage Publications, London.

Index